Something

ESSAYS BY
Gilbert Sorrentino

Said

NORTH POINT PRESS
San Francisco 1984

Contents

Preface

The professional literary critic finds himself in a curious, even awkward position. The rationale for his writing is that it serves to explicate or illuminate the texts of others; it is useful. What a fine ambiguity arises when we read that critic who is most gifted, most serious in sense of his vocation. His writing, as it strives toward the most precise and unique subtleties of revelation in the writing under review, begins, oddly, to detach itself from its cause, and to float free of it. It begins to move, that is, toward the literature that it purports to be "talking about." It is as if it *wants to be* literature too, as if it cannot countenance its function as that of the useful but wishes to approach the condition of the useless. What is most perverse about this phenomenon is that the best criticism is by definition the most useful: it is somehow that which it would prefer not to be. And that criticism that is useless, fashionable, a compilation of gossip, opinion, and *causerie*, criticism, that is, that speaks of everything but the work before it, pretends to be absolutely utilitarian. So we are left with this dilemma: useful criticism would like to be, indeed, strives to be, useless; and useless criticism seems superbly, aggressively useful.

This is by way of saying that my critical writings, herein collected, are, I hope, useful without being "book-chat." I have never had any desire to be creative in my criticism, and it does not yearn, so to speak, for the status of literature. It has been written, unlike my fiction and poetry, with an audience in mind, an audience, moreover, that I wished to influence by any number of rhetorical and argumentative means. Writing it has been an enormous luxury. Collecting and publishing it may also be a luxury, perhaps a foolish one, since there is usually no way that diverse pieces written over (as in this case), a quarter-century can, in any absolute way, cohere. Rather, the mind that issued these utterances can be seen to move, can be graphed from point to point of its prejudices, ignorances, its variegated failures. In short, this book is probably a mistake, but since everything a writer does is a mistake in that it is never "right," never final, never the only way it could have been, I publish it with, as the old song has it, no regrets.

I no longer hold many of the positions taken here; many of them are, in a word, embarrassing. They are, however, intact and unchanged; that is, I have resisted the urge to alter the past. I say this not as an apology but as a caveat to the reader who hopes to "find" me in these pages. On the other hand, I flatter myself that I have sometimes been accurate in my judgments, and, perhaps more interestingly, on occasion right for the wrong reasons, or for reasons that now seem inadequate or unimportant.

This, of course, is only my opinion, and the reader may find me inaccurate as well as wrong for the wrong reasons, since he will act as my critic. And if he writes and publishes his critique, he in turn submits to criticism. The process is, of needs, interminable and leads me to believe that the exercise of criticism is at best—in that delicious old phrase—a mug's game. The critic is either subsumed in his criticism, the latter becoming, relentlessly and imperceptibly, a kind of natural effusion of the collective intelligence; or he is forever identified as "the one who said that . . ." and reviled for such rank stupidity. Either way, he is denied his reality, becoming in the first instance a public idea that everybody held all the time, and in the second, an idiot whose pronouncements are contemptible when they are not hilarious. It is a strange enterprise and one that I am happy to be involved in only at its periphery.

2 February 1984

No sooner is something said than something else must be said to correct the tendency of all that is said to become final, to insinuate itself into the imperturbable realm of objects.

Maurice Blanchot

Something Said

1

The Act of Creation
and Its Artifact

No poem is intended for the reader, no picture for
the beholder, no symphony for the listener.
Walter Benjamin

I don't think that it has been fully acknowledged, or even admitted, that
the writer's finished product, the artifact, is not as important to its maker as
it has been made out to be by critics and scholars; or, to be more precise,
that its importance to critics and scholars is infinitely greater than it is to
the writer. This is a state of affairs that is totally at odds with the idea of "the
job well done" as that idea exists in professions or vocations other than the
artistic. This latter concept is often almost the entire rationale for a given
job's being done at all; and, indeed, the so-called empty job is usually described as that one which has no end product that can be identified with
the labor that went into making it, or the job that has no tangible end product at all. I set aside the profit motive, since what a man is paid for his
work most often only accidentally reflects that work's value. But, curiously
enough, for the writer, the end product, the artifact, but testifies to the fact
that he is once more unemployed. It is a truism that the successful completion of a poem or a work of fiction leaves the writer with a feeling of relief
mixed with a sense of loss and anxiety, but I would go further and say that
this completion also leaves him abashed, disgruntled, even in a state of what
might be called intellectual despair. A writer discovers what he knows as he
knows it, i.e., as he makes it. No artist writes in order to objectify an "idea"

3

already formed. It is the poem or novel or story that quite precisely tells him what he didn't know he knew: he *knows*, that is, only in terms of his writing. This is, of course, simply another way of saying that literary composition is not the placing of a held idea into a waiting form. The writer wants to be told; the telling occurs in the act itself. And when the act is completed its product is, in truth, but a by-product. The bringing to conclusion of a work guarantees the writer nothing; that is, he cannot, because of the artifact's presence, know if he will ever produce anything as good as that which he has just produced. Nor does the artifact preclude the question: Is this as good a job as one can do? These things are answerable only in the act of writing. By some subtle contradiction, the finished work attests to the writer's reality only in the eyes of its audience. It is, for them, since they had no hand in its making, almost the writer himself, or at least a legitimate surrogate for him. The writer's reality is, however, proved to him only in the act of composition. His finished work is before him as it is before anyone else; he, indeed, is usually as much in the dark about it as the reader who comes upon it for the first time, with the burden that it often proves far inferior to his intention. Eliot, in "The Use of Poetry and the Use of Criticism," writes: "What a poem means is as much what it means to others as what it means to the author; and indeed, in the course of time a poet may become merely a reader in respect to his own works, forgetting his original meaning—or without forgetting, merely changing." There is a story told of the late Jack Spicer, reading proofs of one of his books with friends, who pointed out to him that one of the poems in the book was exactly—word for word and line for line—the same as another poem in the book. To which Spicer replied that the poem had to stay because it was written at a different time and was, therefore, a different poem. This is only truly understandable in light of Jack Spicer's practice of writing poems by the process of what he called "dictation," which I will return to later. We may go back to the middle of the twelfth century, and discover Marcabru, the Provençal troubadour, writing:

> I'll take him on as critic,
> who'll call the meaning, in my song,
> of each word,
> who's analytic, who
> can see the structure of the vers unfold.
> I know it'll sound absurd, but
> I'm often doubtful and go wrong myself
> in the explication of an obscure word.

I think these comments on completed work, by three totally different poets, writing out of three totally different traditions, help point to the fact that the act of writing has, for the writer, little to do with the product that issues forth from it: for him, the act itself is the product. When the writer reads his own work he sees, as it were, *through* it, not to anything so shifting or profound as its meaning, but to the fact of his existence as *the one who wrote*. The work does not testify to his existence, but to the recollection of himself in the act of writing: for the writer to be alive as a writer he must re-create himself or discover his reality again and again. Pound's disavowal of his early poems as "stale creampuffs," Dahlberg's refusal to acknowledge the worth of the remarkable social-protest novels he wrote during the thirties, Joyce's impatience with people who wanted to talk about *Ulysses* after he had begun work on *Finnegans Wake*: these are not examples of eccentricity or perversity, but instances of candor. The finished work is, for its maker, a kind of intrusion into his life, almost an affront to it. It marks a full stop and guarantees nothing but that which is self-evident: that his work is over. What is most disturbing to him, as I have suggested, is that this completion does not presage anything in the way of future work. The well-known state called "writer's block," and the equally frustrating state in which the writer writes, but writes badly, are bitter and destructive, not because they obtrude between the writer and the finished product, but because they cut him off from the process of creation itself, that process which tells him that he is alive. Perhaps most unsettling of all is the situation that obtains when one has written with excellence, for excellence does not foreshadow as great or greater excellence to come. The idea that an artist's work becomes increasingly more sublime as he grows older and, if you will, wiser, is a critic's idea, a neat method whereby one may judge what critics like to call "growth" or "development." Writers know better, and it is not at all uncommon that a work of great power and beauty is succeeded by a lesser work. Literary style is not sharpened or refined by diligence. Rémy de Gourmont writes, with his usual unsentimental clarity: "So little can be learned in the way of style that, in the course of a lifetime, one is often prone to unlearn: when the vital energies are diminished, one writes less well, and practice, which improves other gifts, often spoils this one." To retreat into a cliché, for the writer each work, each phrase and sentence, is new, and he is as much working by feel when engaged with new work as he ever was in the past. It is quite literally the fact that the writer's controlling motto is "Scribo ergo sum": and the verbs of that sentence are always in the present tense.

In Baudelaire's great and harrowing prose poem, "À Une Heure du matin," he writes: "Dear God! Grant me the grace to produce some beautiful lines that will prove to me that I am not the basest of men. . . ." The grace that he asks for is the grace that will enable him simply to work, to prove to himself that he is real, that he is what he is—a poet.

If what I have said has any value, then there must be something particularly ecstatic, mysterious, and sublime in this act of creation, something so

infinitely finespun and elusive that no one, including the artist, has ever
been able satisfactorily to describe it, much less describe the reasons for its
power over the artist. No one has ever been able to isolate and analyze the
link between this act and the artifact that it produces. Why this word and
not that one? Why this startling and defining image? Why this metaphor,
so blinding in its clarity that it remains unforgettable, and, indeed, often
colors the way we see and think of whole areas of experience forever after?
When Yeats writes:

> But Love has pitched his mansion in
> The place of excrement

he has, in eleven words, isolated a bitter, unidealized, and absolute fact
about sexual love, the kind of carnal love that the Greeks called ἡ ἄτη,
delusion and madness, what love was understood to be by the Greeks, and
Romans as well, before its idealization as courtly love and its further trans-
mutation into romantic love, which concept still possesses our modern spirit. Yeats, in two lines, recovers 2500 years of pre-medieval Western thought
and, more importantly, allows us to see ourselves in its mirror. And when
Yeats writes:

> Locke sank into a swoon;
> The garden died;
> God took the spinning jenny
> Out of his side.

he encapsulates epigrammatically the cultural, ethical, moral, economic,
and sexual changes wrought by the industrial revolution on a society that
had no idea of how to cope with it. These poetic truths are carried to us by
metaphors, those sudden flashings into the light of what has hitherto been
hidden from our understanding. Poets know that metaphors are not literary
ornaments that give the poem a pleasing surface polish; they are the very
bones of the poem, ways of translating what is unknown or inchoate in the
poet's mind as it has absorbed the data of the world. St. Thomas says:

> Now these two—namely eternal and temporal—are related to our knowledge
> in this way, that one of them is the means of knowing the other. For in the
> order of discovery, we come through temporal things to the knowledge of things
> eternal, according to the words of the Apostle (*Rom.* 1.20): *The invisible things
> of God are clearly seen, being understood by the things that are made.*

And it is the metaphor that allows us to understand "the things that are
made." Our word comes from the Greek μεταφέρω, to carry from one place
to another, to transfer. And metaphors come, by and large, unbidden; they

are part and parcel of this mysterious creative act; they are, indeed, sometimes the entire creative act, for some sublime works of art are, in their entirety, metaphors.

Shelley has said that "the mind in creation is a fading coal, which some invisible influence, like an inconstant wind, awakens to transitory brightness." "Some invisible influence." Lest that be considered the purple effusion of an arch-Romantic, here is Wyndham Lewis, a writer whose devotion to classical principles of composition has perhaps no equal in this century: "If you say that creative art is a spell, a talisman, an incantation—that it is *magic*, in short, there, too, I believe you would be correctly describing it. That the artist uses and manipulates a supernatural power seems very likely." Despite the fact that Shelley says that the artist is used by, and that Lewis says that the artist uses, some outside power, both concur that the power is not, in fact, "theirs." All right: "some invisible influence"; "a supernatural power." We may recall Baudelaire's "grant me the grace," in which we hear him asking for the power to create. There are dozens of other comments by dozens of writers on the creative process—from Lorca's belief that the artist at the peak of his powers is possessed by a *duende*, a spirit, that permits him to make his art, to Eliot, at the opposite pole, who denies the existence of a friendly demon who presents the writer with the "gift" of a poem but concedes that the creative act is the lifting of "an intolerable burden" and that it is effortless. His figure is that of a bird who hatches an egg after a long period of incubation but doesn't know what kind of an egg it has been sitting on until the shell breaks. And in Kafka's *Diaries* we read, on his writing "The Judgment," "The fearful strain and joy, how the story developed before me, as if I were advancing over water." Andrew Marvell, in "The Garden," writes:

> The Mind, that Ocean where each kind
> Does streight its own resemblance find;
> Yet it creates, transcending these,
> Far other Worlds, and other Seas;
> Annihilating all that's made
> To a green Thought in a green Shade.

Yeats' "automatic writing" may also be adduced here, as well as Jack Spicer's reliance on what he called "dictation"; that is, that it is the poet's "outside" that is important, not his "inside," and that true poems issue from the former, unclouded by the opinionated ego.

I have gone on at some length about this process of creation in order to make clear my argument: that the process is sublime and that one of the writer's rationales for his vocation, if any rationale is needed, is the recapture, the re-experience of this sublime state. I don't agree with Eliot that creation is the shedding of an intolerable burden; or, I should say, that has not been my own experience. Rather, it has been, for me, a release from a rootless anxiety, the excursion into a state of exhilaration, of freedom, that is explicable neither in physical nor intellectual terms, since it is an uncanny blend of both the physical and the intellectual. It is as if one could think through and into corporeal pleasure, so that the mind might delight in what is rightly the body's province; or, conversely, as if the body could feel the pleasure that the mind takes in thought. It is a curious truth that when everything is going well, nothing is easier than writing. When nothing is going well one cannot write at all. In the first instance, one works, certainly, but one works almost flawlessly; in the second, the work is wearisome and frustrating and fruitless, the language that one thought so familiar and malleable becomes intractable and gluey. At best, one writes, at these times, "decent prose"—grammatically correct, syntactically rigorous, logically cohesive—and absolutely wooden. The work has everything but the one thing that all good writing must have—style. One might almost say that to fight the language is to court failure.

Excellence, stylistic excellence, is somehow achieved by that part of the mind that has nothing to do with thought, as we generally consider thought; nor is it done by that part of the mind that says "good morning," or "pass the butter," or "I love you." It is far removed from linear, or logical, thought and is done in a kind of trance or semitrance state, in which this dark corner of the mind performs quite independently. Proust has gone so far as to posit the idea of the writer as two distinct beings, when he writes:

> Any man who shares his skin with a man of genius has very little in common with the other inmate; yet it is he who is known by the genius's friends, so it is absurd to judge the poet by the man, or by the report of his friends. . . . As for the man himself, he is just a man and may perfectly well be unaware of the intention of the poet who lives in him. And perhaps it is best so.

Proust was speaking here of Saint-Beuve's denial of Baudelaire's genius because of his disapproval of the poet's scattered and wretched life. But the Baudelaire who whined and begged and pitied himself was a Baudelaire who had nothing to do with the poet who wrote *Les Fleurs du Mal*. That is one of the reasons why "À Une Heure du matin" is such a great poem, for in it we are privy to the first Baudelaire addressing God and asking Him to allow the second Baudelaire the grace to write; or, to put it more precisely, we see the poet recognize the fact that his poems come from some "other" part of him and are produced with the aid of some power which he does not normally possess.

I have said that the writer works in a kind of trance or semitrance. I don't really like these words, because they conjure up the image of the artist as a kind of idiot savant, a comfortable image for many people, since it reinforces their prejudice toward the artist as an overgrown child, still dabbling in fantasies. I think it is instructive that the word "fantasy" has taken on a totally different meaning from its roots, which are Greek. The noun, ἡ φαντασια, means *making visible*, from the verb φαντάζω, *to become visible, appear*, from the verb φαίνω, *to bring to light, make to appear*. We have, by denying the etymology of this word, tried to make the artist as discoverer or revealer into the artist as daydreamer. So, instead of using the words trance and semitrance, let's rather define this state as one in which the writer is possessed by the will to make, to the exclusion, during this act of making, of all other things. In a sense, he *becomes* the act itself. In this state, he does not so much invent as *find* what is already there, find, to return to Proust, the "intention of the poet who lives in him." Our word, "troubadour," is the French version of the Provençal "trobador," which means, precisely, "finder." In this state, this magic state, things that are unknown to the writer in his everyday life are *found*, the clearest example being the discovery of metaphors that will reveal to him what he does not know, that will express to him those things that are there, but there in darkness and obscurity. This state is surely what Shakespeare had in mind when he spoke of "the poet's eye in a fine frenzy rolling," if we understand "frenzy" to mean a state of temporary "insanity," and not, as the vulgar would have it, a description of The Crazy Artist, still one of the philistine's most cherished inventions, an invention that reinforces his belief that art, since it is produced by maniacs, who are also, let us remember, children, is not to be taken seriously, or not to be taken at all. To this point, it is interesting to note here that I've recently read of psychological studies that have found links between the voices heard by paranoid schizophrenics and the "voices" heard by writers in the act of composition. These latter are not necessarily "heard," but may be considered to be the power that effortlessly directs the writer's thought or that he directs. When he is not composing, he does not hear these "voices"; or, to paraphrase Jung on Joyce, the artist is different from the psychotic because he can will his return from the state in which the psychotic is helplessly trapped. We might say that the "everyday" man in whom the poet lives never enters that state, but the interior poet lives in it always, waiting to assert himself in the act of creation. It is to the point to remember that *Finnegans Wake* is in essence a world of voices, all of which continually and unpredictably shift into other voices; it is as if Joyce's interior voice has been consciously splintered in order to evoke and reveal a state divorced from what we think of as temporal reality. His methods, as he once said, in elaboration of criticism that called the *Wake* "trivial," are also "quadrivial," an absolute exploitation of the mind's detritus.

But how does this poet who "lives in" this otherwise very ordinary human

being select and order the materials used in the work? How does he go about
setting down on paper specific elements in specific ways?

Writers' minds are as full of trash as is the mind of anyone else; writers are
subject to the same weaknesses and temptations as anyone else; they are, as
is everyone else in the industrialized technocracy that the world has become,
bombarded daily by the same endless and disconnected data. How then,
does the writer, *writing*, work? What happens that permits him to select,
from all this jumble of garbage, the items that go to make his poem or work
of fiction? If he is lucky, information long lost, or partially remembered, or
completely forgotten by the "ordinary man," is held gingerly by the "other
man," the man inside, and released as it is needed. This release of data is
not neat and orderly; the process might be compared to working a jigsaw
puzzle which not only does not have an illustrative paradigm as guide, but
one in which the pieces themselves are continually changing shape.

While it is presumptuous to speak of how other writers compose, and
while it is well-nigh impossible to give a coherent account of how one composes oneself, I hope I may be forgiven if I end these remarks with a brief
account, one that is remembered as exactly and honestly as possible, of how
I composed part of a chapter of one of my books, *Splendide-Hôtel*. The chapter under discussion is the one titled "R." First of all, it is necessary to know
a little about this book: (1) It is an imaginative and critical foray into the
life of Arthur Rimbaud; (2) Rimbaud wrote a famous poem, "Voyelles," in
which he assigned colors to vowels; (3) my own favorite color is orange. I
quote the pertinent passages of the chapter:

> R is a beautiful letter, ultimately deriving from the Phoenician ꟼ, a tiny pen-
> nant. I will it to be an orange pennant, since orange is my favorite color.
>
> • • •
>
> R is a letter of enormous beauty. I take it to be orange. In the context of this
> work it stands for the poet's very name.
>
> • • •
>
> In 1876, the poet, the monarch of colors, sailed to Java. I imagine his slight
> smile as he discovered that the ship that would take him there was the *Prince
> of Orange*.

The tiny pennant, the Phoenician letter that has the exact shape of a
pennant, I have made into an orange pennant, since orange is a color, my
favorite color, that appears elsewhere in this book. Its assigned color allowed
me to partake of Rimbaud's invention of vowel colors by here giving a color
to a consonant. The "R," which is the title of the chapter, gave me the
occasion for permitting it to stand for Rimbaud's name, thereby weaving his
name into his color inventions, and, by extension, into my own, and, by
further extension, into my designation of him as "the monarch of colors."

If the poet may invent colors for vowels, why may he not invent colors for all letters? And if Rimbaud, my subject, did not invent all the colors, I, as his surrogate, invented at least one of them, this orange "R." At this point I stuck. The chapter needed closing, some paragraph or phrase or even sentence that would snap it shut as well as coherently incorporate the elements I had already composed. At this point the "poet inside," if you will, declared his intentions.

The orange pennant, each time it came to mind, presented itself as the sort of signal pennant flown from ships; I have no idea why. It may have been because of my recollection of the Phoenicians as mariners *par excellence*; it may have been because of my memory of the "Death by Water" section of "The Waste Land," in which maritime imagery and language are used for effect and whose figure is that of Phlebas the Phoenician. I submit these data in retrospect, as the reader of my own work; at the time, these shards and bits and pieces of information entered my mind willy-nilly, urging me, it now seems plausible, toward something of which I had no knowledge—or, let me say, toward something of which I had no inkling that I had had knowledge. Buried in the detritus of my mind was the dim recollection of something—but what?—something I had long ago read in a biography of Rimbaud, the celebrated study by Enid Starkie. Its information had settled in my conscious mind as a series of "major facts," but it was not "major facts" that the poet within needed. I was sent from my orange maritime pennant to Professor Starkie's biography to look for something that I was not sure existed; but that "something" was what the "other" Sorrentino knew all about. The poet within knew exactly what he was searching for; I was, as it were, his agent. And then, in Starkie, I read that Rimbaud "made his way to Holland where he enlisted in the Dutch army to go to Java. He signed on for a term of six years and was given a bonus of twelve pounds. He sailed on 10 June 1876, on board the Prince of Orange...." When I saw that sentence, my chapter had what it needed, my orange pennant, which was also an "R," which was also the sign for Rimbaud's name, now flew from this ship, the *Prince of Orange*, on which Rimbaud, the prince of colors, had sailed, taking with him my personal color.

I tell this story to point to the fact that I insisted on my orange pennant being a marine pennant and I went to Professor Starkie's book almost as if I had certain instructions to do so. In this act of composition, what I had forgotten was not forgotten by the writer who knew how to end the chapter. I was, very calmly and aloofly, manipulating, in some way I did not understand, some outside power, one that enabled me to find what I needed. The entire process was exhilarating, an instantaneous release from anxiety. What seemed to be unsayable became possible to say. Kafka writes: "How everything can be said, how for everything, for the strangest fancies, there waits a great fire in which they perish and rise up again." The chapter, as it now stands, written, exists for me as a memory of the act that made it. In a very real sense, a writer's finished work is, for him, a mnemonic device that allows him the recollection of its creation. The finished work is an artifact; and if it gives its maker pleasure to regard it, it is a cold pleasure.

Thomas Middleton writes, in his great tragedy, *The Changeling*:

> A cunning poet, catches a quantity
> Of every knowledge, yet brings all home
> Into one mystery, into one secret
> That he proceeds in.

The "mystery," the "secret that he proceeds in," is the essence of his vocation, made intense precisely because it is as much a mystery and secret to him as it is to anyone else. The artifact that emerges from this procedure attests to the latter's absolute reality but can never explain its workings.

The Review of Contemporary Fiction, 1981

2

William Carlos Williams

REFLECTIONS ON *Spring and All*

If modern poetry, or the new poetry, or the nonacademic poetry, is a return to the essential logic of the imagination (which is absolutely antithetical to the logic of the philosopher, or scientist), and if "one perception must immediately and directly lead to another perception"—as Olson says, then it all started, for American poetry at least—and I conceive of American poetry as that poetry which has most daringly junked the paraphernalia of "the beautiful," as conceived by aesthetes and professors—with the poems of *Spring and All*. To be sure, Pound invented his "new metaphor" and used it well in the Cantos written between 1920 and 1925, but I cannot think of Pound as an "American" poet in the same boat with Williams. The difference is slight, and perhaps impossible to explain; but to a born American, it is there. The savagery, the harshness, the open wounds displayed in *Spring and All*, not to mention the maintenance of the lyric voice, as against the voice heard in the *Cantos*, all set the two apart. Whereas Pound has been a teacher and an influence on a strictly tutelar, or abstract, level, Williams has forced his way into the minds of the poets who were his contemporaries, as well as those who are now young men, by virtue of his absolute rapport with all of us here, Americans. It is the voice of a brother as against that of an inspired evangelist.

So. We have the poems of *Spring and All* before us. Twenty-eight short lyrics, lanced through with light and space, they end in slammed doors, they cover the emotional range of a man intent on recording the mayhem of life in urban, despairing, profuse America of the twentieth century. Nowhere before them do we find such mastery of the gross, such triumphant willing-

13

ness to use the speech so kicked around the gutters. We have heard so many poems like them in the last forty years that we tend to forget what it must have cost, what a risk it must have been to write:

> No one
> to witness
> and adjust, no one to drive the car

The lines almost seem trite, they have been written thousands of times— by all of us who write. I am reminded of young men reading Hemingway for the first time and finding him wearisome and "old." And almost every prose we have developed here since him depends on, at least, the stories. Shaw, Salinger, Mailer, Capote, as well as Selby, Rumaker, and the other younger writers, not to mention the whole "school" of *The New Yorker*, have been deeply affected, either directly or indirectly, by at least "Hills Like White Elephants" and "A Clean, Well-lighted Place." So have the poets been affected by *Spring and All*. Men who have never read it echo its lines.

To me, the techniques employed in these poems start with a poem published three years before (1920) in *The Dial*, "Portrait of a Lady." Here, for the first time in Williams, we get the great opening up of the language, the huge leaps of thought, the daring ability to let the poem have its head. A formal logic is discarded, a gritty insistence on the poetic intrudes, makes the poem dance, explode:

> Your knees
> are a southern breeze—or
> a gust of snow. Agh! what
> sort of man was Fragonard?
> —as if that answered
> anything.
>   • • •
> Which shore?—
> the sand clings to my lips—
> Which shore?
> Agh, petals maybe. How
> should I know?
> Which shore? Which shore?
> I said petals from an appletree.

It seems amazing that the publication of that poem did not start the "revolution" of the new poetry immediately—certainly nothing like it had ever been seen in English before. But, as Williams himself has complained, Eliot had seized on the imaginations of the *avant-garde* with "Prufrock" in 1917.

By the time *Spring and All* was published (1923), the literary world was dancing in mock despair to the tune called by *The Waste Land* (1922) and "poetry was back in the classroom." Who wanted to bother with an obscure American who grappled with the problems of his own language, its cadences and barbarisms, when here was a twentieth-century Laforgue to tell everyone how miserable life is, in elegant verse that could be picked apart with the aid of the dictionary and several reference books? What could one do in a classroom or literary *soirée* with:

> And so it comes
> to motor cars—
> which is the son
>
> leaving off the g
> of sunlight and grass—
> Impossible
>
> to say, impossible
> to underestimate—
> wind, earthquakes in
>
> Manchuria, a
> partridge
> from dry leaves.

Poets were given the gift, the key, to a way *through*, a new voice, a method of composition to bridge the gap between the dull and the specious, and they turned instead to—crossword puzzles and literary anagrams. The most frustrating part of the whole matter perhaps, certainly the least explicable, is that American poetry continued on its dull course all through the twenties, thirties, and war years of the forties. It is not until we come to the early work of Olson and Duncan, and later, Creeley, that we find the energy of *Spring and All* made use of. At this very time, a reading of Lowell, Snodgrass, Booth, Kunitz, Eberhart, Wilbur, Dickey, Hall, Roethke, et al., convinces one that they have never ever glanced at the poems, let alone studied them. What is held in contempt by the "academics" as mere flash-in-the-pan poetry today, is, ironically enough, merely a return to, a pickup of, a valid and tough-shelled technique that lay dormant for more than twenty years. In Lowell's recent book, *Life Studies*, we see displayed a grudging and embarrassed handling of a "new" line, a "new" freedom. The reviews all praised or damned the book because of its trailblazing habiliments. Unfortunately, the book is made up of heavy-handed free verse which shows no aptitude whatsoever for the rhythms of American speech. Yet it was greeted as if nothing had happened in American verse since the publication of *Leaves of Grass*. And one constantly hears the wailings of those who are saddened by the fact that Robert Frost has never received the Nobel Prize—Robert Frost, whose relation to American letters lies in the fact that he sometimes throws the name of a New England state into his poems.

All right, then, to the poems. A careful examination reveals that in the twenty-eight poems there is only *one* use of simile, and that is in "To Elsie": yet even here it is a use of simile that is most valid, not one that takes two concrete things, confuses them, and comes up with a stew, e.g., "clouds like lambs." The simile *holds* to the visible, the real, the comparison strengthens the ultimate image, instead of dulling or diluting it:

> as if the earth under our feet
> were
> an excrement of some sky
>
> and we degraded prisoners
> destined
> to hunger until we eat filth

—the earth does turn to excrement within the lines, and we must eat it in our hunger. The other twenty-seven poems have absolutely no simile, they force their way through to the mind on the strength of absolute clarity. To be guilty of an old cliché, *they mean what they say*. The clean edges of the words glint against each other, the images are exact, the imagination is given its utmost play within the limits of a magnificent concern for form—those poems which seem obscure are so only to the reader who looks for a tract. To one who wishes to be hurled into the open freedom of a great poet's imagination, there can be no obscurity. That is not to say that all the poems can be "understood"—thank God. As poems they are trees that we come upon in the country—or, I remember the first time I ever saw a yak at the zoo. I had never seen such a thing before, but there it was! I didn't try to "understand" it. I *looked*.

Many of the poems are "narrative"—that is, they start at the beginning and move in a straight line to the end. While they are successful, those poems which most excite me are the ones in which the "narrative" line is broken inside the poem, a series of events and/or images is suddenly interrupted by the intrusion of some foreign element, and the poem quickens, the whole center seems to break open, we are confronted with an abyss into which our imaginations must descend.

                Nobody
to say it—
          Nobody to say: pinholes
Thither I would carry her

among the lights—

Burst it asunder
break through to the fifty words
necessary—

            a crown for her head with
castles upon it, skyscrapers
filled with nut-chocolates—
           • • •
Hate is of the night and the day
of flowers and rocks. Nothing
is gained by saying the night breeds
murder—It is the classical mistake

The day

All that enters in another person
all grass, all blackbirds flying
all azalea trees in flower
salt winds—

Sold to them men knock blindly together
splitting their heads open

—and at the bottom of the abyss, a new world of light.
    We are made to see all the world, "the universality of things," in a clutch
of poems that deal mainly with those mundane elements that lie directly in
front of the poet's eye as he walks or sits at his desk. The well-known "The
Red Wheelbarrow" *does* inscribe a world, and so much *does* depend on that
lonely image—all poems do, as does the life of the imagination. If you must
ask "what?," go back to Carl Sandburg. And similar minute worlds exist for
us in the smallest of things, a catch-all utility box, for example:

            What is the end
            to insects
            that suck gummed
            labels?

for this is eternity
through its
dial we discover
transparent tissue
on a spool

But the stars
are round
cardboard
with a tin edge

and a ring
to fasten them
to a trunk
for the vacation—

In the microcosmic world of the utility box, trunk tags glitter in a non-existent sky, but are driven inexorably, harshly back into the actual by the relentless honesty of the last two lines.

In "The Eyeglasses," the static picture on a candy wrapper becomes alive, the farmer is really there, his daughter is really there, the "small yellow cinquefoil" *grows*. It is all

for eyeglasses

to discover. But
they lie there with the gold
earpieces folded down

tranquilly Titicaca—

The poet risks it all on letting the eyeglasses *see* for him—and the risk succeeds.

So, for me, this remarkable book is the beginning of American poetry, *per se*. It is still rewarding, still stimulating, certainly an absolute necessity for anyone attempting either to read or write poetry today in the sixties. Although Williams went beyond this frontier of his own fashioning, it seems to me that here lies the very center of his work. His rhythms and metres are beginning, in these poems, to have the authority that we see full-blown in *Journey to Love*. As a matter of fact, the three-line stanzas of "To Elsie" and "The Eyeglasses" prefigure, in metrics, the "dropped" lines of the later poems.

In a note written four or five years ago on a poem published in 1934 ("Down-Town"), Williams says: "I liked the picture of a man riding the end of a girder because it is masculine, like the skill and audacity of masculine games. I expressed an equal audacity in writing something that could not be understood." It is this same audacity that has infused Williams' poems up to the present time, and which has given contemporary American poetry such a range of daring and vitality. Clearly, the poems of *Spring and All* display the first consistent application of this audacity.

Kulchur, 1962

The Collected Later Poems

New Directions has just brought out this revised edition of Williams' *The Collected Later Poems*, including the *Lost Poems* originally published in *New Directions 16*. Although all those familiar with the life work of Williams are also familiar with the lost poems included in this new edition, it seems that a small note is in order here, one at least celebrating these poems and the man who produced them.

Dr. Williams was a gentle and wise man, as well as a great poet, but he was not, assuredly, a sap. He was a deeply "natural" man, and by that I mean that he had all men's failings. His naturalness was innocent, but that innocence was not naiveté. We have been enjoined for so long to honor him as the simple, small-town physician—who also wrote simple, small-town poems—that we have tended to actually *think* of him as a primitive genius. He was about as primitive as the game of baseball, that is, not at all. His great glory and the contempt in which he was held for so many years are both dependent upon the fact that he just would not be a good fella and stay in the slot that the Untermeyers, the Eliots, and even the Pounds would have him in. He confounded the picture that had been carefully drawn by endless risks, by constant ventures into areas of literary endeavor that were not poetic. To all genres he brought freshness and brilliance. To dullards his poetic was (and is) "arbitrary." So be it. Its very "arbitrariness" has been the major force behind the contemporary American poetry which has redeemed the twenty years of academic merry-go-rounding which still characterizes the "official" poetry of our time. Above all things, he was a professional, he believed in work, he believed in curiosity, his strength is the strength of the people among whom he lived and worked—and I am not indulging in a populist mystique based on that overtaxed term, "the people."

This book shows him in every mood, beautiful, craftsmanlike, fierce. The domestic and artistic problems of his life were, truly, resolved in his poems; or, more importantly, if they were not resolved, the poems *say* so. He was a tough and knowing man, whose toughness never became meanness, and whose knowledge remained clear and without pomposity. He was, simply, a man in the turmoil of millions of other men and things; and he knew this to the very day he died.

The day he was buried began in a pouring, drenching rain. As we left the funeral parlor in Rutherford (those few of us, not his townspeople, who were to accompany him to his grave) the rain stopped, a fresh wind sprang up, and suddenly the dazzling sun of early spring broke out of the clouds. Louis Zukofsky looked up, smiled, and to no one in particular said, "It's Bill's day, after all." Reading this book will give you a slight idea of what Zukofsky meant.

Kulchur, 1963

"ART IS A COUNTRY BY ITSELF"

In a nine-year period, beginning with *Kora in Hell* in 1920 and ending with this—happily reissued—first novel, *A Voyage to Pagany* in 1928, Williams published six books, the other four being *Sour Grapes* (1921), *Spring and All* and *The Great American Novel* (1923), and *In the American Grain* (1925). With this decade's work, the artist all but single-handedly invented modern American literature. *A Voyage to Pagany* is, in a sense, a reprise of the bitter truths Williams came to embrace during these ten years. It is a beautiful novel, unorthodoxly impressionistic, written in that tough yet delicate prose of which Williams was always the master. Among the American novels published during the twenties, it has perhaps two peers—*The Great Gatsby* and *The Sun Also Rises*. Yet it received little or no attention; nor, for that matter, did its author, this greatest of American poets, receive much more until he was sixty.

America eats her artists alive. *A Voyage to Pagany* tells about the European sojourn of an obscure American writer, a Dr. Evans (Dev), who refuses Europe's blandishments and returns to his own barbarous country to live and work in almost complete obscurity. Williams made the same decision for himself, somehow drawing from the air and soil of his small New Jersey city the power to make a granite American art, one that would embody the isolated flashes of beauty scattered and dying in this numbed culture. That he succeeded in making this art has become blindingly clear, even, perhaps, to those who not too many years ago thought of this supreme writer as a "provincial" who "observed" small-town life. Provincial indeed! As provincial as Cézanne.

In *Paterson*, Book I, the poet writes of those American artists who expatriated themselves to Europe:

> a sort of springtime
> toward which their minds aspired
> but which he saw,
> within himself—ice bound

"Ice bound." In *A Voyage to Pagany*, Lou Martin, the woman who leaves Dev in order to marry a rich Englishman, says to him: "Dev, there's something the matter with you. You don't register. What in the world are you about? What does the world mean to you? You don't seem serious. You frighten me. Really, I don't understand you. I want someone I can understand. You are—You should protest more. You shouldn't lie there and take this. Why don't you do something about it? What is the matter with you?" And Dev replies: "To be young, to be gay, to be clever, and not to know where one is going, nor why, nor how? Very well. Less intoxicating is to go differently." The conversation is analogous to others he has in the book with his second lover, Grace Black, with his sister, Bess, with the German girl, "The Venus," he meets in Italy. They are bewildered by him, troubled, angry. There is in him something "fine" that should be allowed to flower—in Europe. Yet there is also that icy core that compels him to insist on returning to America, there to work out his art and his life. He loses all these women, even his sister, with whom he has a relationship bordering on the incestuous, when he decides to go back home: but home is—where? To his sister, drunkenly pleading with him to stay with her in Europe, in France, where the country has somehow a connection with "purity," a purity that can sustain him, he says: "Bess, you don't know what you are talking about. Art is a country by itself."

It was to this country—even in the midst of a life more "American" than most literary Americans could ever dream of living—that Williams exiled himself, working in almost total darkness, by trial and error, to hammer out an art that would express the vitality and vulgarity of the American experience. We see, after all these years, that it is to Williams we must go even to begin to understand just what has hit us. His work allows us to comprehend the decline, here, of the last seventy years. *A Voyage to Pagany* is everywhere dark with the knowledge of this decline and fatalistic concerning it—so that Dev's "country of Art" appears to be that place in which something can be kept clean, saved from the general decay. Yet it is only amid the decay that those "isolate flecks" are to be found upon which the imagination can seize to perceive the reality of America.

Williams' vision is essentially bleak and tragic—not anything so fashionable as pessimistic. Here is America, the artist says. Let us investigate it and see what it is. It is dead. What has it done to its people? They are ruined. Who besides Williams, in the context of the twenties, would say: "The pure products of America go crazy"? He did not mean silly or zany or "freaky"— he meant insane. "As if the earth under our feet were an excrement of some sky," the poet says, "and we degraded prisoners destined to hunger until we eat filth." Yet this writer is continually referred to as "warm"; his brilliant work with a variable measure thought of as "confused"; until ten years ago he was often spoken of as a "primitive"—a kind of literary Grandma Moses;

a critic has recently written of his "child-stance"; others safely tuck him away as a "chronicler" of industrially blighted north Jersey.

I submit that we cannot really face him, for the tragedy he presents to us is the tragedy of our own lives, unique and specific. The corruption of New Jersey's industrial cities is an effect of the ineradicable sickness in America's soul. We must call the poet's terrible clarity provincial or regional to save ourselves from its devastating power. His work is specific—and how can we Americans face that, who are such saps for the grand statement, the allegory, the symbolic gesture, the "truth that lies beneath the surface"? There is nothing but surface, over which the imagination plays: and the master of the imagination is the artist. So that what Williams says must be repugnant to us. Religion is dead, as are politics, business, philosophy—all the gods we serve. Only the imagination can save us by allowing us to see, momentarily, the truth. We see it best when it is embodied in art; therefore, trust the artist. No good American can accept that hilarity. Art, we all know, is irrelevant. So we persist in our "changing" and "reforming" and "bettering"—while drowning in bitterness, our hearts cold.

"Art is a country by itself." Indeed. Which many leave, and others plunder. It is a "backward country." So Williams, and Dev, returned to it. This novel serves as the base upon which the artist built for the next thirty-five years. The naturalism of the "Stecher trilogy"—that supreme investigation of success—as well as the genius of "Asphodel, That Greeny Flower" rest on its structure, and *Paterson* is its ultimate reason for being. Nothing is irrelevant to its texture; chance encounters and fragmentary scenes set the tone of the book; beyond impressionism, realism, and narrative, it "places" itself as a remarkable modern work. It is not a great novel, but one of the many pieces that go to make up the great art of this master.

The Nation, 1970

THE VARIOUS ISOLATED: WILLIAM CARLOS WILLIAMS' PROSE

In many poor and sentimental households it is a custom to have cheap prints in glass frames upon the walls. These are of all sorts and many sizes and may be found in any room from the kitchen to the toilet. The drawing is always of the worst and the colors, not gaudy but almost always of faint indeterminate tints, are infirm. Yet a delicate accuracy exists between these prints and the environment which breeds them. But as if to intensify this relationship words are added. There will be a "senti-

ment" as it is called, a rhyme, which the picture
illuminates. Many of these pertain to love. This is
well enough when the bed is new and the young
couple spend the long winter nights there in delightful seclusion. But childbirth follows in its time
and a motto still hangs above the bed. It is only
then that the full ironical meaning of these prints
leaves the paper and the frame and starting through
the glass takes undisputed sway over the household.

Kora in Hell (1920)

William Carlos Williams' neglected "Stecher trilogy"—*White Mule, In the
Money*, and *The Build-Up*—is the best fictional treatment of the immigrant
"success story" that we have in American letters. Its power, its secret power,
one might almost say, lies in its ability to release the absolute meaning of
cultural and financial success in the context of a narrative that is neither
comic, tragic, nor satiric. This is no small thing, for the detailing of the
failures of the American dream has always demanded, so it seems, a kind of
educated and knowledgeable *comment* on the part of the American novelist,
lest he seem to be taken in, duped by what appears to be contentment or
happiness. So at first glance, or with an eye too used to the patterned assaults
upon this success story, the Williams trilogy looks simple, trusting, innocent—almost naive. "The lovely and uncomplicated past," one might say.
We may even take it to be an exercise in nostalgia, to our utter confusion.

Of the writers of Williams' generation (and one may also include most of
those who came just after it) whose work is purely American, by which I
mean that they wrote of Americans in America, Williams is the sole figure
whose work speaks to us with ruthless and persistent clarity, and with a
vision of American life which becomes more intense as the years pass and
we see what we have come to. This quality is partially achieved by his absolute willingness to forgo "sophisticated" effects in order to discover the
essential qualities of the most obscure events; in other words, in his willingness to appear "simple." His entire body of work is a record of continual
observation, of the revelation of what he calls the "isolate flecks" in which
the whole meaning of a life, or of a cultural milieu, may be contained. Somehow, during almost forty years of the most preposterous ignorance of his
fiction on the part of the critical establishment, he captured, by dint of
perseverance and his own wide-ranging imagination, the meaning of the
shapelessness of American life, buried, as it has always been, in the pettiness
of our daily routine, and the "famous," hollow triumphs that speckle it.

His sensibility was so acutely against the grain that his work, to this day,
is almost unfathomable to many literary people who have been raised in
what has been called the "international tradition" in letters. He does not fit,

he is a maverick, his compositions bulk uncomfortably in the landscape of the classical moderns and almost seem to refute them. Nothing fooled him for long because he refused to let "ideas" govern his work. He is sprawling, confused, unfinished, and at the same time brilliant, succinct, crafted— and unfailingly, unerringly dark. Not dark with the tragic, but with the endless defeats of life and—nonetheless—its tenacity. Without sentiment about God, politics, love, the working man, nature, the family, marriage, or children, he is yet uncynical. People are born and live in recurrent confusion; the overwhelming majority of their days is wholly without meaning. In America, this happens in a specific way, a way which makes us specifically American. The imagination, only the imagination, Williams says, will free us from the waste and despair that America has hidden under its continual smile. It is the flight, or the heartbreaking attempt at flight, of the imagination that he seeks to pin down and isolate in all his work.

In the "Stecher trilogy," Joe, the husband, a craftsman printer whose major interest in life is honest work well done, becomes a rich man, largely through the goading of his wife, Gurlie. Ironically, it is his stubborn artisan's honesty that shapes his success in the corrupted, get-rich-quick business world in which he is forced to move. Thwarted in his desire as a young man in Germany to attend a university, he is disgusted by the admiration that merely earning big money garners in the United States. Joe knows who he is, and stays that way, battling off as best he can Gurlie's constant prodding to be "fancy." Yet at the end of the trilogy, with his older daughter run off with a hopeless, charming painter, his younger daughter married to a young doctor who has married her even though he does not love her, his son dead in a shotgun accident, and his social life in a kind of limbo because of his anti-British stand on the war, Joe builds the mansion that Gurlie has always wanted. What else is there? The excavators run into granite as they begin digging the foundation, and Joe says, at the end of *The Build-Up*, "No matter. Blast! Blast it out! Blow the damned rock to hell and gone. We're going to have a house like nothing in the neighborhood. Like nothing, like nothing in the neighborhood. Expense be damned." Joe, of course, cares nothing about the house, has never cared about it, nor about the expense. The house is the secretion, one might say, of Joe's trapped imagination. Bewildered in his misery, he seeks a place where that misery might go, since there is no place else for it to find relief but in something that he can afford—out of the wealth he does not care for and cannot really understand.

"The imagination will not down," Williams writes in 1923 in *The Great American Novel*. "If it is not a dance, a song, it becomes an outcry, a protest. If it is not flamboyance it becomes deformity; if it is not art, it becomes crime." Joe Stecher is only one of the characters of the trilogy demeaned and emptied by the tyranny of "reality."

Where does the artist go to find these bastards of the thwarted imagination? He goes down the street, or around the corner. He takes a ride in his car.

The fact that Williams had everything under his eye, that his laboratory was something so uneventful and banal as the American small town, gave rise to the critical dullness that has always thought of him as a primitive, or a *naïf*, or an "experimental" writer, i.e., one not to be taken seriously, as in "Robert Duncan is an experimental poet." Or, more charitably perhaps, but no less foolishly, as an Eastern Sherwood Anderson. But Williams was a great artist whose creative powers neither flagged nor became ancillary to shifting fads. As *Paterson* is the culmination of his poetic genius, so the "Stecher trilogy" is that genius's most thorough prose expression.

Novels are cluttered with all kinds of signals, flashing and gesturing so that the author may direct our attention to a particular configuration of character or plot in order that his work, such as it is, may be made simpler for him, and for us. One thinks of the work of John Cheever, Capote, Norman Mailer, and the master of the technique, John O'Hara, whose characters are presented for inspection and understanding in terms of their very luggage or the brand of cigarettes they smoke. Indeed, in an O'Hara story, "Exactly Eight Thousand Dollars Exactly," these signals are manipulated in reverse, so that the character with whom we expect to be in sympathy turns out to be the heavy. I like to think of this as a writer's joke, or perhaps as an indication of O'Hara's awareness of his own progressive decline as an imaginative writer. Such signals assure us that we are here, oh yes, in the world that we understand; what we "understand" are the signals. When the signals are crassly or obviously used, we are given the popular novel, or the Western or mystery; when deeply or subtly placed, it is a good bet that we are in the presence of the well-crafted, talented, and often slick novel; if the signals are all, they become symbols: we think we are learning something, we are seeing "beneath the surface" of things, but we are seeing nothing at all. Symbols function secondarily: if a work has no power on a primary, nonsymbolic level, the most assiduously laid-on symbolism will not rescue it from the inert.

Readers are so passive before this assault of the conventional that they often look for these signals: when they are not there, they feel abandoned, they feel that the work is difficult, or gauche—they feel, perhaps, betrayed. At such times the novel is often forced to yield up that which it does not possess. Those novels that have no symbols at all, nor that can be squeezed to release a few, critics have misnamed "naturalistic" or "realistic" novels.

But signals are gimmicks, elements of craftsmanship, or the lack of it. They allow the writer to slip out from under the problems that only confrontation with his materials can solve. Novels are made of words. The difficulty in writing fiction is that the words must be composed so that they reveal the absolute reality of their prey, their subject—and at the same time, they must be in themselves real; i.e., they do not have to stand for a specific meaning. Here, one may think of Wittgenstein's "Man possesses the capacity of constructing language, in which every sense can be expressed, without having an idea how and what each word means." In *A Novelette*, Williams suggests that even conversation in fiction can be so composed as to remove itself from what characters are "saying." He writes, "The solidity of the pure lends itself by pure design. . . . That would be a writing in which the conversation was actual to the extent that it would be pure design." And further on, he says, "To be a conversation, it must have only the effect of itself, not on him to whom it has a special meaning but as a dog or a store window." (It is, incidentally, this conception of conversation that gives to Williams' characters, in the trilogy, the curious flatness of speech that is often mistaken for accurate transcription—which it is not.)

The words must also have, in their composition, a texture and design we call style. The novel must exist outside of the life it deals with; it is not an imitation. The novel is an invention, something that is made; it is not the expression of "self"; it does not mirror reality. If it is any good at all it mirrors the processes of the real, but, being selective, makes a form that allows us to see these processes with clarity. Signals in novels obscure the actual— these signals are disguised as conversation, physiognomy, clothing, accouterments, possessions, social graces—they satisfy the desire that we be told what we already know, they enable the writer to manipulate his book so that it seems as if life really has form and meaning, while it is, of course, the writer who has given it these qualities. It is the novel, of itself, that must have form; and if it be honestly made we find, not the meaning of life, but a revelation of its actuality. We are not told what to think, but are instead directed to an essence, the observation of which leads to the freeing of our own imagination and to our arrival at the only "truth" that fiction possesses. The flash, the instant or cluster of meaning must be extrapolated from "the pageless actual" and presented in its imaginative qualities. The achievement of this makes a novel which is art: the rest is pastime.

The novel we think of when we hear "this is a real novel" is filled with people, weather, places, and conversation that we recognize instantly— from other "real novels." We all know that plump, perspiring woman who chews gum, the failing ad man with the shakes in the bar at three in the afternoon, the lonely girl from the Midwest who lives down the hall and who befriends the super. Will any of these people do what we do not expect them to do, save as "irony" or surprise? Will they move the story naturally? Are they anything more than the characters we know from movies, instantly recognizable? Their very attitudes are as frozen as the faces of actors playing character roles.

Williams points out, in a lecture touching on *The Sheltering Sky*, the finely wrought art by which Bowles allows a woman on a train to be stripped naked by a man whom she despises. Her disrobing, and subsequent seduction, are brought about by a series of the most delicately crafted events. It could have been easier, certainly, had Bowles used the "exotic-night-in-Africa" signal; but he shapes a situation that is not what one might expect from the scene presented. In keeping with the tone of his novel, she must not *simply* be seduced; her seduction must anticipate the despair and madness bearing down on her. A dozen writers, more highly praised than Bowles, would have simply got her out of her clothes by means of one signal or another; but this artist does not lead his imagination, he allows it its head. The invented character can only reveal the actual if he is the creature of the novelist's *invention*, not a signal whom we stupidly think is doing something "believable."

There seems to be no established critical apparatus to deal with this "signal-less" American novel. Not even after all these years. We are lost in a sea of manners, or blinded into thinking that "characters" are characters. Hubert Selby speaks of the value of "true people as opposed to the blatant REAL people" in certain fiction—that latter in which we read dialogue as accurate as a tape recording, i.e., false dialogue. They do, these "REAL people," believable things in terms of the novel's development. Are we all mad? Fifty years after Joyce and Lewis, Williams and Ford, we search for "flesh and blood" characters who "walk off the page." Somehow we wish the novel to be a reflection of the world that the news tells us is true. The "facts" are paramount, the imagination is trapped, thwarted, unrelieved, until it must find its release, finally, in trash, or in Anglo-European fiction that lulls us into thinking that it is addressed to us—who have no traditions, and whose best art has always appeared in staggered and lonely configurations that seem insane or deformed.

Doomed as are so many novels to chic caricature, awash with signals and creaking symbolism, filled with accurate conversation, real people, or the pop-art situations and characters that substitute for the imagination in the swill of black humor, what attention can be paid to novels that eschew these conventions? What happens to that writer whose imagination composes not the pseudo-reality, but those facets of reality that bring what we do not know—or do not wish to know—about ourselves into the light? Charles Olson, in his essay "Billy the Kid," defines "misery" as no more than "a characterization of unrelieved action or words" and goes on to say that the history of the United States has stayed, and stays, unrelieved. "And thus loses what it was before it damn well was history, what urgency or laziness or misery it was to those who said and did what they did." He also says: "All we got is what the best men have kept their eye on. No figures, no forms, no known largenesses whatsoever. Zero." Thirty years earlier, in *The Great American Novel*, Williams was saying:

> America is a mass of pulp, a jelly, a sensitive plate ready to take whatever print you want to put on it—We have no art, no manners, no intellect—we have nothing. We water at the eyes at our own stupidity. We have only mass movement like a sea. . . . Ugliness is a horror to me but it is less abhorrent than to be like you [Europe] in the most remote, the most minute particular. For the moment I hate you, I hate your orchestras, your libraries, your sciences, your yearly salons, your finely tuned intelligences of all sorts. My intelligence is as finely tuned as yours but it lives in hell. . . .

It is this unrelieved quality in American life that the best American fiction does, indeed, relieve. It occurs, it is surely clear, in few novels, and these often berated, misjudged, or ignored, e.g., Edward Dahlberg's *Bottom Dogs*, William Eastlake's *The Bronc People*, Paul Goodman's *The Grand Piano*, Douglas Woolf's *Wall to Wall*, Robert Creeley's *The Island*, John Hawkes' *The Beetle Leg*, and Paul Bowles' *The Sheltering Sky*. Williams, in his *Autobiography*, speaks of "the inarticulate patient" who "struggles to lay himself bare for you, or with nothing more than a boil on his back is so caught off balance that he reveals some secret twist of a whole community's pathetic way of thought. . . ." The "Stecher trilogy" is a work of fiction that catches, off balance, by the most precise and deliberate accrual of those "isolate flecks," an entire American family over a twenty-year span, revealing it as well as the particularly American world in which it at once prospers and is subtly defeated.

The prose of the "Stecher trilogy" seems remote from that in Williams' earlier imaginative prose works, *Kora in Hell*, *Spring and All*, *The Great American Novel*, *The Descent of Winter*, and *A Novelette*, all of which are almost gorgeous in their marshaling of expressionist and surrealist prose techniques taken from modern French literature. The same contrast may be noted in the verse, the earlier being packed and convoluted and microcosmically metaphoric, and the latter, as in *Journey to Love*, having the complete mastery of statement which can dispose of all trope and convention, and register the subtlest nuances effortlessly, and in language so "plain" as to defy analysis as to the magic of its power.

It was Williams who first signaled the death of imagism, who broke the ground for the discarding of simile and contrast, who insisted on a verse that would be neither qualitatively measurable nor "free." Contemporary American poetry—I mean the kind that has added an integer or facet to the poetic process, not the kind that scholar-critics like to call "major poetry"—has, as everyone knows, moved away from the image at bewildering speed and has completely done away with simile; even metaphor has become a manifestation of the whole structure of the poem, not one of the components of the engine that makes it go. Jack Spicer, I would say, has shown us most clearly how this poem may be made to work; but it was Williams who wrote the poems from which Spicer proceeded, his "Portrait of a Lady," written in 1920, signaling a whole new methodology in the writing of American verse. It was Williams who demonstrated that if one writes the word "glass" or "sky" or "rose," one has made an "image." Until this, and its formal ramifications, are understood, nothing written about current nonacademic American poetry will be clear or even worth attending.

It was the long period of trial and error in the composition of his verse that brought to Williams his prose style, a style that, in the "Stecher trilogy," defies mining; i.e., there is *nothing* beneath the surface of the words. Williams specifically applied himself to the composition of a prose that functions only as paint functions in a canvas. A conventional narrative is also avoided, so that one has not even a progression of events to deal with; there are no climaxes, no denouement, no tragedy. What does *White Mule* mean? Read it. The signals are missing. The young Stecher family, Joe, Gurlie, Lottie, and the newborn Flossie, does things that cry out for "treatment": at the beginning of the novel, Lottie, when shown her baby sister for the first time, says, "the nasty thing," and slaps her with all her strength in the face. What does this mean about Lottie and the relationship she will have with her sister? Is it possible that Williams will not *use* it to construct a tale of sibling rivalry that can extend throughout the trilogy? He does not. Then it must simply be a "slice of life," a hunk of good old realism from the provincial doctor. What this slap does is show us a facet of Lottie's *mother*, Gurlie. This is done without comment; look for yourself.

It is a flash of the actual. Coupled with many others, it makes the novel. This is Flossie's book; with her birth the Stecher family begins its move toward success and its attendant and almost inarticulate loss, its ordered move, one might say, toward order: underneath which there is the subtlest aroma of sadness and meaninglessness. But never, never tragedy. There is no tragedy in America; there is only that state described by the American phrase "washed up." The nearest we get to tragedy is the situation so precisely limned in *The Great Gatsby*, which, if it be tragic, is so in the most picayune sense, lacking nobility and grace, and founded on the triple American flaws of greed, carelessness, and romantic nostalgia.

We are dull and torpid and because of this look for writers to tell us that these states are tragic, romantically heroic, that our lives are *gloriously* blasted from the start, that our defeats *mean* something, i.e., in some transcendental way. We adore losing the way that Frank Sinatra loses in his songs, but we cannot stomach the loss that Williams speaks of. Our representative fiction is romantic because the natural state of American life is featurelessness; we must give it a face—any face. Who is our ranking official great novelist? Mailer, of course, who else can it be?—a writer who has never written a first-class novel, a man who cannot refrain (he is a supreme Romantic) from putting a coat of paint on everything he sees, so that his America is unrecognizable to anyone who has walked the street. His imagination functions in a world of ideas, which may be why the novel has become almost impossible for him to write—witness his last two attempts. In his novels, tragedy is sexual violence, his heroes lose, and in losing they win—something. The Medal of Romantic Wisdom, perhaps.

But American life is not tragic, it is dull; its losses are almost silent, inexpressible, obscure. Williams tells us this and tells us with such persistence that we cannot stand him. We will not stand him. The imagination, only the imagination, can release us from despair? Who will believe it? We need signals; evil must be given a face or else we will be forced to accept the fact that it has no face, that our corruption is diluted so thoroughly that we all have a little in us, like strontium-90.

Gurlie is a willful woman who nags her husband, Joe, into success because she wants to be rich. What else is America good for? she says. What else, indeed? She succeeds, and by the end of the trilogy, in *The Build-Up*, Joe does not even offer her token resistance. Gurlie is a "bitch," the upwardly mobile, conniving, and mindless wife who pushes her sensitive husband until he is, indeed, rich. So there is your American novel—or is it? What has Williams done with it? Where are those signals we look for when we meet the fictional bitch? They grow old together, they have even been *happy* together. The novel makes no sense! It has no plot! What are we to do with this woman who has tricked us? Nothing happens, nothing *really* happens! It is not even an attack on the middle class, it is—nothing. Under the words there is nothing. It is American success as it is, without tragedy, grace, or understanding.

> as if the earth under our feet
> were
> an excrement of some sky
>
> and we degraded prisoners
> destined
> to hunger until we eat filth
>
> while the imagination strains
> after deer
> going by fields of goldenrod in

the stifling heat of September
Somehow
it seems to destroy us

—Williams says, in "To Elsie." And ends this great lyric:

no one
to witness
and adjust, no one to drive the car

Except for the artist and his relentless and despised imagination.

In *White Mule*, published in 1937, in the midst of a deluge of socially relevant fiction perhaps unmatched for sentimentality and bathos until our own
time, Williams chronicles, as I have said, the first year of life of the baby,
Flossie Stecher, and her parents' initial move toward success: a curiously
detached thing to be doing at a time when more admired and certainly more
famous writers were contributing to the building of the brave new society in
which we are, of course, now living. We read these writers now with the
same curiosity with which we read back issues of popular magazines of the
time; they are more remote from us than are Baudelaire or Sterne. (Some of
Williams' peers—equally detached—have by now earned their deserved
praise: West, Fitzgerald, Djuna Barnes, et al. But Williams' fiction is still
largely unknown.) He might well have been better employed at slicing up
some life for us, or making us indignant; he did neither. What he did do, we
can now see, was to show us where the thirties came from (and the sixties
and seventies as well), and why. The novels take us up to the First World
War, and the Stechers' triumph—and defeat. They are bewildered as to the
hidden nature of their defeat; they really do not know that they have been
defeated.

It is this inarticulateness, this bewilderment in the face of success that has
always been so specifically American, so that novels that detail the journey
"from rags to riches" must need be, so it seems, novels that have a dimension
that we can grasp: the loss and the destruction inherent in American success
must be made manifest in tragedy or protest, polemic or satire, so that we
may trace the figure of decline. Williams chose a way to trace this decline
that has made him, I believe, almost wholly misunderstood. He came to see
that despair and defeat are indigenous and that for us, the tragic is exotic.
There was no language for the revelation of that strange mélange of prosperity and bitterness that Williams found in his own small-town life, and it
was this search for a language fit to express it that dictated the composition
of his trilogy.

As I have suggested, the "theme" of almost all serious American fiction
of the past forty years is romantic loss. Let me go further and say that this

loss is almost always redeemed because we insist on imputing to the losers
the knowledge of their own heroic pathos. From Jake Barnes to Stephen
Rojack, we see the heroic pattern clear. But what can we do with that rarest
American fiction that details the defeat that is neither "principled" nor even
understood to *be* defeat? How, even, is such fiction written? It is still a novelist's problem; in Williams' time, it was the problem entire, since the "little
man" in much of the fiction contemporaneous with his own was a sentimental figure understandable only as a victim of abstract powers of government,
business, prejudice, politics, destiny, etc. Williams had no relation to those
writers whose characters are manipulated by "history," nor was he in any
way akin to those who offered figures whose ostensible success masked ravaged psyches. He was interested in the successful character, the "nice guy"
whose life was, on the whole, placid and stable, and whose imaginative life
was atrophied or dead. He insisted on revealing defeat not in the guise of
success, but as an inextricable part of it—and hence, totally obscured. His
novels are barely plotted, his characters flat and ordinary, the destruction of
their hopes a whisper. These things were all necessary to the realization of
his intent, and he had no models.

His problem was not that the patterns of American life were unobser-
vable, but that a language had to be found to express them, an American
language. Williams' well-known attack upon Eliot is understandable only if
we know that he refused, not his gifts, but his Europeanized mind; it was
this belief in a native art that makes clear what he meant when he wrote,
"Your attention is called now and then to some beautiful line or sonnet
sequence because of what is said there. So be it. To me all sonnets say the
same thing of no importance"; we see what he meant when he said that this
American language came from "the mouths of Polish mothers." The dumb
quality of our malaise had to be given a voice, a "redeeming language" had
to be found that would enable an American to discover, in literature, the
"secret twist" that reveals a community.

It may well be that the waste and violence and loss in American life is
partially accounted for by the fact that we cannot assuage our miseries, no
matter the floods of "hard information" daily tendered us. We know everything, and nothing. We are wild in our dullness, our inability to *do* anything
in the face of this endless stream of news that irritates us without respite.
We look for our relief in the products of the imagination, but we have no
heroes except the romantic losers. When that "secret spring of all our lives"
is tapped, as it is in Williams' trilogy, it is difficult for us to accept it, since
it is difficult for us to accept the truth that our lives make a pattern no more
meaningful than its own shape. "No figures, no forms, no known largenesses
whatsoever. Zero."

The "Stecher trilogy" shows us that a family can be defeated in its success
and still have a reasonably contented life; at the same time, the Stecher

family is revelatory of that larger suburban community that has, in recent years, become an American cliché. Williams explored it when it was in its infancy, and explored it without moralizing, without a point of view, except that, exactly: a point of *view*. Williams sees, and his observation is carried over to us by his voice, an American voice, emerging from a characteristically staid and placid hell, but one in which we are all, nevertheless, burning.

Louis Zukofsky, writing in 1930 of Williams' early collections of poems, notes that "there are poems that will stay though many lines are invalidated by his [Williams'] subsequent criticism. It is salutary that these lines may be omitted and still leave a number of structures. The process of rehabilitating the good to its rightful structure is always possible with writing in which something was seen, a quantity heard, an emotion apprehended to begin with." And Williams, writing in *Kora in Hell*, says: "Often a poem will have merit because of some one line or even one meritorious word. So it hangs heavily on its stem but still secure, the tree unwilling to release it."

It is helpful to bear these comments in mind when reading the "Stecher trilogy," or, for that matter, any of Williams' work, for he was a hurried man, an overworked doctor with a wife and family, who wrote almost continually, in his office, at home, on pads in his car while going from one patient to another. There is much in his work that can be "invalidated" by his own "subsequent criticism": his alternative to writing in this fashion was not to write at all. It was the necessity to write within the harshly defined limits of his own life that somehow drove his style through the tangle of accepted niceties and made it immediate; it was this reliance on the actual, on the power of sight as against "intellect"—his works written in white heat and polished later—that has made so many people speak of him as an imagist. But the "images" are *actual*, redeemed by the careful composition of the words so that they are not "literary"; and they are not photographic.

> By the road to the contagious hospital
> under the surge of the blue
> mottled clouds driven from the
> northeast. . . .

Those lines betoken the demise of imagism.

To catch the whole of his world on the wing, to be its sensory apparatus, and then to compose these impressions so that they would stand free, each to itself, remote, remote from the search for the image that is addition, and *not* what he wanted. He wanted total clarification, a language to catch and hold fast the flat surfaces of the life that surrounded him daily. "That which had been impossible for him at first had become possible. Everything had been removed that other men had tied to the words to secure them to themselves. Clean, clean, he had taken each word and made it new for himself so that at last it was new, free from the world for himself. . . ." Williams wrote that in *The Great American Novel*. Free from the banal, the formulated, all signals discarded, the "Stecher trilogy" justifies this early note—"everything . . . removed that other men had tied to the words. . . ."

POSTSCRIPT

As far as the writing itself is concerned it takes next to no time at all. Much too much is written every day of our lives. We are overwhelmed by it. But when at times we see through the welter of evasive or interested patter, when by chance we penetrate to some moving detail of a life, there is always time to bang out a few pages. The thing isn't to find the time for it—we waste hours every day doing absolutely nothing at all—the difficulty is to catch the evasive life of the thing, to phrase the words in such a way that stereotype will yield a moment of insight. That is where the difficulty lies. We are lucky when that underground current can be tapped and the secret spring of all our lives will send up its pure water. It seldom happens. A thousand trivialities push themselves to the front, our lying habits of everyday speech and thought are foremost, telling us that *that* is what "they" want to hear. Tell them something else.

The Autobiography of William Carlos Williams

No outside program has influenced his social awareness. It is the product of the singular creature living in society and expressing in spite of the numb terror around him the awareness which after a while cannot help but be general. It is the living creature becoming conscious of his own needs through the destruction of the various isolated around him, and till his day comes continuing unwitnessed to work, no one but himself to drive the car through the suburbs, till they too become conscious of demands unsatisfied by the routine senseless repetition of events.

Louis Zukofsky (1930)

New American Review, 1972

AMERICA, AMERICA

William Carlos Williams: The Knack of Survival in America.
By Robert Coles

. . . observation about us engenders the very opposite of what we seek: triviality, crassness and intellectual bankruptcy. And yet what we do see can

in no way be excluded. Satire and flight are two
possibilities. . . . But if one remain in a place and
reject satire, what then? To be democratic, local
(in the sense of being attached with integrity to
actual experience) [we] must for subtlety ascend to
a place of almost abstract design to keep alive. To
writing, then, as an art in itself. Yet what actually
impinges on the senses must be rendered as it appears, by use of which, only, and under which, untouched, the significance has to be disclosed.

"The Work of Gertrude Stein"

Robert Coles is not a trained literary critic or scholar by vocation or avoca-
tion. It may be this salutary amateurism that has enabled him to write such
a clear, intelligent book on Williams' fiction. Certainly, there has been a
quickening in the number of critical articles and books on Williams since
his death, but Mr. Coles' book is a ray of light among them. This spate of
critical attention on the part of the university cannot conceal the fact that
it was not too many years ago that scholars—Americans among them—
were heeding such drivel as:

> He has renounced all the pleasures of the English language, so that he is com-
> pletely American; and he says only the dullest things, so he has won the terrible
> fight to become completely democratic as well.

William Empson wrote that. Is it the Voice from the Crypt, or a remark by
a character in *Zuleika Dobson*? The implication that one writes badly if one
is "completely American" is typical of a petrified intelligence that was at
one time epidemic throughout academe—and note the phrase "says only
the dullest things." After Williams spent over fifty years trying to show us
all that what literature "says" is unimportant, is secondary, trivial. What
work of Williams, in God's name, could Empson have read? When I was in
college in 1950, a professor told me that Williams was one of the "younger
Imagists." At the time he was sixty-seven and had published thirty-one
books.

   Well, times change, and scholars have belatedly begun to attempt a critical understanding of this writer—there is at least displayed the awakening
of curiosity among the tribe. It is encouraging. Some have done outstanding
work: Kenner, Sister Bernetta, Louis Martz—there are a few others. But
most seem to have taken their bearings from Randall Jarrell, who presents
Williams as a notable curiosity, all heart, inspiration, and beer at the ball
game, or from Edmund Wilson, from whom—silence. By and large, critics

of Williams are forever rummaging "between the lines" in a search for "meaning." Between Williams' lines there is nothing but space. All of his work has suffered from this sort of poverty of approach, but none more so than the fiction, particularly the "Stecher trilogy," *White Mule, In the Money,* and *The Build-Up.* Delightfully, it is to this trilogy that Coles addresses the greater portion of his book. Wonderfully free of cant and hot air, Coles' study is a model of intelligent criticism, trusting completely the surface of Williams' work, his words.

I have written elsewhere that the "Stecher trilogy" is the best treatment of the immigrant success story in American letters, and I'm happy to see that in this opinion I have Mr. Coles as an ally. What is most heartening about Coles' study is that he has seen the work as a whole—he has not concentrated on the virtuoso performance given us in *White Mule.* To be sure, that book is an awesome description of the first years of life of the baby, Floss; but it shows, more importantly, the beginning of the striving toward success of the Stecher family, success bought at the cost of a desolation so subtle as to be hardly graspable. It is Williams' triumph that he saw what success in America means, and to Coles' credit that he sees, with fine precision, Williams' painstaking attention to and accretion of details that make us realize finally that for the Stechers success is an alloy mixed of financial security, loss, destruction, and a nameless anomie, a desolation. Coles says:

> Williams was saying in his trilogy that no one can . . . ignore or forget the social and economic circumstances they face and once faced and always will face. Even triumph, he points out in *The Build-Up,* is an obsessive, almost maniacal denial of defeat—rather than a refuge or sanctuary finally obtained.

Everything in Williams' trilogy is plain—there is just enough information or dialogue given in order to make a scene come clear—it all looks simplistic, naive, "naturalistic." But in order to write of people who are not monsters, caricatures, or villains, there was no other way. It is the surface that Williams is concerned with, that surface in which he finds the "isolate flecks" that suddenly reveal the quality of an entire family, an entire community. Such an approach to writing begs to be misunderstood.

The satirist or socially relevant writer, the author of jeremiads must look at but one aspect of his subject, or invent an aspect that can be held up to ridicule or scorn, or assaulted. Williams chose another way, a way so plain, so candid that it is unbelievably subtle. "Tell them something else," he says in his *Autobiography,* other than the "lying habits of everyday speech and thought."

The Stechers are immigrant Americans, here to escape the misery and starvation that their parents and grandparents knew—as Coles points out, they came not *to* something, but *away from* something. In Coles' brilliant dissection of Gurlie's character he shows how Williams cleanly noted the particular American blend of love for this country's largesse for those who will work and struggle in the peculiarly amoral world of business, and hatred for the very thing that enables the family to become successful—that very business world's lying, cheating, and affable ruthlessness. Joe is a wealthy man at the end of the trilogy; but he has become, by the slowest of degrees, everything that he once loathed. But he doesn't really know it—his imagination, thwarted and all but destroyed, can find release only within the boundaries he himself has set up. He is a thorough success.

Williams, more than any other novelist that I can think of, wrote of things as they really are for the American middle class, not as what they "could be" if only—what? If only it were not America. If only this were not the middle class. If only they could "use the money" to buy beauty and culture. But this is the way that it happens. Nameless defeat. Williams understood absolutely the local—it was his laboratory, and for him enclosed the universal. What he has to tell us of this one family floods with light the entire American immigrant experience of this century. "A reply to Greek and Latin with the bare hands."

He saw it all, completely, these seeds of restlessness, discontent, desiccated morality. When Joe, at the conclusion of *The Build-Up*, his children gone, he and Gurlie alone and aging, with more money than they can ever possibly spend, shouts to nobody at all, to the sky, that he is going to build a mansion for Gurlie, "like nothing in the neighborhood," we know that this is not a cry of triumph but of pain, frustration: it is the dying imagination finding an outlet that is meaningless. It pierces the heart. There is no help for it, no help for Joe.

Coles is excellent on this confusion into which the Stechers slide. He sees that Williams does not mean for us to hate Joe and Gurlie, nor hold them in contempt. Why should we? They have worked for the rewards that the vast machine of American business manufactures, they have earned them. Sink or swim was the truth they saw as a young couple. They chose success rather than poverty. Yet Williams has no smeary sentimentalism in his work concerning the "good" poor and the "bad" middle class: at the core of his writing there is a nucleus of ice. He is, in his quiet and unsensational prose, utterly ruthless in his vision. There is nothing wonderful about the Stechers—but the poor are not wonderful either. Both wither emotionally and imaginatively. Coles remarks:

Williams wants us to know that the Stechers were beginning to "make it" at a certain stage in their lives: they were "in the money." There is no great compliment intended thereby; Williams was not a starry-eyed apologist for American materialism. But if the Stechers are no Horatio Algers, or Andrew Carnegies, they are not shown to be decadent, mean, or vicious, either.

A twist here, a falsification there, a reading "between the lines" (which Williams resists tenaciously throughout the trilogy), could easily allow a reader to mark this work as no more than a movie with a happy ending, just as a lazy eye might see Van Gogh's picture of the two crows as a nature painting. But Williams does not allow this—all the information is given, everything is on the surface. It is placid, mundane, ordinary—and terrible.

Robert Coles has written of all this beautifully, in a plain and serviceable prose, and with a wit and energy that are remarkable. He has done a first-rate job with this book, which is, to date, one of the most valuable additions to the growing body of Williams criticism. Let us hope that it will lead readers to this neglected masterwork.

Postscript: Years ago, when I was a boy, I passed each summer over the Jersey flats on my way to vacation in the western part of the state. The train on which I journeyed was the old Delaware Lackawanna and Western. The Passaic, over which the train passed, was, one day, a fantastic rainbow of reds, yellows, purples, and pinks—breathtaking. The colors were, I learned, dyes from the chemical plants and silk mills along the river's banks. Though the waters seemed beautiful to my eye, the river was dead—poisoned by industrial wastes. The men who worked in those plants and the men who owned them were, I am sure, neither devils nor monsters. More than a few of them might have been a Joe Stecher. It is Williams' understanding that success in America presupposes loss and misery and destruction that makes his work so valuable, not only as a self-enclosed and isolated demonstration of his artistry, but as a diagram to show us exactly why America is as it is— not happy, not really sad, certainly not tragic, but desolate.

> as if the earth under our feet
> were
> an excrement of some sky
>
> and we degraded prisoners
> destined
> to hunger until we eat filth
>
> while the imagination strains
> after deer
> going by fields of goldenrod in

the stifling heat of September
Somehow
it seems to destroy us

Partisan Review, 1975

IN THE MODERNIST GRAIN

William Carlos Williams: A New World Naked. By Paul Mariani

The most laudable aspect of Paul Mariani's critical biography of William
Carlos Williams is that it largely succeeds in placing him, in his biographer's
words, as "the single most important American poet of the twentieth century," and though Williams is dead almost twenty years now, there has been
no poet in that time to deny him his primacy. Among his American contemporaries, he had but two peers, Ezra Pound and Wallace Stevens, and
Mr. Mariani makes a strong case for Williams' being "more equal" than they.
He rightly considers T. S. Eliot to be more English than American; and he
hardly glances at Robert Frost, a sign, perhaps, of the whisperings of sanity
in the academic establishment. I agree with Mr. Mariani's judgment and so
need no convincing, but for the reader who knows Williams as the author
of the handful of poems that are predictably anthologized, this book will
come as a revelation.

Paul Mariani is relentless in detailing the shabby critical treatment accorded Williams throughout the whole of his career, a record of intellectual
misprision that invented a Williams who was, and still is—with endemic
regularity—thought of as a kind of amiable primitive, an unsophisticated
scribbler, a simple small-town doctor who wrote on the side, but wrote,
mind you, without quite knowing what he was doing: the literary equivalent
of Grandma Moses or the New Jersey version of *vers libre*'s gift to the world,
Carl Sandburg. Mr. Mariani shatters these idiocies by a careful examination
of Williams' work in poetry, fiction and criticism, setting it against the general somnambulism of the time. In a sense, this book may be read as a kind
of graph of the reactionary shoddiness of the American critical mind in the
face of a modern master, and I half suspect that Mr. Mariani intends us to
read it this way because of the attention he has paid to this facet of Williams'
career.

Paradoxically, the "fault" might be laid at Williams' door. As early as
1917, he wrote: "Ignorant people use the most idiotic words sometimes with
a dignity, a force of feeling that makes them glow and flare. I listen in profound silence . . . later I try to imitate. I almost always fail." In 1917, no

English or American poet made or even thought of poetry this way. Williams' nascent ideas of a vernacular American poetry, which were to flower in the great poems of *The Desert Music* and *Journey to Love* forty years later, had sealed his fate. He didn't yet know this—he soon would.

Three years later, Williams published, in *The Dial*, "Portrait of a Lady," arguably the first *absolutely* modern American poem, one that locally develops the techniques of European, especially French, modernism, an extention of the Apollinaire of *Alcools*, written in those "idiotic words" that "glow and flare." It was Williams' first wholly successful demonstration that there was an American idiom, that its rhythms might be formally controlled, and that it could be turned to metrical patterns that are not those of the "natural" English iambic. It begins:

> Your thighs are appletrees
> whose blossoms touch the sky.
> Which sky? The sky
> where Watteau hung a lady's
> slipper. Your knees
> are a southern breeze—or
> a gust of snow. Agh! what
> sort of man was Fragonard?
> —as if that answered
> anything.

This miraculous poem, *in toto*, is a paradigm of Williams' technical concerns. We note a perfectly balanced iambic hexameter, distributed over two lines, suddenly mocked and broken; an elegant alexandrine pulled up short; and a recurrent aborting of causality and logical development. Nothing like it had been seen before in English or American poetry, but Mr. Mariani does not note that it occasioned any comment. Williams was working in the shadow of Eliot's "The Love Song of J. Alfred Prufrock," and would soon be eclipsed by "The Waste Land," the poem that enraged him because it seemed a betrayal of a new American poetry in gestation, as well as a portent of the return of poetry, as he put it, "to the classroom." He was, of course, right.

In 1949, by which time Williams had published, among many other books, *Spring and All* and the first two books of *Paterson* (which should have been enough to secure his reputation), James Laughlin asked Randall Jarrell to write the introduction to the inexpensive New Directions edition of Williams' *Selected Poems*, the book that was to have served to broaden his audience. It was a mistake. Mr. Mariani tells us that "Williams—noting Jarrell's waverings—had several times confided to Laughlin that perhaps he should have done his own introduction or had someone else do it. But Laughlin's instinct was to go with an introduction by a recognized poet and critic." This introduction petrified, for the rest of Williams' lifetime, and well beyond his death in 1963, the general critical attitude toward his work. In effect, what Jarrell's unenthusiastic introduction did for Williams was to present him as unlettered but well-meaning, and lacking in poetic intelligence and craft; in short, a good-hearted rube, not to be mentioned in the same breath as Eliot, Frost, or Stevens. Mariani continues, "the sense one was left with [was] that one was dealing here with a circumscribed and minor talent."

It is tempting to suggest that Jarrell's attitude stemmed, in part, from the kiss of death bestowed upon Williams by Eliot in a 1936 Harvard lecture. In this lecture he referred to Williams as a poet "of some local interest, perhaps." Eliot's dominance of the Anglo-American critical world was already well established by that time, and he easily succeeded in putting Williams in his place. The ranks closed, the New Critics—or, as Kenneth Rexroth trenchantly called them, "the cornbelt metaphysicals"—were in the ascendancy, and Jarrell's response was almost predestined. But he had help.

In 1938, after the appearance of the Complete Collected Poems, Babette Deutsch complained in The Nation that the poetry lacked a central, all-informing myth. Time magazine praised the work, but praised Laura Riding's poetry more. In The New Republic, Philip Horton, Hart Crane's first biographer, argued that Williams could not be called an important poet and that his poems eliminated the visionary plateau. And R. P. Blackmur, writing in the Partisan Review, said that his work was devoid of any tragic dimension and without the deeper significations of human experience that other poets of his generation had offered. We seem to be located in the world of Hermann Hesse, where poetry is made of Serious Ideas.

Mr. Mariani puts it well in his preface when he writes that this biography came out of the work that he did in the early seventies "in an attempt to determine why the critics had for so long either dismissed or tried actually to destroy Williams' poetic reputation." The "why" is made explicit throughout this biography. Williams himself gave, unwittingly, one of the reasons when he wrote, early on: "The goal of writing is to keep a beleaguered line of understanding which has movement from breaking down and becoming a hole into which we sink decoratively to rest." Writing is almost always most admired when it is decoratively resting—in our time, the more comatose, the more static a mirror image of "reality" the better—and at least three-quarters of the writers of any era employ language and techniques inadequate to deal with that era; they are, in effect, decorators. Williams was a troublesome artist who was always starting anew, and in the despised language that he found, as he said, "in the mouths of Polish mothers." The critics, bemused by "deep thoughts" that shuffled along in stale iambics with the occasional tinkle of rhyme to wake them up, were having none of it.

What could they have possibly said of a man who wrote, in 1950: "To me all sonnets say the same thing of no importance. What does it matter what the line 'says'? There is no poetry of distinction without formal invention," a terse gloss on the classic modernism that has its roots in Flaubert.

Williams' life was outwardly uneventful. Born in 1883 in Rutherford, N.J., he died almost eighty years later a few blocks from his birthplace. At the University of Pennsylvania, where Williams began medical school at age nineteen, Pound, Hilda Doolittle, and Charles Demuth were among his friends. He interned for two years at the old French Hospital in New York and, with a special gift for pediatrics, decided to take another internship at Child's Hospital. Well on his way to a lucrative New York practice, he lost this opportunity because he refused to cooperate with a hospital scheme at Child's involving the misappropriation of funds, and resigned. He began practicing in Rutherford and the grim towns of northern industrial Jersey among the immigrant and black poor, spent almost a year in Europe with Flossie, his wife, where he associated with Pound, Joyce, Hemingway, Gertrude Stein, and most of the other members of the international avant-garde, then returned to the United States for good. He earned little money as a physician because of his unwillingness to press his poverty-stricken patients for payment, and his writing earned him less. Indeed, at the age of 53, in a talk he gave at the University of Virginia, he said: "For the past thirty years I have never been able to get one first-rate poem published in a commercial magazine. . . . I have never been able to get a single book of poems, no matter how small, published except by paying or partly paying for it myself."

Beginning in 1951, he was the victim of a series of increasingly crippling strokes, and in 1953 was hospitalized for severe depression, after terrible "loyalty process" difficulties with the Library of Congress over his appointment as Consultant in Poetry, a position he never assumed. He wrote much of his work in whatever time he could spare from his practice and his family—late at night, between patients in his office, even in his car. His wife was the remarkable Flossie Herman, a courageous and intelligent woman whom, we learn, Williams married on the rebound, his first love being her older sister, Charlotte. The marriage was rocky and often troubled because of Williams' countless liaisons with other women, but it endured. His American contemporaries of note—Stevens, Cummings, Moore, Nathanael West—were friends and colleagues, and were balanced by many other writers whose names are not now very well known—Alfred Kreymborg, Emanuel Carnevali and Robert McAlmon, a tragic man whom Pound always insisted was a better prose writer than Hemingway. Williams was, as they say, in the thick of the new movement, part of its cutting edge, but always, and insistently, "local" in his concerns. This "localism"—in which

Williams insisted that one would discover the universal—coupled with his radical disruption of outworn forms and a consistent sabotaging of "content" as meaningless was to carry the innovations of the European avant-garde into the American climate. These innovations were seen by most of his readers as provincial and inarticulate. It was Williams' vision of what a true modern American literature could be that was behind his reference (in the 1918 "Prologue" to *Kora in Hell*) to Eliot as a "subtle conformist," a startling remark in the light of that era's view of Eliot, and Mr. Mariani traces the mutual antagonism of the two men to that comment.

In the thirties and forties Williams knew and met with a younger generation of writers—Louis Zukofsky (who served for years as Williams' informal editor), George Oppen, Edward Dahlberg, Carl Rakosi and Charles Reznikoff—and in his last years befriended poets as diverse as Robert Lowell, Theodore Roethke, Allen Ginsberg, Gary Snyder, Robert Creeley and Charles Olson. He continued to contribute to the little magazines that had sustained him and provided, often, his only outlet for years. Toward the end of his life, there belatedly came a measure of recognition for his achievement—the Russell Loines Award, the National Book Award, various honorary degrees—yet at the 1951 Dinner Meeting of the National Institute of Arts and Letters, he was booed and heckled throughout a talk he gave on "The American Spirit in Art," in which he championed the work of the Abstract Expressionists. In 1955 he published *Journey to Love*, which includes "Of Asphodel, That Greeny Flower," one of the great poems in the language, of which Robert Lowell wrote, "He delivered to us what was impossible, something that was both poetry and beyond poetry." Yet John Montague, the Irish writer, reported that Williams was "made fun of" during a reading he gave that year at the Iowa Writers' Workshop. The idea of Williams as barbarian had deep roots; Robert Creeley, referring to the literary climate of the fifties, wrote that its arbiters "were dominant in their insistence upon an *idea* of form extrinsic to the given instance. . . . Auden [was] the measure of competence."

I have presented this book narrowly, but it may also be read as a record of the ultimate vindication of an artist who worked all his life against the grain of his time. But this sort of grinding combat is not exhilarating to those who are engaged in it. Had Williams found a commercial publisher earlier than 1934, when he first published with Laughlin's just-begun New Directions, his enormously important early books might have remained in print. One of Williams' lifelong problems was that most of his work was always out of print, so that there was little opportunity for the creation of a body of intelligent critical discourse to be built up around this work. He might have been able to give up his medical practice earlier, and thereby find the time to organize and elaborate the scattered notes, remarks and essays that he wrote on "the variable foot," a theory of American prosody that is a kind of modern variant on Thomas Campion's seventeenth-century experiments with, and ideas on, the role of quantity in an accentually stressed poetry. He might have published in easily obtained literary journals instead of having to place so much of his work in fugitive magazines. His life was, as they say, all uphill, and it exhausted him and finally burnt him out.

Mr. Mariani calls his life one of "complex tragedy and brilliance." How complex, how tragic, and how brilliant, his biography fully explores. Had he not been a man of such stamina and courage, such stubbornness, or had he not had, perhaps, what Pound called in a 1917 letter "enough Spanish blood to muddy up [his] mind," he would have been silent by the mid-thirties. As it was, he persisted. He says, in "The Pink Locust":

> I'm persistent as the pink locust,
> once admitted
> to the garden,
>
> you will not easily get rid of it.
> Tear it from the ground,
> if one hair-thin rootlet
>
> remain
> it will come again.

Yet his persistence cost him. Writing to Zukofsky at seventy-two, he says of a postcard on his desk: "It shows four old musicians walking poorly clad in the snow. . . . They are all scrunched together their instruments in their hands trudging along. I mean to keep the card there a long time as a reminder of our probable fate as artists. I know just what is going on in the minds of those white haired musicians."

Indeed he did.

The New York Times Book Review, 1981

POLISH MOTHERS AND "THE KNIFE OF THE TIMES"

> The language, the language
> fails them
> They do not know the words
> or have not
> the courage to use them
>
> *Paterson One, I*

It is obvious that when Williams remarked that his American language came "from the mouths of Polish mothers," he was not speaking merely of a language whose patterns, inflections, syntax, etc., were those of the imperfect tongue spoken by immigrant women. The comment should be construed to mean that American is made up of linguistic elements that are quite different from those of English—native locutions growing out of "the weather," sketchy and distorted syntax, a "revised" grammar designed for rapid communication, unorthodox verb placement, suffixal prepositions and conjunctions, heavy doses of a constantly changing colloquial, and an expressive slang whose older examples often survive as instances of irony or mockery. A great deal of this language is never written down or "formalized" in any way at all.

Williams' short stories, with the curious exception of "The Knife of the Times," employ this spoken American language. The language of "The Knife of the Times," however, is false and works to prevent the communication of anything other than the superficial, the removed or twice-removed. In Williams' hands it acts brilliantly to reveal the divorce of its users from the reality of their feelings, to deny these feelings except insofar as they are located on a plane of unreality or stale fantasy.

Many of Williams' strategies of construction are deployed in the story, e.g., a third-person narrator whose voice is neither omniscient or limited, but is that of what can be termed an "absent" first person; a nonfunctioning past—time is ignored or foreshortened, so that all the action develops in an "eternal" present; a lack of description or characterization; a contempt for "realistic" motivation—the characters *are now*; and great forward momentum, made possible by the eschewal of standard transitional devices. But the language of the story in its discrete words and those words in varying combinations is very different from that of Williams' other short fiction, so much so that it may be thought of as foregrounded: it is so relentlessly wooden and artificial that it directs continuous attention to itself. Yet the entity presented has no "style," neither is it a parody of a style—it floats free of a recognizably literary tradition. An examination of the story reveals three distinct modes of language out of which it is composed. But first, let us look briefly at the narrative.

The theme of the story is that of one character's (Ethel's) growing lesbian desire for another character (Maura), over a period of years which has seen them, after a childhood friendship, separated and gone into conventional married lives. Ethel's passion is projected through the mails, with her letters growing progressively and, to Maura, disconcertingly more amorous. Maura hides the letters; and after twenty years (!) they meet at Ethel's insistence, have a brief but decidedly sexual moment together, and go back into their normal lives, with Ethel's invitation to Maura to visit her so that they may finally sleep together controlling the last sentence of the story: "Why not?" That we don't know whether this is Maura's question to herself or Williams' question to his story is a precise example of Williams' use of the ambiguous narrative voice. A simple story, and one that would be expected to attract Williams. But the story is not important to Williams; or, more clearly, Williams is not interested in *what happens* or *what will happen* to his characters. The story is a constant, outside time, inflectionless. This static infinitive is embedded directly in the failed language used to tell the story, and this language reveals a social and emotional malaise at once caused and unrelieved by it. Williams' cavalier treatment of the conventions of the fictive temporal erases any notions we may have that the passage of time is relevant to the overwhelming emptiness that the story generates—nothing that *happened* makes the slightest difference to what *is happening*; and what is happening will make no difference to what *will happen*. Ethel and Maura are frozen in time, buried in a present that is created of a language insufficient to permit them understanding or relief. They are inarticulate, "speechless," and hence sealed in misunderstanding and confusion.

Ethel and Maura are void of imagination and cannot understand each other or themselves because of their poverty of language. The story is not written in Williams' usual brusque "short-hand" American since it is emblematic of impotence and has separated these two women from their deepest selves. Their responses to all experience are automatic, superficial, and banal. The entire work is composed of words and phrases distinct from a speech of even the most common denotation or perception, a speech incapable of the delineation of actuality: it is a false language, one that, paradoxically, the intensity of their secret relationship has given birth to, that it has, in fact, made obligatory so that the intensity may be *mistaken*. Williams has constructed this language with exquisite care to show that the impossibility of contact between his heroines is caused by their chosen language's destruction of the imagination. They can be neither lovers nor friends; they cannot confront the fact that they cannot be lovers or friends. The reality of their predicament is unrecognized by them because they have no language with which to plumb it other than one that connotes the spurious: a language of the void. Their words have both invented and stranded their lives.

As I have noted, this work is made of three distinct modes of language, each separate from the other; each at best inadequate, at worst, sham. Carnal passions and fears are presented in a rigid and dead etiquette of the verbal. Let us look at these three modes:

a) Automatized language.

b) Polite or refined language.

c) The language of popular romance-fiction.

The first mode is used without thought, and is the language that enables us to get through the usual business of day-to-day living, to convey and receive necessary information; it is a "transitive" language that, as Valéry has it, disappears after its message has been carried. An example from the story: "And both began to bring up families. Ethel especially went in for children. Within a very brief period, comparatively speaking, she had three of them, then four, then five and finally six."

The second mode is learned, as manners are learned. It is an affected speech, designed to reveal the speaker's sense of the niceties, the sort of language used at funerals, weddings, etc. My mother, contemporaneous with Williams, called this, as did her peers, "refined" language—even the word "refined" was refined. It is a *special* language, brought out on particular occasions, and is dissimilar from the first mode. To use it is an effort of the will, and it is usually intended to gloss over the reality of the situation that calls it forth—it homogenizes what it touches. Essentially a language of concealment, it acts as a figure that concretizes the *social* understanding existent among those who use it. Signatures of this language are often its stilted verbs and verb forms, its penchant for the passive voice, its polite and exhausted idiom, its many inversions of normal sentence structure. It is hard to *say* and is meant to be, since it is, in essence, counterfeit speech, a "written" language. Example: "But the steamer was met, the sister saluted; the day came to an end and the hour of parting found Ethel still keeping close, close to the object of her lifelong adoration."

The third mode is that of the romance-fiction of "ladies' magazines" or popular novels of romantic love. Not so incidentally, four of Williams' contemporaries were champions of this genre: Faith Baldwin, Fannie Hurst, Kathleen Norris, and Viña Delmar. Their books are primers of the craft, their pages studded with examples of Williams' third mode in its virginal state. This language is notable for its delicate avoidance of the overtly sexual, which is dealt with by the use of a fixed repertory of euphemism and cliché. It is a strictly codified language whose rule of thumb is that the closer it approaches the sexual the more breathlessly asexual it becomes. Example: "She spoke of her longings, to touch the velvet flesh of her darling's breasts, her thighs. She longed to kiss her to sleep, to hold her in her arms." "Longings," "velvet," "darling's," and "sleep" all serve to defuse the carnal, rendering it risqué and "spicy," rather than erotic or pornographic.

None of these modes is sufficient to define the nature of the emotional complex that these women form; on the contrary, they blur and distort it.

Williams uses all three of these modes (and none other) throughout the story. They are his sole materials. The story develops a supreme resonance of the banal when he combines two or more modes in single or contiguous sentences: "And through it all (a) she kept in constant touch with her girlhood friend (a), dark-eyed Maura (c), by writing long intimate letters (b)."

"Franker and franker (b) became her outspoken lusts (c). For which she begged indulgence (b)."

The interested reader may go through the story and make three lists, by mode, of all the phrases and sentences that make it up. He will discover that he has made three small handbooks of habitualized and empty language.

Three things should be noted about these modes:

1. They are each responsible for roughly one-third of the total language of the story—a nice balance.

2. Each is used to specific effect by its placement in the text; i.e., one mode sometimes persists for two or more sentences; one mode is used to separate two units of another mode; each mode is used in turn; one mode is used to throw another into relief; two or more modes are mixed in the same sentence or phrase.

3. Williams' antennae are so finely tuned that his surface is continuous, so that each mode slides into the next in a process of elision. They begin to blur, e.g., "nobody but you can appease my grief" is an example of the third mode because of where it is placed in the text. It could quite easily be an example of the second mode; and "not a little fear," here used as an example of the second mode, could be an example of the third, and so on. The story is linguistically seamless, despite its separable modes. *All* the language is exhausted and carries with it no clear intentions other than its own impotence.

"The Knife of the Times" then is atypical Williams. In it he partially solved a problem that he poses in his essay, "The Work of Gertrude Stein," in which he writes: "Observation about us engenders the very opposite of what we seek: triviality, crassness, and intellectual bankruptcy. And yet what we see can in no way be excluded. Satire and flight are two possibilities. . . . But if one remain in a place and reject satire, what then? To be democratic, local . . . [the] artist must for subtlety ascend to a plane of almost abstract design to keep alive . . . what actually impinges on the senses must be rendered as it appears, by use of which, only, and under which, untouched, the significance has to be disclosed. It is one of the major problems of the artist."

"The Knife of the Times" fulfills the requirements that Williams set for himself. More importantly, it proved to him that it was possible to write in a debased language without satiric or parodic intent, to write, that is to say, in a language that seemed to have no possibilities for literature. This empty and pathetic story of two human beings caught in a language unfit to assist or relieve them, and unaware of it, is, in a sense, made of the speech of Polish mothers become Americans. It was, for Williams, an act of absolute creative recovery.

William Carlos Williams: Man and Poet, 1983

3

Jack Spicer

Jack Spicer likes Billy the Kid; he doesn't like what "we" have made of him:
but in that dislike he maims his poem with stuff like:

> Will you dance, Our Lady,
> Dead and unexpected?
> Billy wants you to dance
> Billy
> Will shoot the heels off your shoes if you don't dance
> Billy
> Being dead also wants
> Fun.

No real lemons here: no lemons at all if it comes to that. Some, as it's
phrased, "pedestrian verse." But then, we get to Section IX: I'll quote it in
full because it's the one thing in the poem that is really worth the poem:

> So the heart breaks
> Into small shadows
> Almost so random
> They are meaningless
> Like a diamond
> Has at the center of it a diamond
> Or a rock
> Rock.
> Being afraid
> Love asks its bare question—
> I can no more remember
> What brought me here

Than bone answers bone in the arm
Or shadow sees shadow—
Deathward we ride in the boat
Like someone canoeing
In a small lake
Where at either end
There are nothing but pine-branches—
Deathward we ride in the boat
Broken-hearted or broken-bodied
The choice is real. The diamond. I
Ask it.

The ten sections of the poem do not really connect: but that is Spicer's design at any rate, as shown in his *After Lorca*. But we don't have the connection of ideogrammatic fragments as in EP: what we have here is almost total disconnection; these are really ten different poems. And that's O.K., too, except that to be taken as one long poem, it doesn't make it: not that there *is* no connection—but granting that, that there is such a disparity of quality in the unconnected pieces, there is an alternation of flippancy and sublimity, as in the above poem, that the poem really, as a whole, doesn't have the spread for. You can't recover enough, on rereading, for maybe the fifth or sixth time; you start to skip pieces because they bring you down, jolt your mood, or the poem's mood; and then you reach a point at which you don't miss the pieces that you skipped; and then you reach a point at which you don't even want them: O.K., ill-reading? I don't think so: there is a too-great discrepancy in tonal quality here for the length of the work; such ranges of emotional variance need a poem twice as long. However, it's worth reading; one wishes Spicer would get over his "unworldly" posture and publish more: *Billy the Kid* invites you.

Yugen, 1962

Mr. Spicer is a brilliant poet: he not only has an awesome and formidable array of poetic equipment; but, more important, his poems display a rare ordering of an equally rare intelligence. *The Heads of the Town up to the Aether* is comprised of three sections, *Homage to Creeley/Explanatory Notes, A Fake Novel about the Life of Arthur Rimbaud,* and *A Textbook of Poetry.* Each section is magnificent, so much so that on a first reading, one feels that he is being tricked, the sheer dazzle and precision of the surface are overwhelming. But this is far from trickery, as a second and a third reading will testify. I have occasionally spoken of the poet's job—to extract intelligible forms from seemingly unintelligible things: now look at Mr. Spicer handle the apparent, look at the clarity of the words, the clean, classical form—

Sheep Trails Are Fateful to Strangers

Dante would have blamed Beatrice
If she turned up alive in a local bordello
Or Newton gravity
If apples fell upward
What I mean is words
Turn mysteriously against those who use them
Hello says the apple
Both of us were object.

———

There is a universal here that is dimly recognized.
I mean everybody says some kinds of love are horseshit.
Or invents a Beatrice to prove that they are.
What Beatrice did did not become her own business.
Dante saw to that. Sawed away the last plank anyone
he loved could stand on.

—that is "idea" spun out so fine that it, literally, *becomes*, as you read, poetry. It is Williams' "no ideas but in things" extended, further, into: things *are* ideas, and ideas must be, ultimately, things—for the poet. It is, I believe, what Spicer meant when he said that he wanted the lemon in his poem to be as real as the newspaper in a collage is real. And here is Spicer on the "professional rebel" poet, whose inability to be articulate is his claim to his "apartness." It is a compendium of every argument against the spurious.

Surrealism is the business of poets who cannot benefit by surrealism. It was the first appearance of the Logos that said, "The public be damned," by which he did not mean that they did not matter or he wanted to be crucified by them, but that really he did not have a word to say to them. This was surrealism.
But even the business of ignoring the public is the business of the poet and not the surrealism of the poet. The surrealism of the poet could not write words.

Not to belabor the point, but Mr. Spicer is a rare bird among poets these days. He refuses to gesture, to make sweeping statements about Life, and God, and the Tragedy Of It All; he will not act out a role which our time has decreed for the poet; he will not hide banality and stupidity of thought behind a "formal metric." He is, in short, the genuine article, a true poet, without the trappings of either the imbecile Bohemian or the obtuse academic. His work is authoritative and clear; it glitters. Although Mr. Spicer would probably disagree with me, I find in him elements which are the concern of another elegant craftsman, Wallace Stevens. There is the same penchant in both for the treatment of the two opposites of imagination and reality; the same understanding in both that one is not "better" than the other, but that the poet must make reality useful through the employment of the imagination; and conversely, that imagination, to be legitimate, must be inseparably linked to reality. Finally, there is the exquisite marshaling of words which makes the reading of the poems a unique experience.

Every poet and student of poetry should avail himself of Mr. Spicer's book. Its publication is a literary event of importance.

Kulchur, 1963

Jack Spicer says, in his brilliant book *Language*, "No one listens to poetry." Very few people ever listened to Mr. Spicer; and now he is dead at forty; and the poems, which started out as the work of an enormously dedicated and well-equipped craftsman, and ended with the mastery shown in *Language*, are a testament to his devotion to his art. Mr. Spicer, so far as is possible in language, makes real *things*; he has for some time now achieved his own aesthetic, which speaks of a removal from the concept of image as a method for "connection" within the poem; and instead pushes for a pursuit of those essences in the world which may be said to "correspond." To be free of the image, to be free of the machinery of poem as literary game, to place, as it were, the poem in the position of the revelatory—this is Spicer's program. The world is *here*, outside us, the poem is a tool to reveal its co-respond-ences, not by means of simile, metaphor, or image, but by means of language itself. This all, of course, makes for a poem stripped bare of the nonessen-tial—it also makes for a poem which may hold itself tight and secret against the reader who wants it to make some sort of grand "statement" on the world.

> Troy was a baby when Greek sentence
> structure emerged. This was the real
> Trojan Horse.
> The order changes. The Trojans
> Having no idea of true and false syntax
> and having no recorded language
> Never knew what hit them.

Or this simple, stark remark:

True conservation is the effort of the artist and the private
man to keep things true.

Spicer gave us another remarkable book, certainly as strong as anything he
had ever published, perhaps stronger. For years his work was known only to
those friends who were part of his group in San Francisco; his reputation
has always been high there, his abilities as mentor ("censor" Duncan calls
him—not pejoratively) were known to all those engaged with the art of
poetry.

Duncan wrote to me some years ago that "not all poetry serves the Art of
Poetry." Spicer's does and always has. *Language* is a testament to that, a
testament also to love. In the last poem he says:

> Love is not mocked whatever use
> you put to it

and we believe him.

Book Week, 1966

"WORDS ARE . . . NOT MOCKED"

Language. By Jack Spicer

In sense of linguistic necessity, the poet's task, finally, is to make his words
real, make them, that is, things as certainly as things of the earth are that,
i.e., things. The language itself must be the final cornerstone of his strength,
stripped language, a way through image as surely as imagism found a way
through metaphor; or, the dense fabric, that meticulous notation of Zukofsky, against free verse.

There doesn't seem to be anything "wrong" with imagery. It is certainly
useful. But to build the poem around image, or to string images together—
in the sense of that construct of the poem as its articulation—seems to be
behind us, has become a tool, not an end.

Spicer's movement within his poem, here revealed most beautifully and
fully in this book, published the month he died, was away from this concept
of mechanics, the poem built upon image, and toward language as a final
statement, language itself as image, words placed so precisely, attentive to
their syllables, their fall within the movement of the line, the line's weight
within the whole poem—the poem engaged with reality, its structure the
rationale for its being, reality pursued with the hard bare bones of the very
letter, that intransigently formal *sound.*

There are dangers. The most obvious, it would seem, is that one may pursue reality within the poem and end up with description. The poem back into narrative, the matters of prose. So Spicer had somehow to use the words in such a way that narrative preoccupation and movement are both avoided, yet *technique* is avoided, also. To place the words formally in the line, so that their texture, their substance, as both sound and use are balanced in relation to their meaning: what they mean. The obdurate world is confronted, the language becomes, then, not some sort of fence to keep it out of the artifact of the poem; the language turns into a doorway, the world admitted into the poem; the image no longer a concomitant of craftsmanship, but a reality to be used by the poet, in no sense of taking the *place* of the world's things, but *as* thing, new thing. The reality of the sound, the physical it posits, these set off in the line as parts of the world moving within the poem. A poetic reality. The world revealed in language.

Spicer's achievement in this structuring of the poem is indeed notable. He has made a statement that will be hard to ignore, taken an irritation with the image, which I think we have all felt, and tried to work out, within his own poem, the field in which it might be possible to dispense with it, or at least dispense with it as it has sometimes stood: frill.

> I see you cowering in the corner and the metal in my heart
> bangs. Too personal
> The glass and glue in my heart reply. And they are living
> substance.
> You cannot bake glass in a pie or fry glue in an omelette
> "If I speak in the tongue of men and angels . . ."
> The sounding brass of my heart says
> "Love."

I deeply admired and respected the man's work. It seems that he, gifted as well as sincere, such a conscientious maker, might well have made some final statement thought of as "major." But the extant work is solid enough for any man.

> Love is not mocked whatever use you put to it. Words are also
> not mocked.
> The soup of real turtles flows through our veins.

Not "whatever use you put *it to*." That is the nicety of absolute reliance on, and trust in, language.

Poetry, 1966

JACK SPICER: LANGUAGE AS IMAGE

The insignificant "image" may be "evoked" never
so ably and still mean nothing.
William Carlos Williams

It may be that we are so thoroughly inured to the idea that art is novelty or fashion, a titillation, or teasing, of reality, that a poet of Jack Spicer's gifts and intelligence must go among us unheeded. At his death at forty (August 17, 1965), there were perhaps a few hundred people who cared at all about his work, perhaps half that number who interested themselves in what he was up to. This, in some measure, was Spicer's own "fault." He was long wary of publishing, even more wary of being involved in a world in which "poet" is somehow subtly transmuted to "celebrity."

But he is dead now, and it would seem appropriate to make an attempt to set down a tentative critique of his work, a kind of basic appraisal which might be of use to those readers who care for poetry as art. To try to grasp Spicer as an artist seems, initially, quite difficult. His poems resist a fluid reading, his language is of that sort of clarity which forces one to a rereading, his images are really not what we have come to expect of image—that isolate "picture" upon which the poem depends, and around which it sets ("Find the controlling image," they used to say in school).

It is, however, when one reads his published work—five small books— that one sees a clear development of aesthetic idea, which the poems serve to carry. His early work was indeed unsure, he wrote a kind of laboratory poem, intended to serve as *exemplum* for his poetic. But in his later poems he presents the work itself as aesthetic; there is no sense that the poem is a vehicle; it is the total and masterly expression of a unique poetic sensibility. Spicer achieved that rare and difficult feat—he created an art which was at once subservient to, and dominant over, a set of ideas.

What were these ideas? To somewhat economically state them: that the poem is an instance of reality, not a gloss of same; that the language, not its tropes and elegances, is the core of the ultimate poem; that the poet is not an interpreter, but a revealer; that things do not *connect*, neither in the poem nor in the life from which it springs: they correspond. This last is perhaps the true center of Spicer's work. It is the most obvious to the mind as one reads the poems; and the most arresting in that *correspondence* implies his fight against the image—it creates, as it were, the possibilities for a poem removed from a dependence on metaphorical machinery, a poem enmeshed with the reality it "reads."

The above program would seem (seem?) to be a classical one; further, it is a conservative one. Is it surprising that poets, the best of them, are con-servatives? *Conservare*: to hold on to, to save, to keep that from the past which is valuable. What is it to be conservative, particularly in a writer like Spicer, when the poems seem to belie this fact, being as they are, radically different from all those things most associated in the popular mind with stodginess and staleness—different from, in a word, conservatism? Conser-vation in the arts is the belief in the world as a place which yields up its meanings to that artist who has subordinated his ego to its multiplex phe-nomena. It is the absolute opposite of the belief which holds that the poet somehow "imposes" his will upon the things of the world, and "interprets" it; it is an antihumanist position. "Radical" art, upon investigation, more often than not turns out to be bourgeois in its concerns and preoccupa-tions—humanistic—and not at all *radical*.

The world, one learns, is a hard place, and does not take to being "inter-preted." The poet must humble himself before it, must wait for its meanings. St. Thomas says: "For in the order of discovery, we come through temporal things to the knowledge of things eternal, according to the words of the Apostle (*Romans* 1.20). '*The invisible things of God are clearly seen, being understood by the things that are made.*'" And, centuries later, Keats: "A poet is the least poetical of anything in existence: it is for ever, in, for, and fulfilling some other object." And Spicer, writing in his first book, *After Lorca*: "I would like the moon in my poems to be a real moon, one which could suddenly be covered with a cloud that has nothing to do with the poem—a moon utterly independent of images. The imagination pictures the real. I would like to point to the real, disclose it, to make a poem that has no sound in it but the pointing of a finger."

The world, if one is careful enough, and persistent enough, will yield up its meanings; they are there before us in *things* ("No ideas but in things," says Williams), and things are not dependent on the comments of interpreters for their existence. It is the artist alone who makes us see the world. His perfection of method, not the achievement of some vague "wisdom," is his reason for working. This, I hope it goes without saying, has nothing to do with self-expression, and very little to do with having profound ideas about some isolated event. My landlord has "ideas" which, upon reflection, are as "profound" as those of many contemporary poets. But he is semiliterate and has no style, so his kinship with them goes unnoticed. What I am trying to get at here is that the world is a great rock, and that it stays so. The artist's job is not to tell you what he *thinks* about it, but is to tell you *it*. Working within this tradition, Joyce has allowed us to understand the filth of nine-teenth-century Europe, and Pound has revealed the contemporary hell which is its inevitable successor—while Williams has pushed our faces into an America that blindly roared its corrupted and corrupting way while we clambered about Mr. Frost's walls, picked his apples, and thought such claptrap as "the thing that art does for life is to clean it, to strip it to form" an instance of wisdom. Once you start "cleaning" and "stripping" life to "form," you become an arbiter; you inevitably find yourself in the position of interpreter. The chair you sit on no longer is a chair by its *self's* being; it becomes an "old friend." You have attempted, in your arrogance, to make order out of the world's chaos, *by your intervention*—and you have succeeded in adding to the chaos. Worse, you have allowed your egoism to impose a lie on what is *true* chaos.

The world we live in does not depend on us for its life; but the artist, the poet, by the use of language, a record of sensibility, attempts a revelation. There is a tradition—the language of previous artists. "Homer's *the wet waves* not our *the wet waves* but enough association in the three words to make a context capable of extension from its time to the present. Because, there is, tho' meanings change, a linguistic etiquette, a record possibly clear to us as the usage of a past context. . . ." (Zukofsky). "*A context capable of extension from its time to the present.*" And Spicer, again in *After Lorca*: "I yell 'Shit' down a cliff at an ocean. Even in my lifetime the immediacy of that word will fade. It will be dead as 'Alas.' But if I put the real cliff and the real ocean into the poem, the word 'Shit' will ride along with them, travel the time machine until cliffs and oceans disappear."

We have in Spicer's work an aesthetic built around language itself, divorced from the image—the moon in the poem independent of images. The lemon to be real "like the newspaper in a collage is a real newspaper." There is a kinship here with Mallarmé's "The poet must establish a careful relationship between two images, from which a third element, clear and fusible, will be distilled and caught by our imagination." The "third element" may be Spicer's cloud. Mallarmé believed, however, the world to be meaningless; hence, his language became a language of "Book." But Spicer sees the world as a place with meaning, however scattered. His rejection of the image is based on the idea, it would seem, that the trouble with the image, or imagism as contemporary theory, is that it has outlived its usefulness as tool and has come to be part of the poetic paraphernalia; i.e., simile, metaphor, image, etc. It has become technique rather than process, or *techné*, and must be rejected.

Nothing will lead the poet further from a rapt attention to the real than a strait reliance on the mechanics which were, when invented, simple *methods* of revealing that real, were new process. The image, as *techné*, must be used in a different way, extended, much as it itself extended the possibilities of metaphor become trope. It would appear that these concerns aroused the recent interest in "deep image." That was an attempt to extend image, but it insisted upon a looking into apparent reality, to get to its core, its hidden meaning (the World Explained). It turned out, however, that "deep image" was another instance of the assertion of the poetic ego—the core of apparent reality was what the poet said it was, i.e., how he felt about it. And, of course, it was still involved with image.

Spicer has moved in another direction, has flouted the concept whereby meaning comes about through connection—simile, metaphor, with their "as" and "like"; and image, with its still focus on a particular nexus of the objective, i.e., the image connects us to the world, the world reveals itself through the image, dependent always on its clarity. But to contemporary workers in the art, the image, its use, is unfortunately more a concomitant of artifact than it is a way of employing the poem as lever whereby the mind may be moved to apprehend the real. Spicer wants *correspondence*. This lemon as against the lemon in the world, as against the "waxy and white" lemon Lorca speaks of—this wet wave and Homer's wet wave: the tradition—"a record possibly clear to us as the usage of a past context." To *connect* is to muddy and blur; to correspond is to isolate and sharpen.

It may be of momentary interest to speak of Spicer's correspondence and Baudelaire's *correspondances*, the differences between them. Baudelaire's idea is Swedenborgian: this reality is imperfect, the pure spirit may have revealed to him, through an exemplary life, the perfect reality. Spicer is no Swedenborgian, and his world is St. Thomas' temporal one, to be got to in order to understand it, and thereby to understand the eternal *meaning* of the world, revealed in discrete things, things as things. Not Baudelaire's eternal, idealized (Platonic) things: "Chairness." But they have affinities in that their poetics insist on revelation; there is in both men the belief that the world is there, regardless of what we think it is; it is the poet's task to reveal it. This is not to be witty, nor to comment profoundly, but to do one's job honestly.

Some time ago, in a critical exchange over Robert Kelly's program for the "deep imagists," Olson wrote this single comment in reply to Kelly's explanation of the treatment of imagery within the poetic of the program: "ImagE, not IMAGES." Total image, as language, total poem. It would seem to me that this is what Spicer has done in this compelling body of work he has left us: he has opted for a total poem, but a total poem as image (or ImagE), of the real . . . not a poem which has IMAGES, but the poem in which "the imagination pictures the real," in which the poet would "point to the real, disclose it . . . make a poem that has no sound in it but the pointing of a finger." Neither metaphor, nor image, nor connection, but the isolation of things, their *correspondence*. Writing of Reznikoff, Zukofsky says that there may be noted in the verse "the isolation of each noun so that in

itself it is an image, the grouping of nouns so that they partake of the quality
of things being together without violence to their individual intact natures."

As a final remark before briefly looking into Spicer's poems, let it be noted
that all poets are part of a continuing tradition, that all innovation is part
of a poetic process, and that Spicer was deeply involved with both: what
may seem like arbitrariness or obscurity in his work is not such, but is merely
an instance of one man's mind working on the *necessary* problems confronting him as a poet in his own time. He has added an integer to our aesthetic,
has drawn imagism out to the point at which language, bare and flat, may
stand as image, image may stand as poem, and poem may stand as the real.

In *Billy the Kid*, a serial poem of ten parts, we see this example of a battering
of metaphor, a breaking open of the formalized choreography poets find too
easily to hand:

> So the heart breaks
> Into small shadows
> Almost so random
> They are meaningless
> Like a diamond
> Has at the center of it a diamond
> Or a rock
> Rock
>
> •   •   •
>
> I can no more remember
> What brought me here
> Than bone answers bone in the arm
> Or shadow sees shadow

"Shadows," "diamond," "rock," and "bone" are in no sense used as,
though they tremble on the verge of, image. Nowhere do they become so.
The use of the comparative "like," instead of leading us into simile, neatly
and almost imperceptibly takes us away from any such easy connection,
bringing diamond to diamond and rock to rock: we have a total presentation. As poetics, it is a successful foray into that territory Williams set down
in his "Portrait of a Lady." And as gloss on that poem, as well as on Spicer's
position, one may quote Williams to effect: "One lack with imagism, as a
definition of effort, is that it is not definite enough. It is true enough, God
knows, to the immediate object it represents but what is that related to the
poet's personal and emotional and intellectual meanings?"

I fear that I may carp on imagism, but its quite unsteady position in the
poetics of today must be insisted upon. Nothing is served by thinking of it
as a going concern, by thinking of it as end result: Spicer is superficially

difficult because he got beyond image, and beyond it to an astonishingly successful degree. And he is not "experimental"—that patronizing word whereby the serious artist's productions are tolerated, or as harmfully lionized.

In *The Heads of the Town up to the Aether*:

> What I mean is words
> Turn mysteriously against those who use them
> Hello says the apple
> Both of us were object.

"Both of us." Rejection of ego-ism. A turning away from the *self* as a thing of aesthetic interest, matrix. Everyone may be interesting but the poet; he must be interested. It should be noted that in the first section of *Heads*, *Homage to Creeley/Explanatory Notes*, Spicer uses these "notes" as instances of correspondence. They seem to be footnotes, glosses on the poems; but they prove to be themselves poems, not *connected* with the work they explain, but correspondent to them. They set the mind on end, insist on distorting the clarity of their "subjects," and in so doing, extend their apparent limits. In a poem called "The Territory Is Not the Map," we see:

> What is a half-truth the lobster declared
> You have sugared my groin and have sugared my hair
> What correspondence except my despair?
> What is my crime but my youth?

—and as part of the note:

> This is a poem to prevent idealism—i.e. the
> study of images. It did not succeed.
> Edward Lear was allowed to say this some time
> ago in his books for children.

The other sections of the book are *A Fake Novel about the Life of Arthur Rimbaud* and *A Textbook of Poetry*. From the latter, as an example of what I meant earlier when I said that Spicer used, in his later work, poem itself as aesthetic: "It does not have to fit together. Like the pieces of a totally unfinished jigsaw puzzle my grandmother left in the bedroom when she died in the living room.". . . "Not as a gesture of contempt for the scattered nature of reality. Not because the pieces would not fit in time. But because this was the only way to cause an alliance between the dead and the living.". . . "To mess around. To totally destroy the pieces. To build around them."

The Holy Grail is a retelling of the Grail Legend, using its events and people, not as springboard for allegory, but as comment on modern samenesses/correspondences. Its language is as precise as in the former books, but there is a mellowing of the poet's sensibilities; the search, the trial and error methods of his previous work toward an ease of statement, a thoroughly poetic usage of his intellectual equipment, are here almost totally resolved. In the *Lancelot* section:

> Nobody's stranger than the stranger coming to the dinner
> He can imitate anything or anybody.
> "When they start climbing up the back of the old flash" the
>   runner who had simply hit a single almost had passed him
>   "It is time to quit. I'll never play again."
> Almost saw the cup, Lancelot, his eyes so filled with tears.

The maudlin, yet sincere complaint of the athlete (Mickey Mantle could "really" say this), against the failure of the beautiful Lancelot; the time bridged successfully; the corresponding "myths": all show Spicer in complete control of his materials. And in *Galahad*:

> The Grail is as common as rats or seaweed
> Not lost but misplaced.
> Someone searching for a letter that he knows is around the
>   house
> And finding it, no better for the letter.

The Holy Grail is an intensive preparation for a position: inhabiting which, Spicer changed what might be called a rationale for aesthetic into poetic. The legend provided him with a search, *per se*, and a series of possibilities for correspondence in time—carrying the words over time, the realities of legend persistent in language, beyond analogy.

But it is in *Language* that he gets to the bases of his involvement, explicit in the title itself. Here Spicer is at the source and the poems succeed wholly in revealing themselves as totalities: language has become reality. The poems present an almost unbelievably skilled combination of the tender and the wry, and Spicer's absolute faith in the language leads him to such near-impossible successes as:

> This is the melancholy Dane
> That built all the houses that lived in the lane
> Across from the house that Jack built.
> This is the maiden all forlorn, a
>   crumpled cow with a crumpled horn
> Who lived in the house that Jack built.
> This is the crab-god shiny and bright
>   who sunned by day and wrote by night
>   And lived in the house that Jack built.
> This is the end of it, very dear friend, this
>   is the end of us.

And this, which might be cut into some government building of dream:

> Smoke signals
> Like in the Eskimo villages on the coast where the earthquake
>   hit
> Bang, snap, crack. They will never know what hit them
> On the coast of Alaska. They expect everybody to be insane.
> This is a poem about the death of John F. Kennedy.

—which, besides being an *American* poem of great power, is also a "text-book" example of Spicer's poetics-in-action. The negation of image, the positing of separate instances of the real as correspondences, the avoidance of logical conclusion. The poem is a whole image of a corrupted and psychopathic society, without complaint, rant, or moral. It is totally rescued from poetic cliché by its attention to language. Language is real, the poem is real—it is Williams' "redeeming language."

So we had here a poet of great accomplishment, much of whose early promise was achieved. His work is available for the interested to investigate. What sort of final statement he might have come to had he lived is most certainly there, in microcosm, in his extant work—and in more than flashes, fragments. There is enough solid, honest work in these five books to earn Spicer a position as one of the most gifted of contemporary American poets, as well as an aesthetic thinker and mentor of considerable stature. He has indeed made "a poem that has no sound in it but the pointing of a finger"— and the poem is, certainly, a durable one.

For Now, ca. 1966

The Collected Books of Jack Spicer.
Edited and with a Commentary by Robin Blaser

> Now these two—namely eternal and temporal—
> are related to our knowledge in this way, that one
> of them is the means of knowing the other. For in
> the order of discovery, we come through temporal
> things to the knowledge of things eternal, accord-
> ing to the words of the Apostle (*Rom.* I. 20): *The*
> *invisible things of God are clearly seen, being under-*
> *stood by the things that are made.*
>   *St. Thomas Aquinas*
>
> He [Spicer] had said early on in conversation with
> a young poet that one had first to learn to use the I
> and then to lose it. This becomes an attack on the

"subjective aim" and assurance of a whole culture.
And it cuts the ground from under a poetry that
ceaselessly returns to wrap itself around a personality. It was especially costly to a poet who refused
those resolving images of the writer as victim or
hero. In the face of this work, both hero and victim
are humanisms which do not measure up. In an
extreme move to gain what he variously called a
dictation, the unknown, an outside, Jack's work
contradicts them as resolutions or explanations of
anything.

Robin Blaser

It was a game made out of summer and freedom and
a need for a poetry that would be more than the
expression of my hatreds and desires.

Jack Spicer

Jack Spicer died in San Francisco on August 17, 1965 at the age of forty.
Between 1957 and the year of his death, he wrote twelve books, of which
six were published during his lifetime. In this eight-year span of intense
creative activity, Spicer revealed himself as the most important poetic in-
novator of the post-War period, an artist of absolute integrity and brilliance.
His work is difficult to come at, thorny, flat, not "beautiful," and totally
lacking in self-confession. The poet is nowhere to be found in his poem; he
has disappeared behind his words. I should guess that at the time of his death
he had an audience of no more than five hundred readers. The mushy con-
glomerate known as the critical establishment never wrote a word on his
work, nor has it yet. There is nothing surprising about this; on the contrary,
recognition of Spicer's genius on the part of official literary criticism would
be nothing short of aberrant. We are, poets and critics and readers alike,
suffering from a romantic hangover, and have a kind of hysterical reliance
on humanism as a cure for all our ills, social and cultural, an insistence that
the artist is a kind of dazed egomaniac to whom we look for interpretations
of the world that may be taken as revelatory of the world's reality. Spicer,
with his dogged conviction that language is merely the "furniture in the
room" that the poem invades was and is sadly out of the swim. We must
cling to our belief in the hegemony of the mind as the locus of all reality or
face the pain of realizing that the world does not depend on us. From this
position issues the persistent mumbling about the poet as idiot savant whose
"experience of self" is holy and true.

    This image of the poet as the wild man with flaming eye and confused,
imprecise language in which nestle lofty thoughts is, of course, nothing new.
It has an absolute philosophic source. The reader may amuse himself by

tracing the lyrics of the Beatles, the poems of Allen Ginsberg, or the visions of Norman Mailer back to their roots in the thought of Kant and Locke: the former *vis-à-vis* the conviction that objects are rendered intelligible only through the intercession of the mind, the latter with his belief that the poet is a man of wit, not judgment, that he is not to be taken seriously by serious men because he has nothing of value to say—we go to him in order to relax by ingesting his beautiful "ideas." It is the curious canker of the romantic sensibility to agree with the first and to "rebel" against the second by proudly accepting his patronization of the poet as proof of the poet's genius.

In his wonderfully perceptive and profound essay on Spicer's work, "The Practice of Outside," Robin Blaser calls this attitude toward poetry "a kind of counter to that discourse which made a peripherality of the poetic act. A let's-make-up-for-it routine." So that "the poetic can only be a persuasive dressing-up of a system or grid of meanings." But the true poet does not interpret the real for us, nor does he invent a reality that purports to be the truth that lies behind the façade of that which we take to be the real. The poet reveals to us the reality of that which we all see all the time. "Signature of all things written here," Stephen Dedalus says. "Here" is the world. The "signature" is not a cipher; it is written in a language whose alphabet the poet must learn. And Spicer says: "Invention is merely the enemy of poetry." And, speaking of the poet who is not in "the fabric" of his life: "Even the objects change. The seagulls, the greenness of the ocean, the fish—they become things to be traded for a smile or the sound of conversation— counters rather than objects. Nothing matters except the big lie of the personal—the lie in which these objects do not believe." The "big lie of the personal" is the post-Kantian house in which the great majority of our poets live. And the great majority of our critics praise them for living there. Jack Spicer did *not* live there and spent the better part of his artistic life proving it.

He paid an enormous price for his convictions. It is clear to anyone conversant with American poetry since 1945 that his work was, as I have said, critically ignored and virtually unread. Mr. Blaser goes so far as to say that his work killed him, and he is not given to hyperbole. Despite his isolation, his influence on his peers and on younger poets was enormous and seems to grow with each passing year.

His poems, and the aesthetic out of which they were composed, form an innovative whole that strikes one as being as invaluable as the work done by Pound, Williams, and Olson. What was the basis of his poetics? To sketch its essentials:

1. That things do not connect but that they correspond. Connection demands a marshaling of poetic remarks and insights into an already estab-

lished discourse of systems and beliefs; a kind of exegesis of experience. Correspondence implies a silent reverberation that is set up between two poetic givens—a silence that allows the unknown to enter the poem and be revealed; that allows the poet to bring objects across language. Spicer says: "A metaphor is something unexplained—like a place in a map that says that after this is desert. A shorthand to admit the unknown."

2. That the image is unimportant to the poem because it is no more than a picture of something and that the poem, as it finds its shape in language is, in itself, the image. Spicer wanted, as he writes, "to make things visible rather than to make pictures of them (phantasia non imaginari)."

3. That "words are what sticks to the real," to be used "to push the real, to drag the real into the poem," and that they are, in themselves, of no more value than a "rope with nothing to be tied to."

4. This last brings us to his conviction that the real is not within us, but outside of us, and that it can manifest itself only in the language of the poet if he allows it to dictate to him.

This process of dictation is clearly outlined in a lecture given by Spicer in Vancouver some two months before his death, of which the pertinent section is quoted in Blaser's essay. It is there for the interested reader's study and reflection; here, allow me briefly to note its essential tenet: That there is a difference between the poet and the outside of the poet, which outside is writing poetry—that the poem that is written comes into being via the poet, who listens to the dictation and records it as given, all the while fighting to distinguish between himself and the poem as it is being written—between, that is, that outside and the inside. You must, Spicer says, "clear the mind away from yourself" and allow the objects outside to manifest themselves as reality through the words that are awaiting them.

These concepts make for a poetry that is harsh, severe, difficult, and yet, when apprehended, dazzling in its clarity. Spicer speaks of "the blinding light of the poem," under which, he implies, all that is unnecessary shows itself as dross. This kind of aesthetic has little patience for what we are told with boring regularity is "fine writing," all frill and trope. Spicer's poetry is the enemy of all such fine writing as it is the enemy of all poems that suppose the poet's egoistic vision to be the business of the poem. The reader will see the difficulties such a poetry faces in our time. The confessional in poetry is the *dernier cri* and has issued in formal disguise from the romantic attitudinizing of what used to be called the Beat poets. (It is odd that critics do not see the affinities between such "underground" poets of the fifties and the academics of the present day. They are probably and predictably confused by what they think of as differing "content" and "technique.") Somehow, we have found all truth and sincerity in the first person singular. Spicer, grappling in obscurity with the intransigent objects of a world that is not interested in the poet or his personality, presents a poetry that obstinately, ruthlessly, cuts against the grain.

One point that I want to make clear is that Jack Spicer was that rare thing to be at any time, perhaps the rarest of all things in our own, a true poet. A poet does not interpret, he reveals. His intelligence is poetic, not religious or political or social. St. Thomas' "things eternal" are made visible through the revelation of the essence of "temporal things"—and it is the poet who discovers this essence, who reads this "signature." If you believe that what is visible is a weak and shadowy reflection of some Platonic reality, you will not believe in the integrity of the visible. If you believe that the visible is meaningful only insofar as you encase it or layer it with your own meaning, you will see in the visible what you want to see in it. This is the essence of humanism and of the ideology that holds the poet to be a commentator. In order to assure the poet of our belief in him in a crass and shabby time, criticism has attempted to deny him his right to be a poet and has instead insisted upon his uniqueness as a personality—dozens of poets have gone right along. But the poet is an artist, not a seer or an entertainer with a polished and recognizable routine. We must look to him as one who can reveal to us the actual. His imagination cannot be understood in terms of invention—a first cousin to "making things up" and rambling fantasy. The poet's imagination is a developed gift whereby the essence (Aquinas calls it *quidditas* or "whatness") of the real may be apprehended and understood of and for itself. "The imagination pictures the real," Spicer writes. It does not invent images. It does not make things up. It does not fantasize.

Before ending these remarks, I should like to comment on the title of this volume. Spicer did not, after 1956, write single poems. He composed books that are serial poems or that have within them more than one serial poem. This conception of poetry grew out of his deepening involvement with the process of dictation and with his conviction that there is no such thing as a single poem, that "poems should echo and reecho against each other. They should create resonances. They cannot live alone any more than we can." It is a measure of Spicer's success that it is remarkably difficult to quote lines or even whole poems and give the reader a clear idea of the severe, hard perfection of his work. It coheres not only within each individual book but within the collection as a whole. The work is an overwhelming achievement, and that it was composed, as noted above, in eight years, and in the face of an almost total critical silence, is miraculous. Spicer wrote, in *Language*, these wry lines that penetrate to the core of his chaste poetics and reveal his acceptance and understanding of what he knew by that time was their fate:

This ocean, humiliating in its disguises
Tougher than anything.
No one listens to poetry. The ocean
Does not mean to be listened to. A drop
Or crash of water. It means
Nothing.
It
Is bread and butter
Pepper and salt. The death
That young men hope for. Aimlessly
It pounds the shore. White and aimless signals. No
One listens to poetry.

Village Voice, 1975

4

Louis Zukofsky

Privacy is the hallmark of Louis Zukofsky's life. He himself has written, "As a poet I have always felt that the work says all there needs to be said of one's life." That seems clear enough. A note on anyone's life and work, however, presupposes the inclusion of biographical data, so for those who need it: Zukofsky was born on the Lower East Side in 1904, spoke only Yiddish until he went to public school, and began writing poetry in English at the age of eleven. At sixteen he published his first poems, became friends with Pound and Williams at twenty-three, and at twenty-seven edited the February 1931 issue of *Poetry*—the now-famous "An Objectivists' Anthology." He has published almost two dozen books, and this year saw the appearance of the last two sections of his great poem of a half-century's labor, *"A"-1-24*. His criticism is of the highest order; indeed, it may well be the subtlest and most profound criticism of poetry to have been written in this century.

I have been reading Zukofsky for twenty years and flatter myself that I have begun to understand how to read him; his work, as Williams has said, cannot be thought of as "a simple song," rather, his song is more like Mozart's. There is no way of making him simple. As does all great art, his work resists cheapening, and it must be experienced in the full range of its intellect, craft, and music in order to be understood, even a little bit. The dedication is to art as a kind of supreme search for the clarity of the understanding. As with so much art that is not for sale, the drive toward clarity often makes for a difficult end result. We are left, as it were, with no help except from the poet's other poems, the tradition of the art of poetry, and our own intelligence. The handles are missing.

What is "difficult" poetry? On inspection, it often turns out to be that poetry that hides its meaning from readers save those with "keys" to the poem, as if the poem were a puzzle to be solved. Ah, we say, *this* is what "rose" means—now I understand—and the poem then automatically opens to us its mysteries. There is also that poem that seems impenetrable because of the scholarship or esoteric reference invested in its lines. How often have we been told in classrooms that one of the reasons for studying classical mythology and history is that it will help us to "understand" Milton, or Keats. Will it? Certainly, it will help us to understand references or allusions made in the poem, but these things can as well be understood through glosses or footnotes. When all the data have been explicated, we are left with the intransigent poem. But what of the poem that resists the understanding except on its own terms, the Zukofsky poem, a complex song, a sound that is an interpenetration of intellect and music? For instance:

> Little wrists,
> Is your content
> My sight or hold,
> Or your small air
> That lights and trysts?
>
> Red alder berry
> Will singly break;
> But you—how slight—do:
> So that even
> A lover exists.

What does that mean? What, specifically, does "but" mean? There is no symbolism here. The poem is surely more than imagism. The submitted figure is not surreal. The song demands an adjustment of the mind so that the power of the intellect may be brought to bear on it: not a simple song. Or, yes, perhaps a simple song whose difficulty lies in the meaning and syntax of its language.

This is not to say that there is never external information as a ground for many of Zukofsky's poems. My point is that the possession of such information leaves us, still, with the poem. The received data do not make the poem come clear in the sense that we may then discuss what the poet is "saying" outside of the formal structure of his verse. Poets like Zukofsky are rarely taught in literature classes and as rarely dealt with by critics because whatever "idea" may reside in a Zukofsky poem—and by "idea" I mean exactly that part that may be separated out from the poem and taught—is inseparable from it and may not be paraphrased.

It is and always has been Zukofsky's delight to set for himself aesthetic problems and to go about solving them within the poem. We are not required to know what these problems are in order to allow the poem our attention; they are the poet's concern and are almost always invisible. Our knowledge of them, certainly, enhances our pleasure in the work, just as our pleasure in *Ulysses* is enhanced when we are enlightened as to the formal structure that underlies the edifice of each chapter. But this knowledge of the nature of the materials used in the composition of the poem does not explain the poem—or to put it more bluntly, scholarship can neither write nor read poetry.

As a small example of the sort of poetic problem that Zukofsky invents for himself, consider this. Hugh Kenner tells us that the first five stanzas and coda of "A"-9: (1) follow the rhyme scheme of Cavalcanti's "Donna Mi Prega"; (2) use phrases taken from *Das Kapital* as lyrics to this music; and (3) distribute all the "n" and "r" sounds of the lines acccording to the formula for a conic section. None of this prepares us, however, for

> Hands, heart, not value made us, and of any
> Desired perfection the projection solely,
> Lives worked us slowly to delight the senses,
> Of their fire shall you find us, of the many
> Acts of direction not defection—wholly—
> Dead labor, lowlier with time's offenses,
> Assumed things of labor powers extorted
> So thwarted we are together impeded—
> The labor speeded while our worth decreases—
> Naturally surplus value increases
> Being incident to the pace exhorted:
> Unsorted, indrawn, but things that time ceded
> To life exceeded—not change, the mind pieces
> The expanse of labor in us when it ceases.

This simply cannot be licked off the page. It exists in still perfection with or without the reader's knowledge of Marx's economics and Cavalcanti's prosody, available to the intellect that demands that poetry be more than a recording of the adventures of the ego.

Zukofsky, as he has written of Thomas Wyatt, is "thinking a prosody" in his poems, feeling out sound as he composes, not picking up, bag and baggage, whatever is lying around in the disguise of "our heritage." He does not hammer out dead and dying measures, in order to prove, along with Frost, that he does not like to "play tennis with the net down." He does not write "free verse," which seems to exist only in the minds of insolent academics who loathe poetry. (Whether any verse anywhere was ever "free" is a question worthy of consideration.)

When a poet "thinks a prosody" he is, obviously, absolutely on his own, far from the safeties of measure perfected by men who lived in another time and who spoke a quite different English. Yet he is enclosed in a structure that is distinctly measurable. In other words, he has placed himself outside the concerns of taste and fashion and declared an interest in art. As an exercise in comparison, here are two fragments, the first by Frost, the second by Zukofsky:

> The living come with grassy tread
> To read the gravestones on the hill;
> The graveyard draws the living still,
> But never any more the dead.
> *(Frost)*

> River that must turn full after I stop dying
> Song, my song, raise grief to music
> Light as my loves' thought, the few sick
> So sick of wrangling: thus weeping,
> Sounds of light, stay in her keeping
> And my son's face—this much for honor.
> *(Zukofsky)*

The first is a competent manipulation of iambics, not, certainly, the iambic line as we are given it in Chaucer or Herrick, but a pleasant enough ama-teurish takeover on which ride certain "sentiments." (That they could as well be expressed in prose gives us something to think about.) The second shows Zukofsky inventing prosody in a line that is essentially traditional and yet his own. These first six lines of *"A"-11* take their structure from a pre-cisely, delicately, and inextricably entwined composition of image, sound, and the conceptual intelligence, a controlled combination of eye, ear, and intellect. This is willed prosody, apparent in all of Zukofsky's work, the same sort of prosody that Wyatt forged in his reworkings from Petrarch, and a prosody that probably allowed Wyatt both his fluent and flexible line and the charges later brought against him that he had not known what he was doing. But it is best to let Zukofsky speak here as an indication of his critical intelligence and a suggestion of his concern with poetics:

Petrarch's sonnet ["che' bel fin fa chi ben amando more"] entailed counting out a line of eleven syllables, but permitted elisions in attaining that number, while it let accent shift with the pace of the thing said. And conjecture may say that Wyatt was aware of that, but that in his passion to render this prosody as English thought he decided an equivalent measure was a line of ten syllables allowing for all the devices of Petrarch's craft. ["The longe love that in my thought doeth harbar"] Criticized for not achieving Surrey's settled technique, Wyatt's verse easily matches the "irregularities" of Chaucer's which Dryden did not know how to speak. Chaucer was witness to the sources of his craft and it is possible, as some have said, that like him Wyatt may have read Italians earlier than Petrarch. And if Wyatt did, perhaps he had guessed how to speak Chaucer.

Even this brief fragment from *Bottom: On Shakespeare*, Zukofsky's magnificent study, alerts us to the fact that he is a poet for whom craft is not an instance of the use of ready-made forms into which any emotion may be dumped or squeezed. "I believe in an 'absolute rhythm,' " Pound wrote, "a rhythm, that is, in poetry which corresponds exactly to the emotion or shade of emotion to be expressed." Zukofsky's rhythms are absolute in the way that Pound used the word, shifting as his matter shifts, meticulous in expressing the subtlest moods of thought and feeling:

> Daughter of music
> and her sweet son
> so that none rule
> the dew to his own hurt
> with the year's last sigh awake
> the starry sky and bird
>   • • •
> Horses: who will do it? out of manes? Words
> Will do it, out of manes, out of airs, but
> They have no manes, so there are no airs, birds
> Of words, from me to them no singing gut.
> For they have no eyes, for their legs are wood,
> For their stomachs are logs with print on them;
>   • • •
> Old friends
> when I was young
> you laughed with my tongue
> but when I sang
> for forty years
> you hid in your ears
> hardly a greeting
>
> I was
> being poor
> termed difficult
> tho I attracted a cult
> of leeches
> and they signed *love*
> and drank its cordials

always for giving
when they were receiving
they presumed
an infinite forgiveness

The last quote, which is from Zukofsky's version of Plautus' comedy, "Rudens" (which makes up all of *"A"-21*), is an example of the kind of musical intelligence that informs the poet's œuvre, an intelligence that we may find persistent in the poetics of, say, Thomas Campion, for example:

What faire pompe haue I spide of glittering Ladies;
With locks sparckled abroad, and rosie Coronet
On their yuorie browes, trackt to the daintie thies
With roabs like Amazons, blew as Violet,
With gold aiglets adorned, some in a changeable
Pale; with spangs wauering taught to be moueable.

—which may be held against Zukofsky's:

To-day I gather all red flowers,
    Shed their petals on the paths,
Shimaunu-San, in the dawn,
    Red I go to meet him—
Shimaunu-San, my clear star.

To-morrow I tear cherry sprays,
    Wreathe them in my hair and at my temples,
Shimaunu-San will see my head's white blossoms,
    In the dark run towards me
Shimaunu-San, my clear star.

In both examples the attentive reader will see that the last accent in each line almost invariably falls on the antepenultimate syllable, a handling of language that allows the lines to fall away, and gives them an exquisite subtlety. Zukofsky's attention to and success with this prosodic technique is no mere aping of dead matter, but is, as is Campion's use of Horace's measure, a revivification of a particular metrics.

Zukofsky, with his wife, Celia, a musician and composer, completed and published some few years ago a translation of Catullus that must stand as the most remarkable execution of that poet's verse into English that has ever been attempted. Not only do the translations succeed in carrying over the content of the poems and their music, they render into our tongue the actual sound of the Latin. It is a strange Catullus, granted; yet it also is, in a way that is hard to define, truer to him than all the modern attempts at translating his colloquial yet elegant lines—most of the contemporary tries at him have rendered his work into limp slang, a fearful butchery. Here is a small exhibit: the poem is number LVIII. I give first the original, then my own version, and last, the Zukofskys':

> Caeli, Lesbia nostra, Lesbia illa,
> illa Lesbia, quam Catullus unam
> plus quam se atque suos amavit omnes,
> nunc in quadriviis et angiportis
> glubit magnanimos Remi nepotes.
>   *(Catullus)*

> O Caelius, our Lesbia, that Lesbia,
> that Lesbia whom alone Catullus loved
> more than himself and everything else,
> now on the corners and in the alleyways
> fucks the courageous sons of Rome.
>   *(Sorrentino)*

> Caelius, Lesbia new star, Lesbia a light,
> all light, Lesbia, whom Catullus (o name
> loss) whom his eyes caught so as avid of none,
> none else—slunk in the driveways, the dingy parts
> glut magnanimous Remus, his knee-high pots.
>   *(Zukofskys)*

The marriage of sound, measure, and sense are startling—and become even more so when we find that the OED tells us that "pot" is a word first used in 1891 to mean "a person of importance," usually used in the phrase, "big pot." So we can see how precisely the Zukofskys' "knee-high pots" catches the bitterness of "magnanimos Remi nepotes." It shows, this minor touch, the way that Zukofsky makes use of all the materials available to him in order to make his poem, a mastery of language, a "witness to the sources" of craft.

Zukofsky is seventy-two now. It is clear to anyone who is seriously engaged with poetry that his work stands alongside that of Pound, Williams, and Stevens, as among the most authentic body of poetry to have been written by an American poet in this century. Those of his generation who may be considered his peers are Olson and Oppen. He has proffered us an enormous gift; somehow, we have refused to accept it, blundering after false gods and prophets. It is his own gift, pure and intense, his entire life, the rhythm and meaning of it, that is available to us in his books. To "place" him succinctly, then: he always was the real thing and always will be. Apropos Zukofsky, we can agree with Pound when he writes: "A man's rhythm must be interpretative, it will be, therefore, in the end, his own, uncounterfeiting, uncounterfeitable."

Village Voice, 1976

A WORD ON ZUKOFSKY

Red alder berry
Will singly break;
But you—how slight—do:
So that even
A lover exists.

"But"? What does "but" mean? And is "even" an adjective or an adverb? This "metaphysical" nicety of expression, the lyric turning on the most delicate changes in the meanings of words, is as subtle and exact as Donne's great gold/circle imagery in "A Valediction Forbidding Mourning," and gives Zukofsky's poetry its persistent hold on the mind.

Catullus writes:

glubit magnanimos Remi nepotes

—"magnanimos" used with hardly veiled irony. Zukofsky, translating, has it

glut magnanimous Remus, his knee-high pots

which resists sense until it is discovered that "pot" was a slang word in use in the late nineteenth century, usually in the phrase "big pot" to describe a person of importance, as we might say "big gun." Thus, "knee-high pots" out of "Remi nepotes" locates Catullus' irony for the *twentieth* century. Words remembered and rejuvenated. Zukofsky writes: "Homer's *the wet waves* not our *the wet waves* but enough association in the three words to make a context capable of extension from its time to the present. Because there is, tho' meanings change, a linguistic etiquette, a record possibly clear to us as the usage of a past context."

Logopoiea: "The dance of the intelligence among words and ideas. . . ."

> where a curtain
> kept the dust from
> the walls,
> a white
>
> that with most
> things packed shows how
> little one needs

and, in *Bottom*, quoting Aquinas: "No power can know anything without turning to its object, as sight knows nothing unless it turns to color." And quoting Christopher Smart:

> For the colors are spiritual.
> For WHITE is the first and the best.

White . . . shows [itself, its whiteness]; white . . . shows [us] how . . . the verb is at once transitive and intransitive. Which takes us, by curious divagation, back to Fenollosa's "Who can doubt that when we say 'the wall shines,' we mean that it actively reflects light to our eye?"

"Nobody seems to catch on that my true song is my skepticism and inside out or vice (*in all senses*) reversed."—Zukofsky in a letter of June 10, 1976.

> Love has an intellect that runs through all
> The scrutinous sciences, and like
> A cunning poet, catches a quantity
> Of every knowledge, yet brings all home
> Into one mystery, into one secret
> That he proceeds in.
> Thomas Middleton, *The Changeling*

"Love, or—if one wishes to explain—the desire to project the mind's peace, is one growth." (*Bottom.*)

Paideuma, 1978

5

William Bronk

William Bronk's poems have hitherto been brought to my attention in magazines like *The Black Mountain Review* and *Origin* (old and new series), both of which are now defunct. This book is his second collection, and it is beautiful. His poems are "intellectually" oriented, by which I mean that he extrapolates the conditions for his poems from data which are mostly non-"poetic." Many of his images are abstract, are phrases, idea as idea, without the movement of said idea into a physical shape. Sometimes he works with the physical, as image, given, received by the eye. His skills are rare and orderly, the world is a place to be respected, and feared: a little suspect. He drives upon the reader at times with the conceits of the metaphysicals.

> One thinks how
> in certain pictures, envied landscapes are seen
> (through a window maybe) far behind the serene
> sitter's face, the serene pose, as though
> in some impossible mirror, face to back,
> human serenity gazed at a green world
> which gazed at this face.

That sort of perception is worthy of Donne.

He is dry, precise; his poems are short and tight, and constantly throw one off guard—he's always up to something else: either he tersely wraps the poem up in the last line or two, in the manner of the final couplet in the Shakespearean sonnet, or he moves through it leisurely, allowing his form to realize its intent—subtly, but with acute care—where it will. He writes a dense poem, every word takes its place and we are held suspended, the tension is never wholly relaxed until the last word is read. This is not to say that the poems are tracts, homilies for the wall. Many of them flower at their conclusion, there is a ringing, a suspension of the mind: we move beyond the confines of the poem as artifact into that space which the poem has charged with possibility. In a poem called "The Lawn":

> it is as though it defied
> not the curvature of the globe, only, but the curve
> of space itself, went straight beyond the curve
> enough to not follow, and just enough,
> and hung there, overhung it. As though it did.

This is very unfashionable stuff: to say about the world that it is enough, as it is, there before us. "The earth is beautiful beyond all change," he says; and in a poem on Machu Picchu, the Inca wall, he says of its builders and architecture, "we see them say of the world there is nothing to say." In an age in which humanism has been the motivation for the most hideous callousness and murder, this insistence on the humble place of man in the earth is, to me, beautiful.

Poetry, 1965

"GOD SWEETEN THE BITTER JUDGEMENTS OF OUR LIVES"

Not to go into a great song and dance about it, but William Bronk is a scandalously neglected poet, at a time when there are very few poets worth attending to in any way whatsoever. I would even go so far as to say that he might well be in that limbo uninhabited even by "poets' poets," though his poems clearly mark him as a remarkably creative artist. He writes the same poem over and over again, exploring the quality and reality of despair. Each rings a variation on his dark theme.

The poems are salutary, however, and the darker and more intransigent the world they inscribe, the more salutary they become: they are tragic. Precisely so; that is, the panorama of life that these poems illuminate is tragic; there is no other sense that the world can make to a reasonable man. The only writers worth paying attention to are those who view the world as tragic, and those who view it as comic, i.e., those who "laugh to keep from crying." All the rest are in the process of giving one "hope," or worse, they are "changing things." But things change far, far from the artifacts of art. To understand that the world is not ours for the taking, and to understand further that it will not yield up anything that it does not intrinsically possess, seems to me to be the only program that a serious writer can subscribe to.

God damn interpretation. God damn opinion. God damn explanation. If you think that the world is any cookie you want it to be, stay away from William Bronk.

To know that the sun and sea are beautiful, and that as they reveal themselves in these states, men are dying in agony, continually, continually— that is to have a despairing vision. That the world is harsh and vicious does not preclude its loveliness. What is there to say? One might say, as Bronk: "The earth is beautiful beyond all change." Or, of the Inca wall, Machu Picchu, and its builders, "we see them say of the world there is nothing to say." How indigestible such comments are in this time of razzmatazz rhetoric, where all dreams can come true if we can only once again petition, elect, spend, kill, ostracize, wage one more righteous war. Those who believe that men can be "bettered" by such social activities are dangerous and incurable optimists, like Hitler or Guevara or Roosevelt, beings who would rather have choked than admit to a world that is tragic, a world of which there is, indeed, nothing to say. Such men have their living counterparts: all over.

Oh, anybody can be "sad," tragic even, despairing. When life treats one harshly, one is sad. Poets continually confront you with the elation of a new love affair, or with the gloom of a dead one. The rays of the sun, the splendor of mountains, the meadows, etc. "Ecology, and how we love it," they say, these pimps for nature. This all changes as the poet's fortunes change, so that the lovely mountains one day may be the sinister mountains the next, depending on the poet's view of them. One day this entertainer is King Lear and the next Samuel Smiles. Let's gently suggest that this poetry is for people who look through anthologies to find verses to fit their occasions. It is not poetry that has a vision of the world. The world is a rock. Reality is real.

> "Well, of course," he said, "we take a different approach
> to reality." As though it were something that lay
> like a lump in the yard, that anyone could kick.

Bronk is neglected because his poetry is unfashionable, and it is unfashionable because it is uncompromisingly despairing. Men live despite life, he says. The meaning of life lies in the pattern it makes, no more and no less. Nothing is unfair, since unfairness assumes that the world should be "some way." The world is. This is bitter medicine for the modern palate, for people are taught that "action" will solve our misery, or sex, or religion or art, or a belief in the endless and vapid linkages of mysticism. Was it St. Thomas who said that God must have created the world as a joke? It makes no sense, except the sense that Camus' Caligula came to: "Man dies, and he is unhappy."

The wonder of Bronk's poems is that they show, in line after line, that the world has no need for them, that the world will not change a jot because of their existence, that they are parts of the world: they are Machu Picchu. Hopeless poems, hopeless, but like the world, no less real for being so.

Poems like these are often termed "cynical" and are greeted with a nervous silence or the contempt of those who insist that the end of life is the joy of man. But we all know that the end of life is death: no slogans have yet been coined that will remove that strict reality. It is our only abiding fact.

> Geometers, all measures measure themselves,
> none measures the world. Premise and axiom
> are terms of the limited case, to limit it.
> There is no limited truth: there is no truth.

Grosseteste Review, 1972

6

Kenneth Rexroth

A GOOD HOUSE

The Homestead Called Damascus. By Kenneth Rexroth
Natural Numbers: New and Selected Poems. By Kenneth Rexroth

Whether these two books were brought out at roughly the same time in the hope that they would mutually enhance one another is a question I am unable to answer; the fact, however, is that they do and together make a rather handsome package. Rexroth has come a long way from the long, youthfully philosophical poem, *The Homestead Called Damascus*; and the selections from *Natural Numbers* testify to the stopping places along that way.

Rexroth is the kind of poet you take or leave. There's no way that I can see of shrugging him off, or of selecting poems which seem "strong" or "best." He is an honest-to-God classicist: his poems are totally free of bric-a-brac; his images are direct and simple and found only when his movement seems to demand them—that is, none of his poems are built around the image. Along with this, there is an almost cavalier disregard for the niceties of the poetic line, the metres move easily and casually, and rhyme is es-chewed in work as early as *Homestead*. He really wants to get something off his chest, this Rexroth; and his *Natural Numbers* is a sweet, honest book, taking you from *The Art of Worldly Wisdom* (1922) through the *New Poems* (1957–1962). He certainly can't teach you anything in terms of technique, and he is not one to turn a nice phrase; but he can say something like

> At midnight I make myself a jug
> of hot white wine and cardamon seeds.
> In a torn grey robe and old beret,

> I sit in the cold writing poems,
> Drawing nudes on the crooked margins,
> Copulating with sixteen year old
> Nymphomaniacs of my imagination.

—and if it isn't Villon, still, it is good work. What makes a simple fragment like that excellent is the same kind of classically oriented imagination which moves us in the naked, simple lines that end Catullus' fifty-eighth poem, "nunc in quadriviis et angiportis / glubit magnanimos Remi nepotes." This sort of imagination has been regarded with suspicion for a long time now, and many of the reflections in *Natural Numbers* can scarcely be called poetry unless one allows Rexroth his devotion to this unadorned art.

To hold *Homestead* alongside the later poems is to see that Rexroth was a young poet to be seriously considered when he wrote it; but he was obviously deep in books, he rigs a philosophical framework on which the lines are hung, the poem is a three-way "dialogue" and an attempt to tie together Rexroth's knowledge of ideas and the world by the use of unconvincing "poetic" voices. Poems like this suffer terribly at the hands of reviewers, perhaps rightly so; but Rexroth has published this almost as a pleasantry, the poems of *Natural Numbers* giving it stature as bibliography, background. The older Rexroth would never write anything like it, although it contains excellent fragments. The most interesting thing is that his line has stayed as fluid, as haphazardly sophisticated a thing as one notes in the early poem.

> In the deep blue winter evening
> The homeward crowd murmurs and hurries
> And rearranges itself to the
> Color of signal lights and shrilling
> Whistles. Sebastian disengages
> Himself and walks in the cold, smoky
> Twilight of Central Park, spotted with
> Week-old dirty snow. . . .

Although the matured genius of selection and pruning is lacking, there is little doubt that the young man who wrote these lines wrote also

> Skaters on the pond vanish
> In dusk, but their voices stay,
> Calling and laughing, and birds
> Twitter and cry in the reeds.

—lines from the last poem in *Natural Numbers*. I, for one, am glad that Rexroth abandoned the philosophical frame some time ago and has steadily moved toward a "purer" poem. He is capable of writing some of the strongest and surest verse of our era in the next decade or so. "Rexroth is no writer in the sense of the word-man. For him words are sticks and stones to build a house—but it's a good house." That was William Carlos Williams in 1944. Now, twenty years later, Rexroth is still no word-man—and his house is still a good one.

Poetry, 1964

Natural Numbers

Kenneth Rexroth is hard to place in any discussion of modern poetry, simply because he refuses to stand still. By that, I don't mean that he goes off chasing rainbows, but that he has consistently gone out on a limb in his essays on jazz, politics, letters, and all those things which interest the cultured and educated man in our time. Out of a reading of his work, however, there finally comes an attitude—that of a man deeply and sincerely interested in what used to be called, before it became a subject for lame jokes, the "life of letters."

As a commentator on his poetic contemporaries, Rexroth has few peers, as his brilliant essay on the influence of French poetry on American testifies. He is witty and learned and writes a clean, spare prose that is rich with information and opinion without being, for even a moment, boring. I cite his critical prose here because his new book of poems partakes of the same simplicity, the same quiet and candid attempt to make order of his experience, so that he may fully communicate it. The language is stripped to the bone and muscle; he indulges in a "non-style" that he may bring over the emotion in verse unsullied by the lumbering and labored crossword puzzles foisted upon us by the great mob of writers who apparently feel that poetry is an occasion for the monthly quiz.

May I go out on a limb and call him a populist? He'd probably laugh at that but he is close to it, making the common materials of life into straightforward poems, heavily dependent on William Carlos Williams for his attitudes, although nowhere, not even in his earliest work, does one find Williams used as a crutch, or even model. He himself has said it clearly for us, in an interview in *The Sullen Art*: "I've never understood why I'm a member of the avant-garde. I write more or less . . . like the great Greeks and Romans and the Chinese, and so forth. I try to say, as simply as I can, the simplest and most profound experiences of my life, which I think will be of significance to others on a similar level." *Natural Numbers* testifies to that position—forty years of poems, carefully selected and standing as a reflection of a man's inner life over those years.

The literary currents of that span have touched him; his own interest in translation has also made its mark. His handling of the image is sure, but without flamboyance, the image functions. Here, from *The Art of Worldly Wisdom* (1922), we have:

> Nights when the wind stirred this inland water
> Like the sea, piled the waves over the breakwater,
> And onto the highway, tore apart tall clouds,
> And revealed the moon, rushing dead white
> Over the city.

As the poems grow more mature, the use of imagery becomes more and more sparing (as if Rexroth mistrusts this device), the verse pushes outward, becomes more concerned with simple declaration—a poetry that is, in *fact*, what Sandburg's poetry attempts to be. He wants the record straight, has broken with anything which he feels might make the poem mere artifact:

> These words, this poem, this
> Is all confusion and ignorance.
> But I know that coached by your sweet heart,
> My heart beat one free beat and sent
> Through all my flesh the blood of truth.

And in the latest work (1962):

> Look. Listen. They are lighting
> The moon. Be still. I don't want
> To hear again that wistful
> Kyriale of husbands and lovers.

The poems move into you and stay, they are, indeed, records of both the simplicity and profundity of one man's life. Their failures are sincere failures, instances of the poem's inability to match, in intensity, the emotion which occasioned it—such failures are far from being contemptible.

Book Week, ca. 1965

TWO BOOKS

I suppose I've read most of Kenneth Rexroth's essays by now, and *The Alternative Society* is of a piece with all the others. Witty, charming, flashingly intelligent, cantankerous, stubborn, learned, and absolutely wrongheaded—all these separately and together can describe his critical thought. I can't think of another writer his age who has so consistently gone out on a

limb in his opinions, striking, as it is said, while the iron is hot; so that much
of his work, when collected, is seen to be a victim of time. On the other
hand, he is right just as often as not. Curiously enough—since his denigra-
tion of Pound's work over the years is well known—his essays delight and
infuriate in exactly the way that Pound's do. I would guess that the reason
for this is that both of them wrote criticism as working *writers*, not as "critics." So that Rexroth and Pound are more interesting and valuable to read,
even when they are wrong, than, let's say, Edmund Wilson and John Simon
are when they are right. The beauty of Rexroth's work as against the work of
a diddler like Simon is that Rexroth knows everything that Simon knows—
and then knows a lot more; that is, while both men may speak with some
authority on Baudelaire, Forster, Li Po, Eliot, etc., Rexroth can also speak
on Spicer, Bud Powell, Alden Van Buskirk, and The Grateful Dead. He
lives here, you know, *here*, where people who can actually think sometimes
eat Franco-American spaghetti and watch *Star Trek*.

God knows, he's ridden a lot of hobby-horses into the ground, but with
great verve and style. If he says something so ridiculous as that H.G. Wells
was a better artist than Forster, he also points to the genius of Weldon Kees;
if he calls such a watery versifier as Leonard Cohen a major poet, he also
knows *exactly* the cultural differences between bebop and rock; if he suggests
that New York is Fifth and Park Avenues between 59th and 100th Streets—
with the Village and the "East Village" (a realtor's term) thrown in—and
that San Francisco is Athens-on-the-Pacific, he does not explain why for
almost twenty years the most important poets in the Bay Area—Jack Spicer,
Robert Duncan, Robin Blaser, George Stanley, Richard Duerden—were
attended only by a minuscule coterie in that City of Light; nor does he
comment on the fact that ten years ago, when jazz clubs in New York had
already presented such musicians as Ornette Coleman, Don Cherry, Archie
Shepp, Charlie Haden, and Cecil Taylor, San Francisco was filled with the
sounds of what one remembers painfully as "West Coast" jazz, with some
fifties-New York imitations thrown in. And wasn't it Bird who, after the
shock of playing for his first West Coast audience said, "If I ever get back to
the Apple, I'll never leave it again"?

But I can't care about these things: they are all part and parcel of Rexroth's marvelous range and nonpompous erudition. As you take or leave his
poems, you take or leave his essays. His prose is graceful and beautifully
turned, and he makes his points—maddening as some of them may be—
with great precision. Given this particular book, I find that my major dis-
agreement with him concerns his equation of artistic worth with its reception, or lack of it, by the young. If everybody under twenty-five is singing
Bob Dylan and Joni Mitchell songs, that seems to me to be a cultural, not
an aesthetic phenomenon. That only a handful of people that age listen to

Archie Shepp or the late Albert Ayler simply indicates that these musicians have nothing to offer the majority of youth. But "everybody" used to dance to Glenn Miller and Tommy Dorsey, while Jay McShann and Benny Moten were for the cognoscenti. So what? People—the young included—satisfy their "urge toward art" in whatever way they can: none of this affects the artist at all. If one's musical needs are filled by The Monkees, one simply does not need The Budapest String Quartet; if one is moved by *Love Story*, one does not need *The Good Soldier*; if Rod McKuen straightens one out for a week, why struggle with John Wieners? That young people in Peoria know all the words to "Sympathy for the Devil," just as their counterparts on McDougal Street do, seems to indicate something sinister, i.e., that the absolutely hip and the absolutely popular are the same thing. It is a triumph of merchandising. I don't have enough space to go into why I think Bob Dylan is not an important poet; suffice it to say that what he has fills a definite need: he is the equal of Cole Porter or Larry Hart, but he's no Arthur Rimbaud.

As for the translations, *Love and the Turning Year*, they are beautifully wrought, as are those in Rexroth's earlier book from the Chinese. I'm totally ignorant of Chinese and can only judge these poems in terms of the other translations I have read. They are very spare, much like Rexroth's own poems from about 1950 onward, and have the delicate strength I associate with Chinese verse. There are included valuable notes and a remarkably useful bibliography, with brief comments as to the worth of the books mentioned. Both books testify to Rexroth's value as a poet and critic—and to his value as that rarest of birds, a man of letters.

Unpublished, 1970

7

Lorine Niedecker

My Friend Tree

It is distinctly unusual to speak of failure with anything but the rankest of distaste.
Edward Dorn, from the Introduction

These poems are brief records of failure in the overall world which surrounds
them, and in which they exist as brilliant markers. They are clear, hard, and
without sentimentality, they take a classical shape, they exist in "the light
of ordinary day," as Hulme says. Miss Niedecker has the genuine poetic
genius and expertise to speak quietly and truly of absolute, real things and
to make the words of that speech glitter with a quality which I can only call
irrevocable; once she has said something there is no more room to add a
postscript. *What* she speaks of touches any human heart deeply—she makes
me feel the way Snooks Eaglin does on his Folkways recording. These are
such effortless, *true* registrations. Records of failure: without self-pity.

It is one of the hardest things in the world for a writer to speak clearly of
his own failures without either weeping over these phenomena or making
them into something "heroic" or romantic. On the other hand there is the
danger of speaking so bluntly, so simply, that the pathos and poignancy of
these failures refuse to communicate themselves to the reader. When the
balance is achieved, we are given remarkable poetry, as in Catullus and
Emily Dickinson. In our own time we have Zukofsky, and Edward Dorn,
among others. The quality seems to be an ability to simply *say* something
straight out, and then to leave it alone—Williams, of course, has done it
for years. Miss Niedecker does it constantly. It is beautiful poetry.

There's a better shine
on the pendulum
than is on my hair
and many times

　.　.　　　　.　.

I've seen it there.
·　·　·

Black Hawk held: In reason
land cannot be sold,
only things to be carried away
and I am old.
·　·　·

Remember my little granite pail?
The handle of it was blue.
Think what's got away in my life!
Was enough to carry me thru.
·　·　·

He built four houses
to keep his life.
Three got away
before he was old.

He wonders now
rocking his chair
should he have built
a boat

dipping, dipping
and sitting so.
·　·　·

I've wasted my whole life in water
my man's got nothing but leaky boats
my daughter, writer, sits and floats.

Kulchur, 1962

Blue Chicory

Lorine Niedecker, of whom no less an artist than Basil Bunting has said,
"No one is so subtle with so few words," and who is carefully represented in
Louis Zukofsky's shamefully out-of-print A *Test of Poetry* in a group that
includes Keats and Shakespeare, died on New Year's Eve, 1970, at the age
of sixty-seven, in Madison, Wis., not far from Fort Atkinson, where she had
lived for most of her life. Her passing went largely unnoticed except for her

family and friends and a handful of poets who cherished the clarity and precision of her exquisite verse.

It is difficult to think of a contemporary to whom Miss Niedecker may be compared. The spare and harmonious quality of her work is reminiscent of Sappho, of the anonymous poetess of the Greek Anthology who wrote the beautiful and fragile "The moon has set / and the Pleiades" (*Dēduke men a sēlanna / kai Pleiades*), and of Sulpicia, the first-century B.C. Roman poetess who is preserved for us in six brief elegiacs whose plain grace is inimitable. Miss Niedecker's English has the brevity and compactness of classical verse, her syntax carefully balanced in a way usually possible only with highly in-flected languages. She herself called her compositional methods a "conden-sery."

These methods were painstaking and continuously in process and did not make for a prolific output. I should guess that over thirty years she averaged fewer than ten poems a year. Her first verse appeared about 1935, and her first book, *New Goose*, in 1946. It was followed in 1961 by *My Friend Tree*, in 1969 by *T & G: The Collected Poems 1936–1966*, and in 1970 by *My Life by Water: Collected Poems 1936–1968*. *Blue Chicory*, then, is her fifth collection and must serve as her last word until a *Complete Collected Poems* is published by Jonathan Williams' Jargon Society upon completion of the final editing of her papers by Robert Bertholf.

For a model of her poetic methods, the reader may examine this small untitled poem written in 1935. The subtlety of the line-breaks that gives the poem its depth of clarity as well as its ambiguity is notable—something achieved only by the best poets. One sees also that the clarity as well as the ambiguity are matters of how the medium is handled, not of meaning or "interpretation."

> There's a better shine
> on the pendulum
> than is on my hair
> and many times
>
> . .   . .
> I've seen it there.

If the poem were to end at line three, we would have an image; at line four, an image with gloss. The pause, which works as a wordless fifth line, and the flat statement of line six take the poem onto another plane alto-gether: "and many times," so located, functions so as to turn the poem per-fectly on each of three readings, all coherent and absolute.

Blue Chicory reveals these methods still in operation, used, if possible, even more exactly. The last poem of the first section of the book has but one verb; it comes as the last word of the poem and thereby functions as the energy that gives the work its rationale. All the other words wait for the verb to explain them:

> Your erudition
> the elegant flower
> of which
>
> my blue chicory
> at scrub end
> of campus ditch
>
> illuminates

—and when the verb drops precisely into place, we see that it does exactly what it means. The energy that clarifies the poem also illuminates it. There is no fat on these poems and no rodomontade masquerading as feeling.

Miss Niedecker had little attention paid her in her life, none at all by ignorant or malicious arbiters of what is "best" in modern poetry. It doesn't matter much. Her work is here, the product of a true poetic sensibility, faultless and luminous.

The New York Times Book Review, 1976

8

Jonathan Williams

Amen Huzza Selah

Jonathan Williams is an extremely witty and clever poet, who springs from a combination of e. e. cummings, the Poundian definition of *logopoiea*, and Olson's ideas on projective verse. It is an elegant sort of verse, although it constantly hovers on the edge of the merely clever, as in:

> Flogged with a *feruum*,
> young goats
> dance out of
>
> old goat skins
> • • •
> Skin back the year,
> turn over,
>   you new leaf,
>   ewe

Certainly, there is a dedication that lifts this verse out of the so-called "wit" of John Updike's *New Yorker*-isms, or the thin humor of Ferlinghetti. Updike gets by because his readers expect that it *is* that way ("just you and I get this poem, pal"), and Ferlinghetti's readers "know" that it is that way ("we're hip, man"). When Williams fails, he fails obviously and honestly, as in the above quotes. But, at times, his poems complete themselves fully, they remain organic, the tropes and twists of language remain true to what he wants to say: in other words, he is at his best when he stops working at the urbanely elegant:

I cut the stuff,
a whole blue field: figwort
's what they call it

This particular day I put a car thru it,
very fast,
out the gate, second gear, sharp right—

out of ourselves also say,
a few miles only, but

quite out, and up. . . .

There is certainly no other poet that I am aware of who writes in exactly
this vein of wry humor held in place by a heavy reliance upon what words
can do when they are fitted together in unexpected patterns and rhythms
and rhymes. By the way, the rhymes are always used to enforce the ludicrous
intent of what is being said, as if the very tool of rhyme were meant to be
used to poke fun at itself—which is perhaps true for Williams, except that
it limits him strictly to *that* use of rhyme. He has given himself a handicap
here, since the reader familiar with the poems gets ready for a twist of cleverness as soon as he sees a rhyme.

At any rate, Mr. Williams is fresh and funny, his poems turn and change
constantly, and he writes (although this is meant with no pejorative intent)
the finest light verse in the language. I keep hoping, though, for a "return"
to the kind of concern shown in a poem in *The Black Mountain Review* 6,
published in 1956, in which the poet rises above his seeming avowal to be
witty, and uses his talents in a way that is not demonstrated in this book—

We, the
heirs, hear other rustlings (

the grass stirs like an androgyne,
the man in our heart stands
his fear
        on its head,
savagely—
            inversed, nervelessly,
we sweat past each other,
                    unrelieved:
bitter landscapes,
            unlovely

In this unusual departure from his métier, Mr. Williams shows an area of himself that has been too long absent from his work.

The Nation, ca. 1962

In England's Green &

For some years now, I have been trying to determine whether Jonathan Williams is a dilettante or not. This latest collection leaves me as much confused as before, and my only conclusion is a lame one; he is, and he is not. Before continuing, however, I am not using the word contemptuously, nor do I feel that Williams lacks "seriousness." Closer to my usage is the etymology of the term, Italian *dilettare* from Latin *delectare*, to delight. Williams delights in art, in letters, in brilliantly wrought poems that are filled with wit, humor, and intelligence. I have said before that he is the finest light-verse writer in America, and that includes Ogden Nash. His great claim to dilettantism is the fact that his poems are mostly derived from books. Where he does see for himself, he somehow is constrained to find in that thing which he has seen, personally, an analogy, or rapport with another author's seeing. On the other hand, he will on occasion mar brilliant objective limnings of solid images with "wise-guy" or hipster slang, where rigorous editing might have saved the poem or poems in which this occurs. In this book, for instance, he appends two pages of notes which serve, on the one hand, to indicate many of his sources, and on the other, to notify the reader that he knows his stuff. It is not too difficult to imagine a reader's annoyance at this, since the notes assume an ignorance or a disinterest on the reader's part which he might not have.

But sometimes Williams really comes through as a poet, he seizes on an image and places it precisely—

> a white cloud in the eye
> of a white horse
>
> a field of bluets moving
> below the black suit
> of William Bartram

—but then he begins to explain, and the poem falters, although it is almost rescued by the sublime pun which closes it.

high hills,

stone cold
sober

as October

Certainly Williams doesn't have to worry about my carping. His place in
contemporary American poetry is both secure and unique. But I am convinced that there is much of the dilettante in him. His dilettantism, however, is much like that of the minor Elizabethan poets of the Golden Age;
competent, cultured, elegant, and informed of the multifarious phenomena
of the world.

Kulchur, 1963

FOR COLONEL WILLIAMS ON HIS TENTH LUSTRUM

There is very little to say about Jonathan Williams that has not already been
said by people with an interest in good letters. Jargon Books has been, since
1951 or thereabouts, a phenomenon in American publishing. And Jargon
Books is, quite simply, Jonathan Williams. He has published, among others,
Olson, Creeley, Zukofsky, Oppenheimer, Duncan, Layton, Perkoff, Loy,
Patchen, Lowenfels, Eigner, Levertov, McClure, etc., etc. Many of these
writers were published in book form for the first time by Jargon. He published
my own first book, and at a time when I had "credits" consisting of perhaps
a dozen appearances in the smallest of little magazines. The design of Jargon
Books is impeccable, and his covers and illustrations have been done by such
people as Rauschenberg, Rice, Callahan, Dawson, Nakian, Kitaj—the list
is long and distinguished. I mean to say that a Jargon Book is typically a
perfect synthesis of writing, graphics, and design; it is a pleasure to hold and
read. I treasure my copy of Jargon 15, Louis Zukofsky's *Some Time,* which
may be the most beautiful book I have ever seen.

Mr. Williams has read, for years and years, the work of Jargon writers to
audiences in God knows how many burgs and hamlets, audiences to whom
Amy Lowell and Edna St. Vincent Millay are, I suspect, pretty heady stuff.
These readings have served to help him keep body and soul together and to
finance, at least partially, his list of titles. Yet he seems always to be in debt
to printers, and there has been more than one occasion on which finished
books have been held in the bindery until Jargon could come up with at least
partial payment. Grants from here and there have helped, as have patrons,
but the financial pressure on Jargon has been, and is, enormous.

Outside of his (you will pardon the expression) business concerns, Mr. Williams is a poet of exceptional talents, and may well be the best comic poet writing in English. He is as good as, perhaps better than, Stevie Smith, and that is saying a good deal. When he is working at the top of his form, his poems exhibit *logopoiea* with a vengeance and may well be taken as *exempla* of that manner of making. His extraliterary concerns include wild-flowers and other flora, stories and speech patterns of Southern mountain people, jazz, classical music, baseball, and on and on. He is a wit, gentle-man, *bon vivant*, hiker, raconteur, and discoverer of scores, if not hundreds, of artists and craftsmen of this and other centuries, minor but oftentimes brilliant people whom time and fashion have obscured. If he had been born fifty years earlier, one can imagine him publishing Ronald Firbank and Sam-uel Greenberg.

He is a unique man, one to whom everything is interesting; i.e., I cannot imagine him ever being bored by anything that is not fake. I've known him for twenty years and count his friendship as among my most valued.

Truck, 1979

9

Edward Dahlberg

Because I Was Flesh

There is nothing remotely like this book in American literature. Edward Dahlberg, who for years has been a gadfly of gargantuan proportions, here, in his brilliant autobiography, tempers his invective with compassion and writes what can only be called a masterpiece. It is the story of his youth and young manhood, and most especially, of his bitter, exhausting, guilt-ridden relationship with his mother, a woman who is, essentially, totally uninteresting, but who emerges from this work as a figure of unforgettable impact and power.

This, friends, is tough business for a writer. It's one thing to write of your life with the veneer, however thin, of "fiction" to protect you from the Furies; it's quite another to lay it on the line like this, to lay the ghost with the stench of the corrupted flesh still about it. Dahlberg has faced the most painful, self-shattering areas of his life with an honesty and an intensity which is terrifying; that he has succeeded in translating his emotions into a work of art is astounding.

I read with awe and envy. The language is his unique amalgam of the learned, and loved, English prose writers like Browne, Donne, Walton, Gibbon, and the precise idiom of America, its cant and slang. The situations are presented with the verve and exactitude one finds in only the very greatest prose masters. Wild humor, ribaldry, fury, horror, wisdom, the riches of the books which he has read and treasured, all mesh together in pages which are a succession of blinding personal revelation. The book wounds as only the greatest books can.

Although many of us have known him as a choleric and intransigent man, both in his personal penchants and his writings, I can't ever remember his choler loosed upon objects, phenomena, or people not richly worthy of it; he is not a fink, he does not play ball, he does not praise those things fit for the garbage can, no matter the weight of fashion and wealth behind them. What has been a flaw in his work heretofore has been his seeming lack of compassion for those weaker, more willing to bend than he. In this book, his spirit flowers; he moves into the estate of wisdom and patience; he shrives himself in one of the most remarkable, hair-raising, and unvarnished accounts of a life ever written.

His self-deprecation is totally legitimate. He doesn't make of his misery, weakness, failure, chicanery, greed, some noble thing. His acts are not picturesque; his sins are that, sins. His is a noble spirit because he struggled against the filth of his own life. His book is noble because he shows you the struggle as it was waged. How marvelous to be a hero when everyone knows of one's heroism—and how disgustingly futile to wrestle with the banality of one's life with the knowledge that not only is no one looking on, but no one gives a damn about the honesty involved in the struggle.

Edward Dahlberg is a grossly underrated, and a terribly unknown writer. The subtle reasons may be many, but they all come down to essentially one reason: he is not for sale. What a simple statement that seems. He has had, I am sure, many opportunities to say something else, to dilute the impact of his work, to smile at the correct suits and ties, to chat amicably with the proper dentures at the proper cocktail parties. Various combinations of the above activities, mixed with a knowledge of typing, can do wonders for the young writer about town. Truth is something else again. Another simple statement. What does it mean when some lunk of whom nobody has ever asked the right time says that he has never sold out? It means that the occasion of sin was never presented. When one sees the evidence of Dahlberg's refusal, one can surmise that he battled the easy buck with the anguish that only the poor man can know, and from that anguish came his bitterness, at least a good share of it. Not for sale.

Writers are a universally unrespected lot. It becomes increasingly clearer that they achieve respect in direct ratio to their sales, and it is a truism that their sales increase in direct ratio to the lies they tell. Any slob of a dress manufacturer can give you his ideas on literature. Any clod with the money to spend can publish books; he has ideas on literature, too. An editor who might be better off as a dress manufacturer will edit one's work for publication without prior consultation. A writer to them is nothing unless he is respected, which gets us on the squirrel wheel again. How grim to realize that Dahlberg has fought this all his life, and how good it should make any writer feel that he has succeeded in remaining what he has always been, a serious writer, an artist.

I have for some time thought that the three books indispensable to an understanding of where we are as Americans, here in the twentieth century, are *In The American Grain*, *Call Me Ishmael*, and *Can These Bones Live*. To this personal list I must add *Because I Was Flesh*. Reading it is a humbling, grinding experience. It is a work of art of the very highest order.

Kulchur, 1964

A MEMOIR

The first of Edward Dahlberg's books to come to my attention ws the Har-court, Brace edition of *Do These Bones Live*. I still remember the excitement and awe with which I read this beautiful and pure work, so remote from what I had come to think was "criticism," yet critical in the very best sense of that word. That book (and subsequently the rest of Dahlberg's work) seemed such a clear-sighted attack on the chicanery and guile of American life as to literally be its own explanation; i.e., there was nothing to which the work could be compared. I would say, unhesitatingly, that Edward Dahlberg has been a great influence on me, not, certainly, in any sense of "style" or "phi-losophy," but in a broader sense of placing the anguish of the America of the twentieth century clearly in the light.

Some time later I met Edward Dahlberg, during his sojourn in New York, and talked with him many times. I clearly recall one evening, when Edward was visiting at my house along with a number of my friends—all members of my own generation—and I remember how he tolerated us, the only word I can think of to describe his generous stance. Oh, we knew it all in those days! And Edward was a strange throwback to a time when a writer showed respect and deference to his elders: curious aberration. We thought that we had nothing to learn from him and that his presence among us was an in-dication that he hoped to learn from us—who had nothing at all to teach. Now, with humiliation, I see that this very great man had come to us out of loneliness and out of some need to sustain himself as an artist in the company of fellow artists—neophytes though we were—thirty years his junior.

How kind he was. And with what elegance he graced our table. Another poet and I asked him if he knew an ancient song, "Hello Central, Give Me No-Man's Land," a popular tune of the First World War. Without a mo-ment's hesitation, Edward sang the song in a gentle vaudeville manner. It was such an absolute gesture of candor, and love. We laughed to hide our shame at having thought to bait him.

To close this brief and inadequate note, let me say that he trusted and encouraged young writers, he listened to them, and his deviations from what was at that time our literary enthusiasms were salutary. To be absolutely clear

about it, let me accord him what to me is the highest honor one can give a
writer, or any artist, outside useful praise for work well done: Mr. Dahlberg,
as Pound says of the temple, is holy, because he is not for sale.

Tri Quarterly, 1970

POET OF ABSOLUTE INVENTIONS

The Sorrows of Priapus

Let's get it said immediately: Edward Dahlberg is a great writer. It is also true
that his work has been beyond criticism, in a very real sense, for the past
thirty years. He exists as an enormous, stubborn giant of American letters,
largely unread and almost useless to any writer who wishes to learn from him
about technique, direction, even position. His prose is as sublime as Donne's
gold beaten to "ayery thinnesse." He is a sport, or freak, if you will, of modern literature. It is impossible to take issue with such power, with such consistently beautiful prose. Dahlberg is after a pure design in his work, and he
achieves it in book after book. In one of the most astonishing and well-
known turnabouts in American literary history, Dahlberg moved from the
hard-nosed, gut-bucket school of American realism as displayed in such
early books as *Bottom Dogs, From Flushing to Calvary*, and *Those Who Perish*, to the wondrous sonorities and textures of *Can These Bones Live* and
Because I Was Flesh. A comparable change would be to imagine the author
of *The Grapes of Wrath* writing, some few years later, "Canto LXXXI." The
suggested lab test for the new reader is to read *Bottom Dogs* and, immediately
thereafter, *Because I Was Flesh*, two books that mine the same facts yet seem
to come from two different men.

Dahlberg's bitterness and sourness are familiar to many readers, as is his
scornful treatment of writers whose work offends his sensibilities. His near
to comic reactionary positions on anything and everything are equally well
known. But what does it matter, after all? Irving Rosenthal, in his neglected
Sheeper, points out that Dahlberg cannot place two sentences in logical
order, that his invective is scrambled, that his scholarship is of the Marx
Brothers variety. Yet these are the soft grumblings of a lover, for Rosenthal
has nothing but praise for Dahlberg in his essence, because of his style, his
pure, breathtaking style. That is something that only the artistic intelligence can supply, and there are only a handful of writers who have it in the
required degree. Comically, again, Dahlberg despises most of them—that
doesn't matter either. Joyce, Pound, Beckett, to name just three, are men
who cheerfully throw out the baby with the bath water so that a twist of

phrase, a comma, a particular word may take its place in the sentence to make it sing, or snap like a whip.

You can find no meaning in Dahlberg, none that you can't get from a thousand lesser writers. Mailer is a titanic thinker next to him; your mailman or boss has more enlightened or informed ideas. There is nothing in Dahlberg except his greatness: he is the real thing. We flee in terror from him. The neglect accorded him by the world of fashionable or frivolous criticism is infamous. The pashas of this world seek out "meaning" in an artist's work, as if that were the artist's concern, as if he had any more in his head than the placing of a colon or tinkering with the syntax until the sentence stands forth, shining. There are louts teaching English literature who know more about it and about the world in general than does Edward Dahlberg. But they can't write. So let us creep up on the great unwhispered secret: writers have only a fistful of ideas, most of which have long been unpopular. Joyce was a Jesuit who based his life on an invented aesthetic out of Aristotle by way of St. Thomas; Pound a man whose brain was filled with zany ideas about free silver, a Rothschild behind every bank teller, and Westernized Confucianism; Beckett an existentialist who ate Descartes and threw him up mixed with black Irish comedy; Ford thought that knights and kitchen gardens would save the world. And Dahlberg? A man who has made a mythology for himself in the twentieth century, one based upon the mythologies and histories of the past, crammed together in disorder, incomprehensible. Yet we read him and read him again. He brings us a world of beauty. "He will sacrifice any meaning however important he may have made it out to be for any flourish or conceit, and he would sell his soul to the devil and mine too for the power to write one unalterably beautiful sentence," says Rosenthal.

Writing of the translation into Italian of "Anna Livia Plurabelle" by Nino Frank with Joyce's assistance, Richard Ellmann says, "Joyce's whole emphasis was again on sonority, rhythm, and verbal play; to the sense he seemed indifferent and unfaithful. . . ." Great writers are great because of the way in which they compose the language. Who reads Shakespeare for his plots, except fools and directors?

This book was originally issued as two volumes, some eleven years apart, *The Sorrows of Priapus* and *The Carnal Myth*, though they were meant to be two sections of the same work. I'm sure Dahlberg is happy to see the book published as it should be, but it makes no real difference now that the sections are together; indeed, it would make no difference if whole chapters were excised, or if chapters from one section were interleaved with chapters from another. Dahlberg has been writing one book, and it is a mark of his pure artistry that his work can ride out and triumph over any manner of assault upon it. *The Sorrows* begins:

> Man must be classed among the brutes, for he is still a very awkward and salacious biped. What shape he will assume in the future is vague. There are many traits of early man he has lost, and it is plain that he is much more given to falsehood, robbery and lawsuits than the primitive. The first two-legged man scratched himself because he had an itch. Men now lie and steal for this pleasure. Primeval natures wallowed without thought, but as soon as men began thinking how pleasant it was to rub themselves and have deliriums from mud, they employed their minds to achieve what paleolithic mankind did without being lascivious.

And *The Carnal Myth* opens:

> The majority of persons choose their wives with as little prudence as they eat. They see a trull with nothing else to recommend her but a pair of thighs and choice hunkers, and so smart to void their seed that they marry her at once. They imagine they can live in marvelous contentment with handsome feet and ambrosial buttocks. Most men are accredited fools shortly after they leave the womb, and these ninnies are always drunk for women. Sometimes they fall into convulsions over a piece of vermilion cloth wrapped about the bodice of a drab, not perceiving they could have just as well taken for a spouse a swath of red material, and for much less expense and trouble. The salacious zany is enticed by a petticoat or the saffron hair of the pard.

The two sections can be scrambled together in any way the reader desires, and still hold their lucidity of design, their quirky beauty. As with great writers generally, Dahlberg's basic unit is the phrase. When he has that, he goes on to the next, until the sentence is fashioned. Make your own connections, he says. If you don't like it, go and read another book. He will not go one step toward the reader, bless him, with his dense yet lucid prose. The reader does the work; Dahlberg is not in show business.

His book is intensely American, although Dahlberg would not be pleased by the suggestion that he has subtle links with such American writers as Pound, Williams, Stevens, and even Gertrude Stein. Only America can produce this sort of uncanny literature, abounding in contradiction. Ideas exist to be exploited, to be forged into glittering sentences. Like these artists, Dahlberg means what he says, but in the terms of art, not "communication." There are no poses in his work to compound his Jewishness: the latter is biblical, not fashionably urbane in the manner of the wise jokes ground out by Malamud. Dahlberg's statements are absolute inventions, as black paint in a Kline painting is black invented.

American literature is wondrous because of the way in which it confronts the limping and shabby thing that is American experience. Clear in its wild aberrations, its works are executed on a field that must itself be first created. To Europeans, American literature often seems ragged and hysterical because it usually shows only the field it has constructed. Dahlberg has mined and ravaged the literatures of the past, the myths of God knows how many cultures, loony entomologies, natural sciences long since discredited, all to make his field, clear himself a space. Now, after a lifetime of work, he stands in it, free to make the sentences that strike us dumb. He means it: he has forced this America in which he has grown to maturity to distill itself in prose that can lay us flat, an artifact fantastically made, much as the stories of Poe were made out of the odds and ends of sickness, horror, and dead women, so as to match the mundane horror that was his life. Dahlberg has eschewed what we laughingly call reality and invented, first, a world, and second, an art to reveal that world.

His work is magnificent in its contours, bursting with the pearls that he has cast before the critical swine during a half-century of arduous labor. Again, his books do not lead us to reality, nor are his opinions worth any more attention than those of Sargent Shriver. But when we read him we are crushed against the stones of his language; his visions of darkness and doom force their way into us. He is neither more nor less than an artist, as pure and unerring and obsessive as Baudelaire or Cézanne. We don't care to have too many of them, here in Oz.

The only thing that you can do with him is read him. He will repay your least attention with his best, i.e., perfection. He's not building housing projects or leading the people, but he is doing what only a very few men in any century can do: making something unimpeachably beautiful. He's seventy-two now, and the Nobel committee might do worse than award him their prize. It would be one way for them to erase some of their shame for ignoring the late Ezra Pound, another writer who, like Dahlberg, "tried to make a paradiso/terrestre."

The Nation, 1973

10

Paul Blackburn

SINGING, VIRTUOSO

The Journals. Edited by Robert Kelly

This publication proves to us, if we needed proof, what a remarkably gifted poet Paul Blackburn was. It seems reasonable to assume that this is the way his work would have continued to go had he lived, so forcefully and serenely does he move, in this book, into his statement. It is at once a triumph of voice and a triumph over it, a total mastery of his endless and variegated materials in a form that allowed him complete flexibility. I think the word "journals" is a small joke that Blackburn played on his readers, a joke almost like the smile he sometimes allowed himself when he read a poem whose bittersweetness flowered into ambiguity. They are journals only in that they purport to follow the events of the last four years of the poet's life, but the selection of the important elements out of the sea of experience and feelings that must have been his as he moved toward his death is rigorously formal and burgeons into poems that work as a shorthand of the emotions.

It was always easy to think of Blackburn's poems as instantaneous registrations of his contact with the phenomena of the world in which he moved, of "what happened" to him. I remember my shock some fifteen years ago when I realized that his most casual poem, his most "spoken" lines were composed in a language that had as much to do with his conversation as a perfectly made cabinet has to do with raw lumber. God knows, I don't mean to imply that people went about thinking that Blackburn wrote his poems in a kind of dazed passion of white-hot "inspiration." But there was a subtle and unspoken sense among many of his contemporaries that he relied a good deal on his fingertips in the composition of these marvels of seeming insouciance. Certainly, I thought this for some time, until I suddenly saw into the poems, saw the purity of his formal intention. (Now, it seems spectacularly perverse that one could have ever thought that any of his poems were thrown onto the page.) In *The Journals*, this purity is refined, quintessential. It is, quite simply, a handbook of invented form perfected, a book of exclusion.

Blackburn worked at his poems the way novelists work at their prose. He sat down and *worked* at writing poems. That the poems seem, often, the thought of a moment, a brilliant or witty or dark response to still-smoking news, is the result of his carefully invented and released voice, a voice that we hear singing, virtuoso, in *The Journals*. It is characteristic of the man that he never explained any of this, never said that this man that you hear in the poems, this subtly shifting voice, is not Paul Blackburn. It is what he decided Paul Blackburn would be in his song. And the place, the locus from which the voice issued forth, that is what he allowed or invented as background. This is a novelist's province. To place the language in a sternly exclusive landscape. In Joyce's Dublin, there is no such place as New York.

In a time when the confessional poem is everywhere applauded, and, God help us, ransacked for "data," this stringent insistence on formal invention disguised as happenstance may seem to signal a lack of what a lot of people seem to think of as sincerity. But it is only quite recently that readers expected the poet's life to sprawl before them, that the first-person voice in the lyric poem should tell all, like an analysand. Certainly, if we wish to read into Blackburn's poems the private concerns of his life, we may, even though we will not find them there except insofar as they exist transformed; in brief, we will not find that famous truth that facts supposedly proffer. Blackburn's truth is more elusive and difficult to come at—it is the truth of the lyric poem that slips away as we press it to stand still and answer, answer. This exquisite ordering of the common materials of the poet's life is the architecture by means of which he not only deployed them in balanced design within the poem, but by means of which he changed them into instances of artifact. His poems are as artificial as those of his beloved troubadours.

As everyone interested in Blackburn's work knows, his twenty-year study of and translation from the troubadours was, in a very real way, the essential center of his poetic career. He was never long away from this continuing work; and, as I see it, it affected his "own" poetry deeply. Surely, one of the nodes of this effect was his knowledge that the poetry of Provence was highly stylized in terms of its subject matter and the troubadours' response to it. In the *canso*, in any event, the troubadour sang with pointed brilliance of love, that is, courtly love—nonexistent, and with no possibility of existing in real terms with real women. In lyrics of surpassing intelligence, and within verse forms that were fixed by self-imposed schemes, the troubadour implored mistresses and mourned for unrequited passions that never were; by the standards of our own fact-crazed and voyeuristic time, he was insincere. Yet these lyrics—that treat the facts so cavalierly—are among the greatest poems that we have. We know, and yet we surely do not know, the poet; we hear his words as they are spoken by him, but what do his words say? Who indeed was Arnaut Daniel? Who was Paul Blackburn? His poems will not tell us, nor should they. They give us an invented voice that invents.

Blackburn was a gregarious man who lived in intense privacy, open to almost everyone about almost everything—except the core of his life. There are some who have seen this as an indication of his embarrassment in the face of "what matters," or as a sort of proof that there was no core to his life. To me, it was simply the dignity of a man to whom the world is a place into which one *goes*—one does not invite it home to be its confidant or confessor. He was a man of great reserve, disguised most often as an oddly rough-hewn "buddy." *The Journals* strike me as partaking of this quality of the man. Robert Kelly, in his Introduction, speaks of Blackburn's "old world song" and "strange melancholy." It is the song (and the melancholy) of a man who loved the world as Roman Catholics are taught to love God—He is *there*; you are *here*. Such an attitude does not make for the nattering that passes for candor. At that moment, in his poems, when we think we will, finally, be allowed to see the poet, he magically fades away into his voice, a protean voice so perfectly under control that we think it is telling us something true. This book is the work of a man who had come to a perfect sense of his own powers. He has done what all poets who have tried to remain faithful to the lyric must envy. His ego has been disguised, not revealed, by his voice, it has been subsumed. To come to this expertise within a poetic structure that we may call, for want of a better word, closed, is an enormous achievement. To arrive at this position in the poem as "journal," the open poem, is mastery.

At one with this subtlety of tonal modulation is the curious reticence of these poems—and of all Blackburn's poems. It is a reticence built not on a sense of shame or secrecy, or on pride in one's knowledge or perception, but on modesty. Even in lines that might otherwise function to make a reader squirm with embarrassment (as do so many of the gross statements in those poems heralded as self-confronting), Blackburn holds something back; he reins in the voice and makes it step with a true delicacy. In such a mode, it is worth our attention to see how the poet handles sexual and scatological themes and language. They become as fine-spun and sweet as the music of Campion.

I'm going to
die, I'm afraid. O-
kay, I'm afraid, I
shall hold you in Front Royal, Ashville,
Nashville, Memphis, Springfield, Alamosa,
    Aspen even, Rawlings, Boise, Portland,
        other towns to the South.

Our asses, our mouths.
      • • •

The guards
who'd confiscated my camera stayed
down by the *caisse* at the entrance
so I touched all the statues of Venus
cunt, belly and breasts

Somehow—and I don't *know* how—the movement of these lines lifts them above the specific fact of their "vulgarity" into a candid splendor. The matter-of-fact mention of death with the sexual love that will occur before its arrival; the attribution to the goddess and the naming of those womanly parts that she *possesses* as her power over men—in some way, as I say, these things, barely touched on, as it were, thrown away, give to the poems a perfect grace.

The reticence of the poems holds, as they used to say, worlds. Where there might be comment or thematic development, or just embroidery, we have:

    a doomed man planting tomatoes
    backyard of a house he lives in
    belongs to somebody else
        • • •
    Where are the bees? The yard dies, the
    tulips go by, what fun!
    I write letters these days to everyone.
        • • •
    How say goodnite to you all, dear friends?
    Easy.
    Goodnite!

And this ending to the poem "July 23"—its own unphrased question, its own explanation, its own gloss:

    From a far country,
    David Henderson has
    come unto Michigan,

Hermes in shades, to
give us the word, BURN.

(signed) Paul Blackburn

The joke, as they say, is certainly on somebody. But then, on whom? And
is it a joke? The voice fades and is sharpened again to give us—a meaningless
signature—certainly a joke. How ludicrous all this blather of the polis must
have struck Blackburn as being, but it is treated gently, gently. And again,
who is the butt of the joke if it be one? In *The Journals*, the concerns of this
world are at the same time overwhelming and picayune. They are remarked
on with dignity and dryness by a voice that speaks from a strange place
between this sad earth and hell.

This reticence, as I have remarked, is not new, and often it turns a Blackburn poem (as above) into a sudden graph of humor that dies, as we recognize its underside, its ambiguity, as swiftly as it was sketched. From *The Cities*
(1967) we have:

Stay drunk!
that's my motto.
Then you'll never have to know
if the girl love you or no
                    (hee hee hee
                    nor will she

—a poem that hides its barb in doggerel rooted in drunken conversation.
Blackburn was always fond of pulling the string on a poem or stanza this way,
and in *The Journals* he has arrived at a perfection of the method. It is done,
in this book, as offhand remark, slightly different from the patchwork above.
The focus has shifted almost imperceptibly, however. Most of the jokes are
now at the expense of the voice that tells them. The essential absurdity,
almost the embarrassment, of the poet's position is clear. He knows *specifically* that he is going to die; a far remove from the romantic agony. We
discover lines that it must have taken incredible restraint to set down and
then let alone.

and my son wakes up from his nap, comes
to climb in my lap.
kicks the book from the table
onto the floor . what more
can I say? It's one
                    way to begin a long summer. haha.

And this wry comment—for it is always wryness that supplants anger and bitterness and malice in the Blackburn poem—on the kind of fame that had found him after some twenty-odd years of labor:

> Cities and towns I have to give up this year
> on account of my cancer: Amster-
> dam, Paris, Apt, Saignon and Aix,
> (Toulouse I'll never loose), Perpignan and Dax,
> Barcelona and south
>   (or the other way,
>   Catania . I warn ya)
> The hell, I read a review of a reading in January.
> They loved me in Shippensburg, Pennsylvania.

These brief examples from some of Blackburn's poems give some of the flavor, but little of the texture of the work that he has left, and certainly none of his vast range. By range I don't mean his array of subject matter— that was most carefully limited so that his mastered voice could exploit it to its limits—love, friends, travel, and place. I mean the way the poems, over his entire career, return again and again to these things and each time extend their possibilities in terms of Blackburn's deepening understanding of them. And as his understanding deepened, so did the metamorphoses of his expression become more refined and given over to sudden shifts within poems— even within stanzas. Upon a mere handful of objects, if you will, he rang ceaseless and endless changes. It is a triumph of "the quality of the affection."

I have written elsewhere that Blackburn's poems are accepting of the world as given. What kept him sane, I think, and working with steady and "professional" dedication, was his absolute presence in his life. He was a man who cared about the everyday things that are the concern of the most ordinary humans, and who felt them. Because he shared these banal concerns of the "common man," he was allowed into their lives and thoughts. If the ever-fluctuating and precisely tuned voice that occurs within his poems is always just right, exact as to the rhythms that occur in the aimless street- and bar-talk of the workaday world, it is because the poet who constructed this voice out of those many voices knew, from living there, what they sounded like. The more he seems like "anybody at all" in his poems, the more is he the poet. He wore his learning lightly and there are dozens and dozens of poems available to readers of differing sophistication, levels that swim into cognition according to what is brought to bear on the work. But there is almost always something for everyone—he is as accessible as Villon. Perhaps because he does not posture in his poems, holds no extra-mundane "philosophy," he was held cheap, as he was. Kelly says that he was "happiest in the middle of things, a stranger to scorn." I wonder.

There is such a clean simplicity in the language of *The Journals* that one is tempted to say that Blackburn never really wrote like this before. A moment later comes the realization that, about 1950, he wrote, in *The Dissolving Fabric*:

> Returning from the funeral
> I saw her and liked her. The air
> was very quiet
> near spring.

—and, twenty years later, we read:

> Have seen you as woman longer than
> you, yourself have, wonder now at the tenderness
> as we walk about the grass at yr / wedding reception, smoking
> grass upon the grass, yr / hips moving gently, that
> between them all men prize
> blind their eyes—

As I have said, the essential difference between *The Dissolving Fabric* and all the earlier poems and *The Journals* is but the mastery and full control of the lyric voice, i.e., Blackburn learned, through the writing of literally hundreds of poems, and from his study of the troubadours, that the "I" of the poem is as much artifice as the poem it speaks—and yet it can locate itself with such immediacy that it looks like the vehicle for common speech, laden with information from the horse's mouth. The first fragment above, from "The Funeral," surely shows talent: that is beyond question. But in *The Journals* we enter a territory of virtuosity, a blend of attitudes, voices, ironies, all existent as a filigree that can hardly be seen for the overt brusqueness of the basic tone. Look at the way he handles this piece from the last poem in *The Journals*, quite possibly the last poem he completed. The shifts in the lines occur at bewildering speed, the references are both obvious and esoteric, the suddenly collapsing humor mentioned earlier is snapped in and out of the piece, and the fragment closes with a flat click. And notice how the word "momma" is employed: as invocation to his dead mother and to death itself, as casual colloquialism, as a filler or tag line in a jazz vocal. And the whole in what seems to be the easiest speech, the whole "said" by "Paul Blackburn."

> What a gas, maybe
> Louie Armstrong & I
> die, back to back,
> cheek to cheek, maybe the same year. "O,
> I CAN'T GIVE YOU

ANYTHING BUT LOVE,
Bay-aybee"
      1926, Okeh a label then
      black with a gold print, was
one of my folks' favorite tunes, that year
that I was born . It is all still true
& Louie's gone down &
I, o momma, goin down that same road.
Damn fast.

These fourteen lines may stand as *exemplum* of Blackburn's methods in *The Journals*, although they are by no means his only methods. As Kelly says, "He worked hard enough at the trobadors and their prosodies to qualify, had he chosen, as a walking book of meters and 'forms'—but those collected shapes were not the forms that concerned him." His poetic learning was deep and interiorly held and in this book we can watch it at work—changed, flattened, disguised, but worked into the dense fabric of these poems in recollections of gone speech, points of rhyme and half-rhyme, formal notations on weather and landscape. I can almost imagine him thinking of the above quotation as a new way of tearing open the sonnet. Why not? Nothing melodic or prosodic was alien to Blackburn, and when he seems most colloquial and chatty, it is often right there that we may find, buried in the perfectly broken rhythms of his voice, the skeleton of a loved and austerely bounded form.

His sense of his poetics was put, most clearly perhaps, in "R O A D S":

Thus qualified, I
want to write a poem abt / roads
that they are there, that
one travels them & is not obtuse
nor obliged to take anymore in, onto the mind, than
the body in time and space taketh unto itself, the
mind in its holy vacuum
breaking out of   past the fact
to other   FACTS?

What is there, finally, to say? Even lacking a satisfactory collection of his later poems, we can see that Blackburn was one of our most brilliant poets. That he had come to his maturity is obvious from *The Journals*. The neglect that was his during his life will, I trust, be remedied before too long, although I take no bets on it. In all events, to anyone who cares for the life of the poem in this latter half of the twentieth century, Blackburn must stand as a greatly gifted artist who has left us a body of work that is formal, intelligent, and beautiful.

Parnassus, 1973

PAUL BLACKBURN (1926–1971)

In an Andy Capp strip of some years back, Andy crashes what he thinks is a wedding reception and announces that he is "a friend of the groom." He is chagrined and silenced when he is told that it is not a wedding, but a funeral. Paul takes this strip and in a poem that chills the heart, says:

> He t'ought it were a weddin but
> it was a funeral. So?

> > what is the question. or,
> > who is a friend of the groom?

There is a great deal of sadness in Paul's poems, an acceptance of life and its attendant miseries. It is cloaked by the poet's invigorating voice, his novelist's ear for speech, his patient humor. Perhaps sadness is the wrong word—a tragic sense of life might be a phrase more precise, although that seems oddly wrong when applied to a New Englander. But there is a sense in the poems that the world is enough, or all there is, that one cannot do very much about certain things; i.e., secular salvation is limited. Beyond its various benefices, one steps carefully and hopes. It may be a sense of life curiously held by many lapsed, or failed Catholics, as Blackburn was. The world is a rich, varied, absurd, and cold place. The Sacraments do not change it one whit; but there is no mundane substitute for them. One is out there all alone. It is a sense that forms the constant undertone of the Blackburn poem; turned another way it produces the flat, thin tragedy of Camus' existentialism. Paul's poems are chaos reduced to a voice, more wry than anything else. The voice says: "the arrow of love is destroying me and I have no God. Now what?" The "what" is the poem. In *The Power and the Glory*, the whisky priest, reduced to despair, laughs to himself. Blackburn does a lot of laughing too, a gentle laughter it is, without malice.

We first met in 1956 and were friends until he died. There were and are great differences in our work, Paul's poems having a centrifugal force to them, that is, they all seem to be straining to burst outward; my own poems turn in on themselves, like a man pulling his hat down over his eyes. But I can't recall our quarreling over these differences: we simply accepted one another's failings and went on from there. He was at once a cosmopolitan figure and a local one. I can't remember him posturing in any way at all. In his two favorite saloons, McSorley's and the Cedar, he was always himself, that is, Paul Blackburn. He did not assume the masks of either aesthete or common man to please or fit in with his companions.

Time will treat him more generously than have his contemporaries. He was thought of, for so many years, and by so many people, as a good fellow, an organizer of readings, a chaperone and guide for writers newly arrived in New York, a good listener, a man who deferred to the opinions of his inferiors, however shabby or ludicrous. Beneath this easy and patient geniality, the poems were made. He worked continually and thought of writing as a job. Romance in his life as well as his work had the tang and tartness of lemon.

His stories and anecdotes were endless and endlessly embroidered, the punchline always telegraphed long before the finale. I remember him savoring particular turns of phrase almost as if tasting good whisky. He chuckled at twists in the narrative as if someone were telling him the story. Plenty of time, he had plenty of time. Some of his poems are like his conversation, although he had many voices—or, I should say, accents and dialects. Even his failed poems have a sheer gracefulness to them; they refresh with their candor.

I suppose the thing that kept us from becoming truly close friends was Paul's conception of poets as being comrades-in-arms, one for all, etc. To him, the most alarmingly dull scribbler was a compatriot. This was nonsense to me. Paul encouraged and assisted anyone who wrote a poem or even spoke of his intention to write poems, as if a plethora of poetry would change the world. My own view of poets is that they are analogous to ball-players; i.e., there are hundreds of thousands of them, but only 600 in the major leagues. The rest are bushers. There is nothing "wrong" with that—it is simply the fact. The terror of the Pacific Coast League cannot hit the major-league curve. It soon becomes apparent. To Paul, the urge to pick up the bat was enough. I think that this was the reason we rarely discussed the merits of particular poets; it was difficult and embarrassing for both of us. He had his dislikes, certainly, but rarely expressed them.

Somehow he was ignored by that critical regiment that pretends an interest in contemporary poetry, and that is always with us, like gonorrhea. His work was taken for granted. His inspired and brilliant translations of the troubadours have not yet, to my knowledge, found a publisher. To be candid, he was not thought of as a first-rate poet. I don't know why this should have been so. Certainly, he was the equal of his peers, and there are some things that he does in his best poems that have never been done better by anybody. He was always "good old Paul," despite the elegance and intelligence of his work. Well, he lacked ambition and the drive toward success. By his easy geniality and good humor he encouraged those who had not a fraction of his talents to quickly feel his equal or superior. But he was no *naïf*; he was totally aware of the value of his work. There was a great reserve in him that prohibited him from blowing his own horn. Ungraciously, perhaps, I persist in thinking of his inclusion in anthologies as the literary equivalent of "and let's have a hand for Paul Blackburn, too." There are, too, those anthologies that purport to "survey" the American literary scene in which he is not represented at all. The stupidity of editors is everywhere apparent, but the omission of Blackburn from any "representative" gathering of American poets is aberrant.

If you were to meet him at one of those grimly desperate readings at which people drone on and on about their souls and their sexual feats and intersperse their poems with anecdotes about their marvelously interesting lives, he would, more often than not, sit next to you and wordlessly hand you a pint of cheap Spanish brandy (a favorite drink) or Old Mr. Boston Orange-Flavored Vodka; something to get you through the shameful mediocrity of the recital. He had a lot of style, the only thing left outside of talent that cannot be bought or affected. I saw him sink to the floor once, monumentally drunk, and do it with unequalled style.

If that Catholic Purgatory indeed exists, let an indulgence of 300 days that I remember from my childhood be an epitaph: *Merciful Lord Jesus, give him everlasting rest.*

Sixpack, 1974

11

Hubert Selby

Faustus: How comes it, then, that thou art out of hell?
Mephistophilis: Why, this is hell, nor am I out of it.

What is so remarkable about Selby is that he makes us see all these people as real, e.g., what did John Dillinger read in the bathroom—? Jack The Ripper drinking sherry, perhaps: as against the more devastating manifestations of their "public" faces, the small notations of their lives. All these people are so far from enviable, they live in a special hell: the clue to Selby's brilliance is that he has not invested any of them with dreams and/or aspirations which are, for them, phony. They move in the circumscribed area of their own despair—even Georgette's narcotic dream of happiness with Vinnie is only faggoty desire (as a matter of fact, Georgette's page of impossible romantic desire, her "vision" of a love idyll with Vinnie is perhaps the most unerring detection of the vulgar since the scene in the room above the town festival with Emma and Rodolphe in *Madame Bovary*)—although she is on a "higher" level than those with whom she associates; her dreams place her, precisely, in her element, which seems to me a cogent understanding of the homosexual, an avoidance of the adventurous cast in which his world has been so often molded. The look is without pity, but not without compassion. Georgette, after all, really *does* love Vinnie, as well as she possibly can.

The use of cops. "Another Day Another Dollar," the scene with the hoods, GIs, and cops: when that cop speaks, you get chills up your back; he almost clubs you from the page itself. You can see his fat, red face and sloping shoulders, the blue uniform stained black under the arms, the other copper moving sullenly around the edge of the crowd, waiting for someone to say something out of line. (In "Double Feature," the sudden terror which ends a very funny sequence occurs when two cops enter the theater at the complaint of the manager in re: the two young drunks.) If you prove you can't freely conduct yourself, you are forced to conduct yourself according to the laws of a more powerful phenomenon . . . cops, hoods, junk, what have you.

Selby: "My stories are about the loss of control." You can live a total lie out so long as you act as if you belong to the society—in Selby's case, since the society is hellish, brutal, one wrong step and your head is broken—and it begins as a child (the playground scenes in "Landsend"; nobody has a chance). If you allow what is bothering you to get out of control for just an instant, you pay the price of destruction. The police are interchangeable with the society in the strict mechanistic terms of punishment for transgression. If the skillet doesn't fry you, the fire will broil you. A harsh world of pain and horror, the police aid and abet the misery, they don't, in any way, alleviate it.

The world of these streets sheer chaos, love does not exist in a world of violence except in the hokey, campy love of Georgette for Vinnie. She loves him, but in some story-book way based on a future which is not only not realizable, but which doesn't even exist as a vague possibility. Her future is death; she dies on the subway (where else?) in her pathetic dream; if she hadn't she would live to go back uptown, still craving Vinnie, still convinced that their lives together could be beautiful—the ultimate mistake of the orgasm theory.

Important to realize that these people have not wholly been turned into what they are by the society in which they exist—they, in a very real sense, have created this society, Frankenstein creating a monster who hunts down his creator, things interact. Everything is spurious and shoddy but death and pain and squalor which are unbearably real. In "Landsend," nothing is of value, from Ada, whose religion is psychopathological, to Abraham, who starves his children to keep his Caddy going; all is filth and horror. The women in the project's "recreation" areas turn, as the story progresses, into Yahoos, searching each other's heads for lice.

"Strike" is, for me, a masterpiece, possibly the finest short story written in this country in a decade. Every false ideal, every rotting set of values, every cliché we have ever heard about marriage, homosexuality, labor and management, the dignified poor—all are exposed by this merciless flat prose. No comments, ever, in Selby. The prose moves the experience directly *to* you, it is style-less.

That which stands out so clearly in Selby's prose is the fact that none of it is what is thought of as "quotable." There is no "style," no "elegance." He is, by any standards which may be used to measure him, a PROSE writer— nothing at all of the poet in him, the stories are constructed simply, in a horizontal line; the words are true to the narrative they move. And the narrative *moves* forward, the classic climax is reached, the story pitches down, no chance for a reversal, at all. It is like one dull stone piled atop another, nothing remarkable about them in any way at all; and suddenly the mind is confronted by a pyramid, an overwhelming edifice—it won't go away, a new thing has been made and placed in the world.

The ear for speech, impeccable. People don't talk the same way unless they are joined together in some common purpose, have common lives, goals, desires. The great mistake of so many prose writers in their transcription of speech is to record its syntactical eccentricities and habits carelessly; e.g., they'll have an uneducated laborer speak the same way as an uneducated thug. Or, a cop will speak the same way as those he bullies and arrests. The mark of brilliance and honesty in speech transcription resides in the differentiation of language patterns. Only a fool can be misled by the heavy-handed vulgarity of so many popular prose writers who mistake one brand of grammatical aberration and slang for another. Look at the differences, subtle and beautiful, in Selby's work, between the speech of those who are societally close to each other. Cops and thugs, thugs and queers, Italians and Negroes. The speech of Alex, who runs the diner, with that perfect placing of his *scatah!* The difference in speech as the character *normally* employs it, as against the way he speaks when he is placed in a situation in which he is not at home, not comfortable—viz., Harry Black: one, the way he speaks to his wife; two, the way he speaks at the job; three, the way he speaks to the union officials; four, the way he speaks to the queers in the gay bar; five, the way he speaks to his wife after he has become homosexually involved. These are *real* differences, recorded perfectly. As James used speech to move and develop his narrative, his unfolding plot, Selby uses it to denote aspects and/or changes of character, emotional states. Check also the subtle differences in the cop's threats to the thugs and to the GI's in "Another Day." The former a bluff, a "gruff reproof"—the latter loaded with poison, and very real. Finally, the incredible pre-strike speech of the union boss to the members. For me, one of the most precise delineations of the pompous and vulgar I've read in years. Each word set into that speech as a tile, the grammatical mistakes are of the sort that his listeners would never recognize but would consider a mark of being "smart"; there is a veneer of "culture" (after all, this is the *boss*) over the words, as he gives them cliché after cliché. What is more remarkable, they are so placed that one can see behind the words, as it were, discover the gross distortions of fact, the real contempt he has for the rank and file as he patronizes them. They're all "buddies"—he loathes them. It is a parallel to the vulgarity registered by politicians when they smilingly eat, in order, knishes, pizza, and cuchifritos on the Lower East Side. A fantastic contempt for the populace, but the unerring knowledge of the "leader" that his crassest insults, his most flagrant patronization seem like unity with them. Even though they *know* he's a son of a bitch, they fall for it when he kisses a baby; how many Puerto Ricans voted for Rockefeller because he speaks Spanish?—Words are weapons; when joined with the properly related acts, they are formidable weapons, viz., Selby's intrusions of remarks describing the boss leaning "wearily" on the lectern, his "worn" face, his "humble" stilling of applause.

Again, Selby has a perfect eye and ear for strata of society, their beliefs, values, the things they cherish and desire. In "Tralala," he sends her, after she realizes that her body, and especially her huge breasts, are real sexual assets, out of the filth of the Brooklyn neighborhood in which she was born, to Manhattan, to search for more lucrative trade. To anyone who knows people like Tralala, with their ideas of elegance and the big time, the bar he sends her to in order to hustle registers with a shock that is so acute one forgets how absolutely perfect a spot it is: The Crossroads. Exactly the right combination. Someone like Tralala would know the bad rep of joints like the Eighth Avenue bars (to which she eventually gravitates), would never move into a hotel bar (an impossible field of action for a Brooklyn slut, better send an East Harlem junkie to Brooks Bros. for clothes), and the small, expensive traps in the East Fifties would never see her—significantly, *not* because they are expensive and chic, but because, being in the Fifties and outside the area of Times Square, they would never seem to her places where she could hustle well-paying customers. Tralala would select exactly what she does select, The Crossroads; the perfect example of vulgar pretension, strictly for the tourist, who thinks that New York begins at Forty-second and ends at Rockefeller Center; apropos of this, I wonder how many tourists think of Times Square as "seamy"—I would hunch less than fifty percent. One must remember that Tralala is one of the millions of Americans who live out their lives in the belief that a nightclub looks like a Hollywood set of the thirties, complete with Fred Astaire; if she ever went to, say, The Blue Angel, she'd think somebody was putting her on; what, *this* is a nightclub? Selby is completely aware of this. What is mediocrity and vulgarity to an expensive whore is the zenith of "night-life" for Tralala. Selby's power is partially explained by this exhaustive, painstaking attention to details. See also, the cars the hoods talk about in "Another Day"—not a Ferrari, Mercedes, or Rolls in the lot. These people are real because their acts are acts which are utterly true to the environment they inhabit; they explain it, and vice versa.

Part of the fascination Vinnie feels for Georgette lies in the fact that he thinks of her as cultured. She seems to hold out to him a world so far removed from his own experience of slums, violence, prison, etc., that he can't resist finding out what she knows, or what he thinks she knows. So, too, the rest of the guys in the queer party uptown. The fags are hip, the hoods are not. A less penetrating writer would have Vinnie a bebop fan. But people like Vinnie were *not* bebop fans. They listened to popular music and do so today. Maybe today a Vinnie might listen to "soul" music or the Bossa Nova, but you'd never catch him with a John Coltrane or Ornette Coleman record. There are such subtle gradations of difference in the "lower" classes, and Selby is aware of them. One thinks of the fantastic inaccuracies of reporters who write that kids say "hep" to each other, wear levis and sweat shirts, and greet each other with phrases like "hiya Gate." These guys are always at least ten years behind what's happening, and their confusion of present values (real) with present values (imagined) sullies their reportorial accuracy as concerns both the present *and* the past. Selby is deadly accurate. Vinnie is amazed by Bird. Of course—Vinnie knew as much of Bird in the mid-forties as Miss America did. Maybe less. Bad, or careless, or popular writers are not *only* that, they are immoral as well. They extrapolate cultural values from economic levels on assumption, thereby confusing whole segments of society with other segments. The stories, the intellectual "sets" created out of such confusions enable great lies to persist, viz., the white middle class, as well as the black middle class conception of the lower-class Negro and his "tastes." Or, check the fantasies apparent in this confusion: the mistaking of "bopping" gangs with those who listened to the music, bebop. Boppers (the rumbling gangs) were called that after bop was dead; they listened to R & B, rock 'n' roll, mambos. Or the confusion, still apparent, of beatniks with hipsters, hipsters with junkies, junkies with beatniks, beatniks with artists. Bad, dishonest writers play on the public's desire to be deluded, and they prosper thereby. Selby wrenches things back into context. The lie can become so great that even the actual inhabitants of the various social strata may be duped; e.g., many beatniks think of themselves as hipsters, while there are no hipsters at all today, at least not in New York; again, vocals in the Sinatra-Darrin-Damone style (the Las Vegas syndrome), with finger-snapping and big bands orchestrated mostly for muted brass behind the ancient bebop 4/4 splash cymbal, are thought of (by apparently thousands) as

"hip." Only a writer with a passion for delineating his time and environment
can explode this kind of garbage in thought. As well as being a finished artist,
Selby is a meticulous student of the lower class, the underworld, the dispossessed. The people he writes of are not the one or two who are weekly sentenced for murder and extortion—they are the hundreds who are daily sentenced (or not sentenced at all) for assault, Sullivan Law violations,
disturbing the peace, etc. They are the men who don't break out of Alcatraz
and Quentin with Bogart and Cagney, but who cop pleas and draw one to
three in such unknown and unprepossessing spots as Coxsackie and Elmira.
The difference between robbing a car and a bank, between mugging and
armed robbery, are *real*. The exact separation of one sort of criminal from
another makes clear whole pockets of society. Dante put his various sinners
in different *bolge*; he made a *moral* separation. Selby does the same in his
mundane hell.

Selby presents his homosexuals as people whose lives are not particularly
glamorous; nor are they sordid, given the world in which they move—they
are essentially futile. Most literature has tried to depict the homosexual as
someone to be laughed at, shocked by, or pitied. Not in these stories; they
are essentially vulgar and their lives are a scramble to avoid the world of the
john, although the john is preyed upon and laughed at. One of the great
miseries of Harry Black in "Strike" is that he is never accepted by the other
queers as queer. When they met him he was a john; but though his homosexual proclivities become more active, more pronounced, he remains in
their eyes what he originally was, the same john; or, worse, he is thought of
as a "dilettante" queer. They refuse to consider him as someone who wants
to *love*; he eventually bores his lover when he runs out of money near the
end of the strike. His value as a john is over; he has discovered that he now
is in a position which is neither homosexual nor heterosexual, and cannot
handle this fact, cannot "adjust" to the fact that the queers think of him as
someone who is simply square. The ultimate placing of the homosexual in
"Strike" comes in the drag ball, which Harry attends, and where, incidentally, he is not attracted to the queens but to the other "active" (male)
queers. The queens are not presented as immoral, or evil; the situation is
not really sordid, but grotesque; there is a kind of bizarre humor about it
which becomes more bizarre because the participants are not at all aware
that they *are* so. Their frenzied dancing in women's clothes is what it is,
ridiculous, as men in women's clothes always look to a nonpartisan eye.
When the dancing queens' genitals fall out of their lace panties, it is certainly not an occasion of eroticism, but one of hilarity. It is to Selby's credit
that he refuses to ornament such situations. Harry is pitiable, but the queens
are gross. While their lives, when they are "straight," may be a constant

whirl of *riposte* and wit, when in drag, they take their places in the ludicrous world which Harry Black skirts the fringes of, and to which they have barred his entrance. He is a john, while they are hip. A finely drawn comment on the narcissistic qualities of the hermetic group.

Some more on the homosexual in Selby's work: In "Queen," one of the fags screams in disgust when the girl upstairs is rushed to the hospital in advanced labor—"you're bringing me down!"Also, one of the favorite epithets one queer will use against another (or against a queer-baiter) is, "you rotten fairy"—and in "Strike," the fag who dances with Harry in the strike HQ was at one time a bricklayer and takes delight in squeezing Harry's hand between her forearm and biceps; a grim gesture toward a world of virility and strength which she has long ago abandoned. What seems to come through these instances is a double-edged "set" toward the heterosexual world, a sort of hatred inextricably wedded to a feeling of superiority; e.g., "even though I'm gay, I'm more of a man (or woman) than you are"—or, as above, in "Queen," a feeling of revulsion and apathy toward the normal functioning of the woman, as if childbirth is somehow "square." The most salient example of this duality, this love/hate occurs at the end of "Strike" when Harry, who is left bloody and beaten in the lot after making advances to a small boy, shouts (in his mind) "God sucks cock!" A hatred for a God who would allow him to suffer such implacable despair, along with a real desire, a need, that God be a homosexual. The statement is, at once, both blasphemous and adoring.

Harry is, absolutely, a *schlemiel*: without that word's humorous connotations. There is no area of his life in which he is successful. As husband and father, he is inept and psychotic. As worker, he is sloppy and lazy. As shop steward, he is a patsy, used by the union. The management simply wants him fired as a condition for acceding to the strikers' demands. As a rather hopeless example of the john, he fails miserably because he thinks that his homosexual lover will really *love* him. And, finally, when he succumbs to his desire to become an overt, active homosexual, he picks on a little boy in his own neighborhood. A loser, a suicidal character all the way.

The movement of the background, the social aspects of "Strike," coincide with Harry's movement from a partially "controlled" existence to a shambles of acts and emotions which bring about his destruction. He can be neither normal nor homosexual. Another reason why the fags he meets have contempt for him is that he hasn't enough strength to shun his "daytime" world or his gay world. In the gay bar he thinks he's impressing the queer at the bar when he tells him he's a shop steward, in charge of the strike; and of course, he is secretly laughed at. A shop steward is, simply, a john, but Harry doesn't know this; he never knows it. The homosexuals go along with him

so long as he has money, though, and so long as his vulgarity and naïveté
are amusing, which seems a fairly lucid statement on the *lumpen* qualities of
sexual desire, both homo- and heterosexual; again, no world of adventure,
no superior and "dangerous" existence as limned by the homosexual writing
of our time. This is simply how it is. An insistence on the equality of gross-
ness shared by both arenas; a fat, pimply whore as against a beard disguised
with face powder—both quite ugly. Selby has shined a strong light on areas
heretofore lost in shadows. The stories, without comment, comprise a manual of candid distinctions.

"Landsend" is the last word on the low-rent housing project—it stands as
the bitterest and fiercest indictment yet written on this contemporary phenomenon. Needless to say, it will probably be thought of as an antihuman
attack, whereas it is actually an anti*humanist* attack. Here, Selby intimates,
is the upshot of that Renaissance dogma that man stands at the center of his
world. These people *are* at the center of the world; the housing project is a
utopian concept, e.g., give the slobs better housing and they'll be good. Not
a start toward understanding the individual problems of the poor and sick.
What is ignored in this cynical bureaucracy is the fact that these people are
striving for those values which are essentially useless, if not evil, values of a
world devoid of humanitarian feeling, while drenched with the idea of the
individual. Perfectible man is moved a notch further toward perfectibility
by putting him in "better" housing—no matter the damage to him by this
sterile and vicious institutionalizing. So long as one puts up a little "recreation area" every block or so, complete with backless benches and leafless
trees, the middle-class conscience is assuaged. If the emotional bankruptcy
of living in such cells bursts out in destruction and violence, these same
minds simply set it down to ingratitude, the ingratitude of the bestial poor,
the minority which isn't "ready" yet to take its place in the pursuit of happiness the rest of us are apparently engaged in (and one may note that only
the American Declaration of Independence speaks of the "pursuit of happiness"—presumably the "happiness" attainable by those who were granted
the franchise). The simple violence and bestiality of the poor are condemned
by the people who display the identical traits in a more subtle, complex, and
"sophisticated" way—the former is called criminality, while the latter is
labeled rugged individualism. The distinctions are implied in "Landsend,"
the frustration and misery of being a tenant in this cynically and carelessly
"given" housing bursts from these people in section after section, a horror
of despair, ugliness, violence, and stupidity. But is it any more culpable, any
more putrid than the drug firm which sold thalidomide even though it was
known to be dangerous? Is that Chairman of the Board in Coxsackie? The
populace of "Landsend" will see plenty of jails for acts which are certainly

no worse: but, they are "ungrateful." Why weren't they happy in their nice concrete rooms, with their nice iron stairs, and their lovely leafless trees? The middle-class mind will apparently never understand the difference between a vicious crime and a crime caused by a day-in, day-out environment of viciousness. The inhabitants of "Landsend" are indeed enthusiastic followers of the *Zeitgeist*; they're going along with the values that the "better" elements have prescribed as correct—their methods are cruder, and they can only expect a state-appointed defense, so they rarely come up smelling like a rose as does, say, Charles Pfizer. Or, look at it this way: these people do their best to live up to that old tried-and-true (and patently un-Christian) aphorism, "God helps those that help themselves." Which, incidentally, is a proverb which was first seen in *Poor Richard's Almanac*, by that most humanistic and bourgeois of the founding fathers, good old Ben Franklin— which seems to prove something about the red-white-and-blue God we have invented here. He's a conservative. The only trouble is that they usually get caught "helping" themselves. It's a toss-up between jail and welfare, even though these poor citizens are following the accepted prescription for the good life: but no matter where they wind up, the Goldwaters and the Mitchells seem to assume that their crimes stem from some evil flaw, which in turn stems from a vague and unexplained un-American and un-Christian attitude. Even Luther would roll in his grave to see what has been made of him. The idea that the poor deserve their poverty is not so discredited as one would like to think.

Selby is a moralist, although not one in the sense that he intrudes on his stories in order to let you know what he, as a writer, thinks. The stories are perfectly clear, without any comments from him. Or, as Allen Tate, at the defense of "Tralala" in Provincetown, said, the moral of the story is "the wages of sin is death." Selby's people, as I have implied, are perfect examples of democratic people—they live in a world which has raised to staggering importance the dictum of the individual's importance, his free will, his freedom of choice. Their choices, however, given the environment which somebody *else's* free choice has handed them, or forced them into, are invariably the wrong ones; and they suffer for their acts. It's important to point out that the odds *against* them making the choices they do are staggering. Selby's stories, although they are not "social," are a perfect delineation of the effect of environment on character; conversely, they limn the oftentimes forgotten concomitant of that—the impossibility of character functioning properly in an environment which *actually* gives it no selection of choice at all—so it is a kind of hypocritical democracy these people partake of, much like that of Negroes who try to register to vote in Mississippi. When Tralala opens the captain's love letter to her, it is to check and see whether there is any money in it—she tears it up in disgust when she finds there is none, just his protestations of love for her. What kind of love could she know? Where has her "wise" selection of possibly proffered loves been exercised? She, as the old song says, "don't know what love is." The most meaningful example of her worth, the one thing which she can draw on to prove her value as *herself*, Tralala, a woman, not a cipher, is her sexual ability, when, at the end, she offers to take on the whole neighborhood in a gang-shag. This seems to me so utterly sad, so crushing, that it is unutterable. She doesn't do this as a "gag," or for money, she does it (God help us) out of a feeling of pride in herself, her worth and "know-how" as a whore. In her mind, she has not defiled her body, nor do those who take advantage of her offer defile theirs. She triumphs over those she feels contempt for; she has taken her choice (and what other?). Also, see Harry's end in "Strike," as counterpoint to these remarks on the cast such a meager selection of choices in such a world will put on any act. Originally, Selby had Harry dying at the end: to enhance the force of his degradation, his tragedy, he allows him to live, the implication of what his future life will be in such environment as he inhabits is obvious—he is ruined, just as effectively as John Profumo was ruined. One must remember that the world of Harry Black is not one which may be deserted at will; Harry can't move to another neighborhood and "start fresh." His "choices" are strictly limited. One enters this world of necessity, and one dies in it unless an economic event of almost-miraculous proportions takes place. It must be stressed that the change in the ending is one of kind, not degree, of "wages."

Selby's style: nothing is ever described in terms of physical characteristics. Which places him in the position of being forced to give us the truth—occasionally clothing is described since in a world such as Selby proposes, clothing is a badge of situation or intent. But it is never used as a gimmick, but as a fact. Some writers, the best, let's say, of the "popular" writers, use clothing and "taste" as an indication of what to expect from the character—this will occur in Fitzgerald, more especially, O'Hara. But they are concerned, of course, with the clash of different segments of society. Many times, they are totally out of touch, as, O'Hara's conceptions, in stories written in the last five years, of the Village, painting, the new poetry and fiction. These are conceptions that are fifteen or twenty years old. Again, O'Hara will use a description of a vulgar character's tasteless clothes as an indication of that character's inherent vulgarity: the reader is clued as to what to think. Occasionally, as if to show you that it's nothing but a gimmick, he'll write a story like "Exactly Eight Thousand Dollars Exactly": one character is held against another; the reader is given over to the movement of the story in terms of these characters' appurtenances and acts; and at the end, he turns the tables on you, a writer's joke. Which certainly indicates that he knows that these tricks are simply that, no more. It's almost a confession that he's aware that his great failures are failures of character delineation, though they are cloaked in a dense, pointed résumé of social appearances. Fitzgerald, of course, never understood the poor and confused poverty with vulgarity. What's worse, he confused "family" money with "breeding." Which, in a bizarre way, is his great value—he demonstrates that in a world of fun and games, it is possible, even probable, that one may *learn* to climb the ladder: which is a useful, though oblique comment on said move. *Gatsby* is a classic manual on this process and proves that Fitzgerald understood, thoroughly, the world of the *parvenu*. But his mentality was middle class; he thought this world, for all its failings, was better than the world of the poor; and I don't mean that in an economic way; it was, simply, better, morally and ethically. The dullest Midwestern boy and the most vapid Southern girl, so long as they had position and money, fascinated him. If his bitterness had only come to him earlier, we might have had a literature of the affluent which would have stood as clear as Selby's does on the rejects. But he is often embarrassing, he didn't even know how the poor speak, and the words he puts in their mouths are as hopeless as Henry James' conception of a Boston cop's syntax. When he uses such speech for "comic" effect, it comes out like Amos 'n' Andy. Selby never uses these superficial things to move along his narrative. His ear, as I said, is incredibly acute. There is a section in "Queen" in which perhaps eight people are talking; and the reader knows, absolutely, who is doing the talking: a precision of recording, for narrative effect and character placement, not to show how "good" he is. Dialogue used, not as a *verbatim* transcription of the language people use, but as a revelation of their positions within the hellish society they inhabit. Of course, Selby doesn't employ anything resembling a "clash" of societies in any of his stories. I would guess that his idea is that if one society is presented in all its facets, a reader may gauge his own against it, illuminating his own particular area of life. In totally presenting this world of the wretched and violent, Selby implies a truth, or truths, for those who do *not* live in it, but who live on a higher plane, socially, morally, or economically. Their movements may be gauged against the movements of those who are not so fortunate, or so good.

At the risk of rehashing the absurdities of the *Provincetown Review* trial, I feel a few remarks might be in order re: the "obscenity" of "Tralala." The old banality holds true: anyone who could be excited by "Tralala" is in bad shape to begin with; again, none of the sex scenes in Selby are exciting in the pornographic sense of that term. The smattering of love that one finds in his stories is always sullied by the terms of its actuality: it's either love on one partner's part—the other thinks of it as lust, or gratification—or, the partner is disgusted and/or terrified by it. These few "love" scenes are the only ones which might possibly enclose the never-never land of pornography where women are nymphomaniacs and men are capable of countless orgasms. The other sex scenes in Selby (those totally devoid of love, or "tenderness") are, in a word, horrifying. The gang-shag in "Tralala," the fierce and pathological rape that Harry commits on his wife in "Strike" (who doesn't *know* it's a rape, or pathological—there's a comment on the quality of that marriage for you!), the fumbling and giggling excitement of the queers over their rough trade: all these things are so far removed from the excitement of pornography as to seem self-evidently nonsalacious. They lack the eroticism of love and the eroticism of simple lust—in Selby lust is most often revealed as the opposite of love, not a concomitant. To call these stories obscene or pornographic seems to me to be an indication of idiocy or neurosis . . . but not really. Selby's people do, say, and think what people like this (and not *necessarily* like this) really do, say, and think; everybody looks alike in the sex act, the variations being learnable and exhaustible. Selby's sex episodes seem to terrify those who would ignore the fact that a human being's sexual knowledge really has very little to do with soft lights, sweet music, and the smell of expensive perfume. He speaks of this trite aspect of human life in an off-hand, matter-of-fact way, bluntly, as he speaks of all the events he wishes to delineate. It may be his matter-of-factness, his candor, which enrages the good people concerned with public morals. His is not only not *erotic*, more significantly, he is not *exotic*. None of the other contemporary writers (with the exception of Genet) whose names are most often associated with "writing about sex" can totally avoid that latter term. Burroughs, Miller, Durrell, Mailer, Rechy, Baldwin—all occasionally turn on the orange lights and cover the bed with black silk sheets. In their work, lust occasionally becomes attractive; for Selby, lust is the crushing price one pays for not possessing love, or for being ignorant or mistaken about it. Nathanael West looked at it in somewhat the same way, but his vision was cynical and not so intransigently uncompromising as to push the idea to its limit. Selby pushes it all the way, and then over the edge.

Selby has told me that the prose writers he most admires are Swift, Crane, William Carlos Williams, Isaac Babel. Among his contemporaries, Rumaker and Woolf. An even cursory examination of the work of these men compared with his own will reveal the same essential attention to the minute detail, the "flat" word, the simple declarative sentence, the absence of bizarre syntax: basically, the attention is directed toward *what* is being said, the experience, the emotion itself—as removed from the glittering icing which is so praised in our time (*v.* Updike). And not a simplicity raised to the conscious level of "style"—as in the latter work of Hemingway, or the imitations of popularizers like Shaw and Jones. For Selby, as for the writers he admires, "style" is malleable, not something which, once achieved, may be used as a container for varying shades of emotion, as trademark. The style is transparent, not noticed, as one notices it in Updike, a virtuoso of the banal, whose style is so labored that one may be momentarily blinded to the fact that he is saying nothing; his emotional registrations are phony, Euphues reincarnated. His work is a *trompe l'œil* of letters: wow! that really looks just like an old poster and a rusty nail! On Tad Madison's knotty pine wall, or: *The Tragicall Historie of a Copiewriter.*

I can't recall ever before seeing a technical device such as Selby employs in his stories so masterfully. I speak of the rapid change within the paragraph, and sometimes even within the sentence, from one voice to another, usually the first person to the third, and vice versa: in "Another Day Another Dollar," to select one model, we have: "The cop stepped over to the soldier and told him if he didn't shut up right now he'd lock him up *and your friend along with you*" (italics mine). What we are given here is a remarkably versatile device enabling the narrator to remain in the third person, but overcoming the sometimes restrictive necessities of that position, by being able to identify, at will, with whatever speaker happens to be holding forth in a story at a given time. What is so useful concerning this device is that it precludes the necessity of inventing a first person narrator who would necessarily be *part* of the story, another character; or of slipping in James' "invisible observer." Selby is able to remain aloof from the story, remain the writer as writer, not character, and yet at the same time he can enter the story as whatever character's voice he chooses to assume, as in the example above. This seems to me to be an extremely liberating technique for a writer of prose, giving him total freedom within the action of the story, but allowing him the omniscience that a first person narrator could not have *(Gatsby, The Good Soldier)*. It tends to give the prose a quality of strength and speed and drive, a genuine support for the older discovery (which Selby employs) that one need not say, "he said" and "she said" so long as the dialogue is precise to its characters. I've heard people say that this is an indication of Selby's "primitive" qualities, which serves as an indication of the perception of the gentle readers. The more intimate one becomes with these remarkable stories, the more one realizes that Selby has taken great care with each word: another reason why the stories are lacking in "quotability." Each word builds to the end of the story; the stories are *wholes*; none of them can be excerpted from without an almost total loss being suffered in the quality of the excerpted section.

That Selby's prose is full of technical brilliance is a truism. What is more, none of it is gratuitous, but all contributes to what is happening in the narrative. The use of upper case letters in the Vinnie and Mary sections of "Landsend" is not a "humorous" invention: Vinnie and Mary converse normally in a shout; one finds them all over New York—they are what Italians call *cafone*, people lower than the lowest peasant. The page after page of upper case come across, finally, as an irritant to the reader: they are meant to be so. Note, also, the change in sentence structure and length from the beginning to the end of "Tralala," coinciding with the change in Tralala's fortunes, from isolated events of the sordid, to the overwhelming wave of bestiality which her life becomes, no one thing differentiated from the other, a total degradation, homogeneous. None of these things are instances of "style," *per se*. They are organic to the "content," both narrative and emotional, of the stories. Selby's exactitude of knowledge concerning the aesthetic tastes of his characters has already been touched on, and one may add another instance found in "Queen" where Georgette reads, in the light of flickering *black* candles, "The Raven." What else?

Edward Dorn, writing of Burroughs, says that he is an author who considers his readers a city dump. I would suggest that Rechy thinks of his readers as yokels; Gelber, perhaps, as those folks around the corner who don't know that on the avenue people are turning on. I select these writers because they stand as three of the noted "tough" writers of the moment. Selby may be placed against them with no loss to him. His is an art which might be described as an attempt to get beyond the concerns of these men *with* the world of the sordid, *to* the world of the sordid, an art which registers the emotional mutilation possible (and probable) in a segment of society where all values have been totally corrupted in the name of progress and law and order. It is not a world of romantic criminality, nor is it a world of the consciously alienated hipster. It is a world where crime is a fact of everyday life, not an event which one nervously partakes in, "beat" style, turning the overt criminal act into an "assault" upon the state, or the prevailing "current of opinion"—crime not as an instance of *épater le bourgeois*, but crime as an instance of, say, belching—ho, hum, it's Tuesday, let's go break a couple of heads. The innuendoes of the work seem to imply that none of this is remediable, given the context of society in which this subculture functions. I'd guess that Selby thinks of his reader as someone who might possibly want to know the truth about a real, living hell which exists in our own time, in the city of New York. He has succeeded in professing this truth with great artistic distinction, without patronization, without romanticizing its facets: most importantly, he has done it without egoistic remonstrations or possible "solutions." He is, in my mind, one of the most powerful prose writers now working in America, as well as the best commentator on the urban poor since the Crane of "Maggie" and "George's Mother." In short, an artist of unmistakable brilliance and authenticity.

Kulchur, 1964

ADDENDUM 1981: AFTER *Last Exit to Brooklyn*

> But any judgment one wishes to make on a work should take into account primarily the difficulties that its author has set himself.
>
> Paul Valéry

The Room is rooted in "Strike," taking the claustrophobia of that great investigation into moral, ethical, and social collapse a step further. In "Strike," Harry Black's interpersonal traffickings serve, curiously, to drive him and his chapter inward; the more he pushes outward into a milieu that he cannot control or influence, the more closed and airless his world becomes. The effect is furiously centripetal. At the end, he is talking to a God that he has invented out of despair, a kind of ultimate blasphemy.

Everything (but that terrible pimple!) in *The Room* exists in the thinker's mind. As his fantastic scenes of torture are invented, so may be his reconstruction of his adolescence and young manhood; as the careful vulgarity of his courtroom scenes are patched together out of the detritus of debased art (the scenes a kind of cento of the various corruptions that inform kitsch, Hollywood, trash fiction, etc.), so may be the circumstances of his unjustified (of course) arrest and incarceration. But whereas Harry's social life exists on the same plane yet is separate from his terrified inner life, the social intercourse and interior life of the thinker in *The Room* are an inextricable mix of buried psychopathological symptoms. Indeed, his social intercourse *is only* interior, and must be taken with a grain of salt as to its actuality.

The Room is a tour de force of linguistic devices, although the slapdash criticism—both pro and con, that all of Selby's work has received—speaks of his language (when it speaks of it at all) as some sort of "natural effusion." *The Room* is developed on at least five planes of language:

1. The hallucinatory rape and torture scenes are described in obsessive detail (the thinker as classic psychopath) in much the same way that Sade meticulously sets the stage before his characters indulge in their orgies of sex, torture, and death. These are masturbatory refinements: the fantasist must know where every lamp, table, and door is before he begins deploying

his characters, lest, in the middle of a scene of carnality, he is forced to stop the action and invent the lamp, table, or door.

2. Scenes of youth are, for the most part, rendered in a soppy, callow, naive language (the thinker as innocent).

3. Youthful sex is given as reportage: unerotic, plodding, mechanistic, matter-of-fact (the thinker as cool exploiter).

4. The arrest is presented in language that reveals the thinker as frightened citizen. It is wounded, indignant, eminently sane, bewildered yet noble (the thinker as exploited).

5. The courtroom scenes turn on the thinker as objective sage, spirited defender of humanity, brilliant legal amateur, relentless cross-examiner (all these masks, in the scene of his judicial defeat, falling away to reveal the rage that is at the core of the novel).

This language, as noted above, is a mélange of contemporary slop-talk: the thinker emerges from a speech culture whose hallmark is decay, a decay so ubiquitous that there is, in a sense, no reality, since the linguistic means by which to measure it are nonexistent. These five planes mix, break apart, recombine, as the thinker creates new realities for himself. It is the interior language of impotence.

In *The Room* then, we know nothing of the thinker but the thinker's mind. We don't even know what this man thinks of himself, nor if he knows *what* he is. This returns us to Harry Black, a man who is not only not what he seems to be, but who doesn't himself know what he is. Harry's construction of his character is overt, though it is a mystery to him. In *The Room*, the thinker denies and accepts a whole battery of characters—as himself—through fantasies, reconstructions of events, and memories; but are the latter two true or false? We can't know because the thinker doesn't know, and the thinker doesn't know because Selby won't "tell" him. All we know in this book is what language tells us, except that this brings us to a problem that is, it seems to me, formidable. If we only know what the language of *The Room* tells us, and that language is everywhere corrupt and fake, what do we know? Linguistically, *The Room* is not satiric, parodic, realistic, vengeful, propagandistic, defensive, expository, attacking, didactic. It is debased and unable to evaluate reality; as a matter of fact, it is language that cannot even represent itself: it slips and slides; and, when it is at its most realistic, it is most false. It is satanic language and *The Room* may be hell.

The Demon gave critics trouble, since the main character (Harry White this time, an intentionally obvious irony) is not a member of the underclass that inhabits *Last Exit*, nor does he indulge in the byzantine thought of the thinker of *The Room* (a man in jail). But he too may be traced to Harry

Black. He is not what he seems. He doesn't know what he is. There is, apparently, more "air" in *The Demon*, yet all the scenes that detail Harry White's descent into horror are sudden and, to his family and friends, inexplicable manifestations of interior tortures and obsessions.

Harry White's language is dichotomous. His speech is banter—manufactured out of cliché, the very stuff of cliché, his jokes and small talk (as well as his "serious" talk) taken from commercials, newspapers, movies, all the empty bits of *lingua franca* of the white-collar worker, the automatic speech of men whose intellectual sustenance derives from profit. It is the quintessence of these things; and it is also discreetly, even puritanically, wary of sex. Harry's interior language, however, is that of madness: foul, profane, murderous. Harry White's articulations show forth the materialist zombie; his inner voice is that of the void. That Selby should have been denigrated by critics because his successful, financially well-fixed, and conventionally married young executive is also a paranoid schizophrenic who is truly "possessed" is an instance of cultural prejudice as well as a variation on that old tune whose title is "Selby the Realist." No one had any trouble believing in Tralala's abasement; but that a man "on the way up" should want to sleep with filthy, lousy whores and steal office equipment could not be countenanced. But Selby is *not* a realist, and Harry White is as "believable" in terms of this author's body of work as are Georgette and Harry Black.

The sections of *Last Exit* other than "Strike" are those that should be considered as the bases of *Requiem for a Dream*. In this novel, we are "outside" again, and doom is of the same kind that destroys Georgette in "Love's Labors Lost." Most notably, *Requiem* engages the world of drug addiction without resort to sentimentality or romance, and without even a hint of the "outsider" pride that seems to cleave to so much fiction dealing with this material. It can be argued, in fact, that the sentimentality, romance, and perverse pride in the "calling" of heroin addiction, when indulged in by the characters (not the author), accelerates their destruction. The characters in this novel see their world as do Tralala, Vinnie, Georgette, Abraham: they are convinced that they can manipulate external reality and come into the good life. Their daydreams, like Georgette's, are set in counterpoint to the reality that destroys them. Like Emma Bovary, they mistake a false vision of the world for the world itself, while the latter, relentless as ever, rolls over them. Sara, Harry's (!) mother, is equally obsessed with and addicted to a false vision, and, like the other characters, is doomed. Her innocent desire for "happiness" is rewarded in the same way as the other characters' cynical and base desire: defeat.

These remarks are not intended to be complete, but I hope that they may be helpful in moving criticism of Selby off that spot on which it has been comfortably settled for more than fifteen years; I mean the spot marked "realism." Selby simply is not coherent in terms of objective reality. His narrative approach tells us this; his episodes tell us this; his dialogue tells us this; his austere selection of *what* he wants us to know tells us this. All of his work is as it is by design. He is writing of vulgarity, vulgarity of different kinds, I grant you, but vulgarity all the same. To write of it he has elected to write in the language of vulgarity. His characters' speech, his narrative devices, his third-person attitudes and points of view are vulgar. Nowhere does he suggest that he is better than his characters; nowhere does he hint that he can write differently, if he chooses; nowhere does he create "beauty." As I wrote of *Last Exit*, a Selby sentence cannot be excised and held up as a model of "fine writing." Selby's sentences simply blow away when divorced from their context.

This achievement is absolutely remarkable. Selby has done, in these four novels, what it is well-nigh impossible to do: he has made major literature out of the kind of language that Valéry calls that which "does not outlive understanding." But Selby's, because he has put all his faith and energy into the composition of works in language that is that of everyday cheapened discourse, and *without calling attention to the fact that he knows better*, does "outlive understanding." He has disappeared into his books, and his books proffer an art made out of trash and garbage. He gives us no commentary, no opinions, no ideas. He gives us—and this is what constitutes his uncanny power—*no comfort*. He "is" the specific vulgarity, cruelty, and madness that relates, in a vulgar, cruel, and mad tongue, the vulgarity, cruelty, and madness of his closed world.

The Review of Contemporary Fiction, 1981

12

Coleman Dowell

PERVERSE STORY

Too Much Flesh and Jabez

This novel is a meticulously and subtly composed tour de force on the imagination, that of Miss Ethel, a seventy-year-old spinster schoolteacher, now retired, and the author of *Too Much Flesh and Jabez*. She has written, as Mr. Dowell states in the "frame" within which her novel rests, a "perverse story"; what a delicate ambiguity suffuses that phrase! Mr. Dowell—like all writers whose intelligence rummages through the minutiae of life, turning and sifting them until he has isolated some few things that will not be reduced—writes prose in which meanings shift just as they appear to assume some clarity. Whatever is "perverse" in this story is so only because it is a symptom of a general emotional decay—its effluvium, so to speak.

Miss Ethel's private *roman à clef* is the tale of a dirt farmer, Jim Cummins, his bitter marriage, his first and only love affair, and his seduction of and by Jabez, a strange, near-hermaphroditic boy who comes to stay at a farm down the road during a summer drought in the first year of World War II. The fictional Jim is Miss Ethel's invention, made from the real Jim, who at one time had been her star pupil, a marvelously intelligent boy whose brain "she saw as abnormally large, an organ too large for his own good," in this town of stupid "good old boys." In her novel Miss Ethel transforms this brain into a monstrous phallus, a transformation precisely apt for the story that Mr. Dowell wishes to tell through her story. We have here, of course, the materials of a dirty joke, and, like all good dirty jokes, its heart is cold and empty.

Miss Ethel is ignorant of sexual love—ignorant, for that matter, of all the modes of love—and so her novel, quite beautifully, embodies an oddly chaste and off-center pornography. What we are permitted to see through her fantastic and crippled opus is her imagination's desperate attempt to come to terms with her own loneliness, her desolation of spirit—the plight she has survived all her life. Mr. Dowell's peculiar talent allows him to reveal this state in passages that are bloodlessly erotic or infused with a comic sense that is both sour and cruel.

A case might be made that in this novel Mr. Dowell is sketching out once again a treatise on sexual freedom as fulfillment, the sexual act as panacea for emotional ills. I cannot for a moment see it this way. It seems clear that had life granted Miss Ethel sexual release, it would have been the counterpart for the furiously cynical experience she imagines for her characters; and if we are tempted to view Jim's release with Jabez as the magic that will free him from his marriage, we face the reality of Jim's presence as an invention of Miss Ethel's thwarted desires. Although she does not, certainly, say so, she would agree with Baudelaire's "*la volupté unique et suprême de l'amour gît dans la certitude de faire le mal.*" It is this "mal" that she stirs into her pages with ignorant and pathetic lust; it is what makes her imagine herself as Jabez, who takes Jim into himself not in love, or even lust, but in rage.

The novel is "perverse"—to return to that word—in that it belies, as it displays, its subject. It is not a novel about Jim, or his wife, or Jabez. It certainly is not about homosexuality. It is not, finally, about sex—which is used as the base upon which its formal structure is built. By a deft sleight-of-hand the supposed theme of sexual fulfillment that Mr. Dowell makes his book turn on, almost as if he were giving the reader a comforting addendum to what he already believes, is perceived as the clear pane through which we may discern the terrible loneliness and waste of a human being. The characters Miss Ethel has spun out of her despair are absolute extensions of that despair—victims, as is their creator.

The New York Times Book Review, 1977

SOME REMARKS ON *Island People*

... threads, leading nowhere. This labyrinth is
sealed with lead.
                                    Island People

How can we linger over books to which their authors have manifestly not been *driven?*
                                    Georges Bataille

Island People is a rich and complicated work that employs a small complement of techniques for its effects but employs these techniques with unsettling brilliance. It deals, I think, with the idea of salvation through the act of writing, although who is saved is a question that the book never answers. It is, in essence, a ghost story, or, more accurately, a book of exorcism. One of the many ghosts (who may all be one ghost) exorcised is the ghost of self. Perhaps "exorcised" is the wrong word; "banished" may be nearer to what Dowell has in mind.

We might fairly say, then, that *Island People* is a work in which the ghost(s) of self are banished through the act of writing, and banished so completely that this self no longer exists, as author, persona, or invented characters. The reader is left with no sure grip on the text since the text of *Island People* doesn't exist: we have a book that might be titled "*Island People.*" Its creator invents a writer who invents a character; this character takes possession of him and forces him to create an alter ego for himself, and it is this alter ego who attempts to write a novel called *Island People*, but who never does.

Dowell so arranges it that we are never really certain exactly *who* is writing *what*, or if the *who* that we suppose to be the writer of any given *what* is the author, the narrator's narrator, or the character who has taken possession of the writer. What we hold in our hands as *Island People* is a book that has avoided being the *Island People* of the alter ego. Through this act of multiple evasion, this willed ambiguity (for instance, there are journal entries that purport to comment on the developing novel but that may very well be part of this novel's text), the ghosts, who could, perhaps, have emerged from the pages of a conventional narrative, i.e., one which "reflects life," are denied presence, are banished to the pages of an "unwritten" book, the house that they may haunt forever.

These ghosts are lured, so to speak, into the house of the text we have by means of curious, quasi-archaic passages that simply *appear*; that is, we have no evidence as to who might have written them: they are not documents, or pseudodocuments, but brief fictional episodes. These passages act as a literary ouija board, and the personages they call up are a nineteenth-century family and its involvement in hatred, violence, and murder. They are called into the present so that they may be banished to the book's pages.

Tricked by a narrative that has as its author *not* its author (nor do we know who its author is); whose chapters turn out to be not chapters at all, but a series of short stories by or about the narrator (invented by an invented character who in turn has been invented); that marshals a population of characters who are really mirror images, distortions, inversions, perversions, and caricatures of each other, the ghosts have no purchase on the real world *outside* the novel. They are imprisoned forever in the text called *Island People*. This may also be viewed as Dowell's commentary on the novel as a closed system; i.e., real ghosts have been rendered powerless by trapping

them in fiction, fiction deployed so that its artificial nature cannot be mistaken.

Island People functions as a medium whereby real ghosts are called up by
a shifting and multiplex character whom they haunt; he rids himself of them
by turning them and all the characters they have possessed (which characters also haunt him) into fiction, wherein they are trapped, so that he may
be free. The techniques of the work are ways of foiling the ghosts: There is
no discoverable narrator; the island is everywhere and takes many guises (the
scenes are claustrophobic and, even when laid outdoors, are cut off from
everything else, "isolate"); the characters are images of each other, masked
by age and sex and name, all of them not only vaguely or overtly similar, but
also curiously like the figures of the nineteenth-century family—so that
they, in effect, are ghosts of ghosts.

None of the ghosts can cross over via the medium of the text, since it is,
indeed, a "labyrinth sealed with lead," whose "threads" lead "nowhere."
They may haunt its pages, but there is no *self* to haunt. The ghosts have
been banished to the text, and the self to a myriad insubstantial selves that
disintegrate and scatter. Only this work of pure invention remains, a work
whose center cannot be found, as it exists somewhere between the artifact
and its creator, and neither is "what it is."

I do not for a moment suggest that this is the only way to read *Island
People*: it may even be a wrongheaded or eccentric reading, since this work
is, as are all works of great authority, inherently mysterious: it has no *inside*.
One thing seems clear, however, and that is that *Island People* is a work that
its author was "manifestly driven" to write.

The Review of Contemporary Fiction, 1982

13

Michael McClure: Artaud

"For Artaud"

To break through the façade of this poem, the difficulty. It is there, the solid core, but getting to it presents the reader with problems—not all his fault; viz., a list of the nouns presents nothing for the *eye* to seize upon. To a generation brought up on Pound and Williams, this is a new experience. Let us see, on the first page alone, we have: "nets," "heroin," "peyote," "interiors," "battlegrounds," "quantity," "air," "beauty," "light," "base," "slack." The one clearly visual words, *nets*, is not such when we discover McClure's usage. And certainly, no one thinks of the physical objects when "heroin" and "peyote" are read. So the confrontation.

McClure's main "body" delineates an investigation—the inner being and the outer reality—though this is no place for a prose restatement. The poem is to be read. Thoroughly. Many times.

What can be talked of is the form: the poem sits upon the paper, symmetrically; a sense of ocular balance is achieved, but the stance upon the page has little to do with its rhythms—nor do the capitalized lines serve to rivet anything into the mind of the reader that lower case would not do as well. We do not shout the lines to ourselves as we read, and the capitals occasionally bring bad lines into salience: "OH BEAUTY BEAUTY BEAUTY BEAUTY BEAUTY BEAUTY IS HIDEOUS" is merely bad oxymoron; "STOMACH BRAIN AND BODY ARE THE ROOMS OF OUR LIVES" too obvious to allow into the poem, perhaps, let alone, capitalize.

But things work—and well. McClure at his best is as good as anyone writing today, there are lines the suggest the Elizabethan crispness: "What is my sickness and my vacancy? / I care/for love and will not/serve it" (the caesura at "care" almost mutilates the line but its choriambic movement is unassailable). And "The face is love—the head is clouded by the smoke we make/of it," where the caesura works and justifies the geometry of the lines' construction.

The closing lines I call particularly to attention because after a poem dealing with abstractions, the "black interiors" of the self, we are brought sharply and beautifully into the mundane with: "But icy light icy dark and green wet leaves/above."

Essentially: for whatever flaws the poem displays, it is a brave one; the matter comes across; there are lines that stay in the mind as music—and, most important, McClure is working toward a form to fill, in his own poetic, the gap left by the pulling down of traditional prosody. His realization of that, and its concomitant, that chaos is a poor substitute for exhausted regularity, is enough in itself to commend the poem.

Unpublished, 1959

14

Max Finstein

One of the first poems of Max Finstein's that I read has the lines, "with care/
it is made."

That is Finstein's poetic fulcrum, I should say, envinced clearly by the
poems you are about to read. No thick gobs of verbiage to clutter the poetic
line, nothing in the way of the poem, as it moves gracefully toward its end,
viz., "gracefully," with grace, not, that is, icing, false pirouettes of wit and
meaning; not, in short, the virtuosity of the poetaster. If the poem is a machine, then Finstein's is perhaps a punch press, the die cast truly, the product
exact to calibration, dross on the floor—for the porter.

A solid bite into the emotions, albeit limited, each rendered skillfully—
a controlling image dominates—"the white/edge of the dollar bill/an indispensable tool." If there is doubt that this is the hand of the craftsman, you
are not concerned with verse.

O.K. Let's say verse and get away from the unsure thinking caused by the
word "poetry." How much verse as against how much poetry being written
today forces the delineation.

Finstein writes poems—he also writes verse. That is, the poems have
form, they exhibit a poetic concern, there is not a TRUE CONFESSIONS
aura above the words. The emotion become art, love settled on a blue
whale's heart, a yellowbird, billy the kid and his baggy pants. The artist is
foremost here. It is a fine book. Max Finstein operates the press truly and
the poems: with care they are made.

Savonarola's Tune, 1959

138

15

Ron Loewinsohn's
Watermelons

Some poems, like Robert Creeley's, take you into a little box, or better, room, in which secrets known to the poet are communicated to you, these secrrets to be taken with you back into the world, and used as tools to help in the steady grapple with experience. They are closed poems, their world is in them only, their relation with the "real" world only in the way their image remains when in that world.

Loewinsohn is not this kind of poet: he is a working man's poet; perhaps he loves freedom as only one who works at the tedium of a job can love it; the blues feeling in there, not in technique certainly, but there in the whole tone: "Weekly tedium of supermarkets./What's needed here's/the Death-Defying Perskys." That's it, and no bad thing, at the least—which that fragment is.

William Carlos Williams once wrote me that he was glad that I was working steadily again, because, he said, that was good for my art; that some of the energy needed to sustain one's self on the job slopped over into the writing and made one steadily industrious. This is certainly true—work is debilitating to a poet if he is one who flutters at the edges of the art; that at least is my justification of the daily boring round into which my circumstances have forced me. Loewinsohn too, of course; the poems are full of allusions to this grind, and the blessed escape from it into art and sex, love, the things that keep us whole in the coldness of an industrial world.

It is not too farfetched to compare Ron with the seventeenth-century Jacobean poets, the metaphysicals, if you will have it that; they were so involved in the world as men of the church, commerce, etc., etc., that all of it slopped over into their art, their images were strong and connected with their own steady push through the years. This too Loewinsohn's strength:

> :Rosy gas station summer eve
> a whole crowd of old spades
> working on a big Buick
> up on the rack showing
> nervous complications of cable
> girders, humps, wire, oil
> the whole scene too dark, almost,
> to see anything . . .
> one of them pausing in his labor
> to look back into the deeper black
> of the lube job cave,
> yells at his buddy who's hungover
> & trying to goldbrick—"Hey Zorro!"

This is *not* Walt Whitman's all-embracing identification with things of which he had no knowledge whatsoever—the romantic looking *with* his eyes instead of *through* them. Creeley has turned the world to account in one way; Loewinsohn has taken a way which can be death to a young poet, obsessed with categorizing, and has made it loose, flexible, has given us the world back, not distorted, but made realer by his vision.

Kulchur, 1960

16

Measure of Maturity

The Jacob's Ladder

Denise Levertov has always been a meticulous writer, one whose poems exhibit a great degree of care and polish. In this new volume, however, she adds to her usual excellence a measure of maturity that has not been seen before. It is a long journey from the "pre-Williams" poems, when she was still working in England—

> A painted bird or boat above the fire,
> a fire in the hearth, a candle in the dark,
> a dark excited tree, fresh from the forest,
> are all that stand between us and the wind.

—with its almost regular iambics and staid progression, the "argument" resolved with the passive "are" as verb, through

> let it scissor and bounce its denials
> on concrete slabs and black
> roadways. Flood the streets.
> • • •
> vague skies, the tedium
> up there.
>
> Under scared bucking trees
> the beach road washed out

in which the voice, the tone, the measures are all American and very heavily laced through with the Williams influence; to, finally, in this new volume:

one knew
that heart of fire, rose
at the core of gold glow,
could go down undiminished,

for love and
or if in fear knowing
the risk, knowing
what one is touching, one does it,

each part
of speech a spark
awaiting redemption, each
a virtue, a power

in abeyance unless we
give it care
our need designs in us. Then
all we have led away returns to us.

She has come into her own movement; the words are charged with meaning;
one must read the poem carefully or the beauty escapes. There is a great
tightening up of the "margins" of the poem. That is, she has almost given
up the concept, so explicit in the second quote, of breaking the sequence of
idea and image, and jumping from one block of words to another. It seems
to me that this is all to the good, for her talents are not in that direction.
She is at her best when the poem moves quietly from the first line through
to the last, without the sudden breaks learned from Williams.

The book has many fine poems, and some failures, but they are never
absurd failures. I disagree with the blurb-writer who lauds her sequence
"During the Eichmann Trial": here she uses her above-mentioned talents
for a direct movement *through* the poem, in a narrative fashion, without
imbuing the words (in the first two sections, at least) with poetic power. In
other words, there is a very thin feeling here—not emotionally, but poeti-
cally. The poem does not carry its own weight, and we have

he scales the wall
enters the garden of death
takes the peach
and death pounces

mister death who rushes out
from his villa
mister death who loves yellow

who wanted that yellow peach
for himself
mister death who signs papers
then eats

—a kind of loose prosy manner that is like the papier-mâché verse of Prévert or Ferlinghetti.

The book, however, is almost totally successful, and the indications are that Denise Levertov is taking her place as a solidly important American poet.

The Nation, 1962

17

Charles Olson: *The Distances*

It seems to be an unfortunate rule in American letters that those poets who are most strongly the "shakers and movers" of their times are precisely those who are most ignored by the literary "officialdom" in power during those times. To be privileged to read a book like *The Distances* and to simultaneously realize that it has been ignored (it was published in 1960) or currishly dismissed (I seem to recall one lout, in an academic quarterly, who spoke of Olson as an aging beatnik) by these powers is enough to make even a nincompoop like David Susskind question the authenticity of the so-called American "cultural revival." It is certainly not in my power to grant Olson a fellowship or a prize, but it is in my power to point out to anyone who clearly cares about poetry here in the United States that Olson is an authentic major poet, and, outside of Pound and Williams, the leading figure in current American verse.

I submit that the most salient poem in this volume, and, by this, I do not mean the "best" poem, is the one entitled "The Librarian." For a reader, it is an excursion into the poet's mind at its most brilliant; for the poet, it is an awesome use of the materials of dream, magnificently unencumbered by the charlatanry of analysis. "The Librarian" is the dream re-created, the dream made mordant, solidified into the viable, the usable structure which we call "poem." It is the most telling use of those materials I have encountered in English, save perhaps for the Yeats poem "The Second Coming." We have the avoidance of the mere "telling" of the dream, we have the avoidance of the even more damaging "explanation."

> In this night I moved on the territory with combinations
> (new mixtures) of old and known personages: the leader,
> my father, in an old guise, here selling books and manuscripts.

and:

> His previous appearance had been in my parents' bedroom
>   where I
> found him intimate with my former wife: this boy
> was now the Librarian of Gloucester, Massachusetts!

and the ending:

> There is no light
> east
> of the Bridge
>
> Only on the headland
> toward the harbor
> from Cressy's
>
> have I seen it (once
> when my daughter ran
> out on a spit of sand
>
> isn't even there. Where
> is Bristow? when does I-A
> get me home? I am caught
>
> in Gloucester. (What's buried
> behind Lufkin's
> Diner? Who is
>
> Frank Moore?

It is significant of Olson's integrity that the question which ends the poem *works*; that is, there *is* an answer—as against the rhetorical questions which end many poems and with which the poet wishes you to share in his "profundity."

This man, it becomes clear, has all the equipment. There are no fake poems; there are no easy outs; each poem is a complete attempt to wrestle with experience, to make some sort of order out of its jumble. The preoccupations are many, but the outstanding concern seems to emerge as that one which has to do with a man's remaining honest to this unnervingly difficult art of poetry. As against the "homely" rhetoric of the fifth-rate Frost, with his "The land was ours before we were the land's"—which had the cultural idiots of our time nodding sage approval—we should have at least the dignity to set Williams' "The pure products of America go crazy." Olson inhabits this same ground; he too has the America that actually exists, and has existed, in his "the lethargic vs violence as alternatives of each other for los americanos." But this, of course, is not "official" poetry. This is the poetry of a man who has seen his land "advertised out" of nobility, as Williams has seen the Passaic turn purple and polluted with the chemical wastes of factories. Being poets who are not interested in making witty remarks at the White House, they embarrassingly say so, while Frost retires to those dear old Vermont woods and makes vapid comments on some damn fool's wall or tree or pond (in his tried-and-true democratic/humanistic shuffle) in poems the language of which is insufficient to carry the "message" of even a *New Yorker* story.

I am sick of it all, and I must say so. I cannot for a minute conceive of writing a review of Olson without saying that his neglect is shameful. While men like Alan Dugan win prizes, while men like Robert Frost are honored, while imbecilities like the works of Carl Sandburg are published with cynical regularity, the beautiful work of Olson in *The Distances* is not only shunned, but degraded. And degraded by those most involved in what can only be called the "snob" culture of this country. Here is Olson himself on this culture in his "Letter for Melville 1951":

> For you will have to hear one very bright man speak, so bright
> he'll sound so good that every one of you will think
> he knows whereof he speaks, he'll say such forward things, he'll tag
> the deific principle in nature, the heroic
> principle in man, he'll spell
> what you who do not have such time to read as he
> such definitions so denotatively clear you'll think you understand
> (discourse is such a lie) that Herman Melville
> was no professional, could not accomplish
> such mentality and so, as amateur (as this clear neuter will
>   make clear)
> was anguished all his life in struggle, not with himself, he'll say,
> no, not with when
> shall i eat my lunch Elizabeth has set outside the door so quiet
> it was not even a mouse, my prose today
> is likewise, the cows, what a damned nuisance they also are, why
> do i continue to extend my language horizontally when
> i damn well know what it is
> a water-spout

Yet these "clear neuters" exist and flourish in the literary community, some insane Edward Bellamy world of happiness and culture, in which the "topics of discussion" have the most tenuous grasp on what is actually happening, like an infinite *Open End* program. This, I fear, must seem like a paranoid rant, but it is assuredly not so; one has only to read *The New York Times Book Review* to discover that world, or at any rate, its manifestations. Front page reviews of Robert Frost and Herman Wouk; "serious" reviews of books of poems by hacks like X. J. Kennedy and Paul Engel; absurdly incompetent remarks about *major* volumes of poetry—I recall seeing one "review" that spoke of Duncan's *The Opening of the Field* as being indicative of the influence of William Carlos Williams and his (Duncan's) dislike of the academy. And this is essentially *all* that was said of one of the most remarkably fine books of poetry published in the last decade. This is not fantasy, this occurs every day. At best it is ineptitude, at worst, stupidity. As Pound never tired of saying, businessmen who pursued their affairs on this level would be put out of business as bankrupts. In the world of letters, however, any "opinion" is all right, so long as it issues from the right mouth—"discourse is such a lie."

But, of course, how can one expect Olson to be honored, or even reviewed, when the poets in which he roots himself so deeply, Pound and Williams, are yet to be accorded the honors they deserve in their indisputable capacity as the two greatest poets this raw land has yet produced? Pound is doomed because of his politics and his "contempt" for the reader (whoever that evanescent personality may be). Williams is safely enclosed in the Wisdom-Gentleness-Patience bin, labeled "Kindly Doctor." The dullards in power have slowly come to accord him his "place" but they still refuse to *listen* to the man, and they refuse, more significantly, to treat his insistence on a new poetics with any seriousness. When one reaches Olson, the dismissal is more poisonous, since he is dismissed as the imitator of two men who have been dismissed for decades. But this is not imitation:

> ya, selva oscura, but hell now
> is not exterior, is not to be got out of, is
> the coat of your own self, the beasts
> emblazoned on you And who
> can turn this total thing, invert
> and let the ragged sleeves be seen
> by any bitch or common character? Who
> can endure it where it is, where the beasts are met,
> where yourself is, your beloved is, where she
> who is separate from you, is not separate, is not
> goddess, is, as your core is,
> the making of one hell

His range, his interests, his capabilities are overwhelming; the book is rich with words and cadences; the mind is filled with a new thing, a beautiful thing;

> Hail and beware the dead who will talk life until you are blue
> in the face. And you will not understand what is wrong,
> they will not be blue, they will have tears in their eyes,
> they will seem to you so much more full of life
> than the rest of us. . . .

That is the line that is reached through one's ear, it attains its length because it must, it is as musical as Campion, or Homer. It is not arbitrarily long; it takes the shape that the thought of the poem demands; against it we may place:

> After 47 years this month
> a Monday at 9 AM
> you set I rise I hope
> a free thing as probably
> what you more were Not
> the suffering one you sold
> sowed me on Rise
> Mother from off me
> God damn you God damn me my
> misunderstanding of you
>
> I can die now I just begun to live

Allow his tours de force, allow his complaints, allow his slighter gestures; this is a world of beauty we are confronted with; and who, outside of this man, has so grappled to form it, so triumphed, and so been denied his victory save the few other artists who have not, or who will not, sell out to one fashionable camp or another? This work, these poems are certainly a part of "what we needed most." But what a slender and despised body of work stands with them to answer the final question of that poem which concludes:

> Yes, mouths bit
> empty air
>
> > They bit. What
> > do they bite,

now? what we needed most
was something the extension of
claritas: what do we have
to report?

Kulchur, 1962

18

Andrew Hoyem:
The Wake

This is an extremely impressive book; I might even say, to go out on a limb, a brilliant book. I know nothing of Andrew Hoyem, nor have I ever read any of his work before this; but on the strength of this small collection, I shall look forward to anything he may publish in the future. This man has the ability to make poems so stinging in their contours, so dazzling in their language, that I went back over some of the lines again and again to make sure that what I thought I saw the first time was really there. He has a freshness of expression and a gaze so steady that each poem emerges like a flower, exquisite. It is the quality of the language which carries his strength, his talent consists of the ability to speak precisely—you've got to *read* the words. In this, he has affinities with men like Creeley and Spicer, although his vision is his own.

What do you do with a poet who makes metaphor? With a poet who makes the image new? *Makes*, I said, not sloshes around in his mind and glues disparate things together, the more discrete the more revered, the more he is scraped to, bowed to, held up as a visionary giant. I'll tell you what you do with him. You ignore him, you slight him, you stick him in the black book along with Louis Zukofsky, H. D., Charles Olson; there's no sense in it, to list, make lists; in our time we have a great republic of the dishonored, which republic, I am certain, Mr. Hoyem will soon be naturalized into. That men can so ignore this, so stand, dulled to the fact that the language is the only thing that will save us from complete doom as men, and the poets are the keepers of the language. Here we have Hoyem, his cutting lines, his passionate, inventive verse; and where will he wind up? Remaindered, or in the hands of a few, or as Olson said, "the few who still read." Olson also said, you can't fool that few; which prevents nothing.

All right, look at this. I don't care if you're a poet, a critic, or simply an innocent bystander, I beg you to look at this and gauge it against the rubbish that passes for the good, the fine, and which is a ticket to our final sellout as a people.

> My lips could part, the tongue cleaved to the palate
> or was loosed to cleft by a hollow pop.
> A teat would not fill it, nor could words.
> The sayings from my mouth
> strung out for miles of messages,
> thin paper ribbons,
> ticker tape from my clacking tongue
> showering out skyscraper windows
> over the street, floating confetti down
> upon some parade or other.

Read that again. It says, "help!" Quietly. Further, "The Texas Poem," the whole thing, is beautiful. It shuttles from constructions so intense in their use of language that one is almost unaware that language is involved, the language is a weapon to attack you; shuttles from that to flat statements the prose qualities of which are impeccable. I don't want to quote any of it; the poem is too beautiful as a whole; perhaps, though, one beautiful image (and this is what I mean by making images) of the banal phenomenon of the moon reflected in water.

> while overhead those mallard ducks take off so serene,
> teach me all pedalling the smooth moon to pieces,
> disturb the surface, not the moon, not the moss,
> nor the turtles down deep, nor the dead,
> nor neither neap me.

It seems so late, so very late, and so futile to begin talking again about image, and metaphor, and what they mean. Williams has said it clearly for us, speaking of some poets he met some short time before his death, poets who looked to Europe or the East and the past for their impetus—"but they can't metaphorize upon that of which they have never heard." And one may add, nor can anyone construct an image which does not reveal a timeless aspect of the thing imaged. *Not* pretty pictures, not labored constructions, not well-turned phrases. We've had enough of all that, it seems, to last us another thousand years. And each well-turned phrase leads us further into the muck out of which modern poetry always seems to be slogging. Who is the enemy? Is it really the completely bathetic disasters of the sincere, or ignorant hacks, who simply do their well-paid work, or is it the snide cleverness of the literate who pass off their manufactures upon a likewise clever audience? In the middle of the rubbish, lost to all save those who care, not for "poetry" but for poetry as *art*, stand the works of people who look upon the verse around them in terms of its (how embarrassing a word) honesty. Mr. Hoyem's work in this book qualifies itself as being of that blazon.

We live, if we are poets, in a world which has become increasingly less possible for us, the irony of this being that this impossible world recreates itself in time, in direct ratio to its lionization of poetry, and poets. As George Oppen has said, the only possible casualty in the battle between Philistia and Bohemia is the artist: the two exhibitionist antagonists remain, forever. One fact stands: the poet looks to his productions, he looks to his words, the more he is praised, the more he wonders *why*, the more he investigates *who*. Don't tell me that it isn't easy to sell out; I've seen it done I don't know how many times, by I don't know how many people of diverse talents, over the past five years. How many of that great horde of writers who worked at that time are left; and out of them, which have demonstrated, in their work, that they are concerned with the words they use, that they are obsessed with honesty? I look around and out of the hundreds of men, my contemporaries, at least in age, who were glittering with promise, there are, what? Maybe fifty still seriously at work. To this small body Andrew Hoyem is most decidedly welcome.

The poem, not "poetry," survives only insofar as the poets' integrity, there is no other way out of it. Poets need each other's work, here in New York we need more of the work of Andrew Hoyem, not to mention Spicer and Duncan. And where is Robin Blaser's book? And where is the new work of Edward Marshall, and Dorn, and Kelly, and Creeley and Jones, and George Stanley? I mean accessible *bodies* of work. Auerhahn tries hard—it is one of the few small presses still functioning fairly regularly—but we need more, we need more magazines, there's just too much work around that no one ever sees. Hoyem's book is a visible chunk of the iceberg, that's all. Nobody can do this but the poets themselves; we need no help from the campy hipness of slicks like *Esquire*, which should have stuck to haberdashery, nor do we need the self-righteous drum-banging of our commercial publishers who shock and astound us with their half-dozen or so "fearless" publications a year. In this hideous wallow of backslapping, handshaking, and asskissing, the poet turns to the one thing his talents may control, his language. Or, as Mr. Hoyem says, to conclude *The Wake*,

The rhythms and sound structures of language are to be considered as measures or direct indices of a man's sinuous, washboard, branching, spiral course of life.

Which statement, as far as I'm concerned, is clear as it needs to be.

Kulchur, 1963

19

Neruda:
Residence on Earth

Pablo Neruda is doubtless the greatest poet that Chile has ever produced, and, along with Lorca and Vallejo, one of the great modern poets of the Spanish language. It is precious to say so, but nonetheless true, that there has never been a satisfactory translation of Neruda into English. Mr. Eshleman deserves commendation for his really strong attempt, his book, comprised of selections from the great volumes of *Residencia en La Tierra*, setting itself up as the best Neruda I have heretofore seen.

The great difficulty in translating Neruda is getting what I can only call the unabashed power of his language, the grim anguish of his vision. There is really no one like him in England, most English poets of today being a shamefaced lot whose verse runs the gamut between watery versions of Williams and equally watery concoctions based upon our "beat" poetry. In America, we have Allen Ginsberg, the only poet I know of whose best work has the same passion and despair as Neruda's. This is a rather strange state of affairs, since contemporary Spanish poetry is very close to contemporary American poetry; that is, there is the same grasp of the ultimate truth of modern life in both; viz., it's impossible, and the best one can hope for is an even break. What is even stranger is the fact that the translations have been uniformly weak. The volume of Neruda's translations published just before Eshleman's was by Ben Belitt, the same man who raped Lorca's *Poet in New York*: his attack upon Neruda is as total. The poet appears as a rather effete "wit," the power and devastation of his poems become almost funny. There is, believe me, nothing funny in *Residencia*. Perhaps Belitt was influenced by Bennett Cerf's admonitions. Well, this is no place to put the boots to Belitt, it's Eshleman that we must investigate.

The great failing (to speak first of the negative aspects of Eshleman as a translator) of the book is the "speeding up" of Neruda's lines. By that, I mean that Eshleman has dropped commas, repetitions of conjunctions, repeated verbs with different objects, all these things being a definite part of Neruda's *style*; it's not that these things won't work in the English, it seems that Eshleman is worried that *he*, as a translator, will appear old-fashioned. But much of Neruda's power comes from this method. Take a look at the supremely great "Walking Around." Eshleman says:

> Happens I'm tired of my feet and my fingernails
> my hair my shadow

while the Spanish develops a driving force with:

> Sucede que me canso de mis pies y mis uñas
> y mi pelo y mi sombra

—ending the stanza with the opening line, "Sucede que me canso de ser hombre." Eshleman, by the way, renders that line beautifully and simply, as "It happens I'm tired of being a man." Then why, later, does he start the stanza noted with "happens"? Power is lost. Later, in the same poem, Eshleman has: "everywhere, umbrellas poison navels," where the Spanish reads: "hay paraguas en todas partes, y venenos, y ombligos." Even an absolutely literal translation, following the Spanish construction, gets that line better: "There are umbrellas everywhere," (then, as if looking around in disgust, which is what the syntax implies, viz., an afterthought) "and poisons, and navels."

However, tackling "Walking Around" is no mean feat, and Eshleman has acquitted himself well in many lines. There are some mistranslations here and there; but they are not, on the whole, too bad: "muriéndome de pena" is given as "drained with anguish," when it means, simply, "dying of sadness," or (mental) pain. Also weak are constructions that are schoolboyish, making out of good Spanish, bad English, viz., "toallas y camisas que lloran/ lentas lagrimas sucias." The rendering has it as "towels, and shirts that weep/ slow tears of dirt." That possessive "of" can, with profit, be eliminated to make the line read "slow dirty tears."

Eshleman also leaves some lines out; why, I don't know. Possibly because he thinks that they are not germane to his translation, or because he thinks they are too tough to get into English. Whatever, this is not good practice for a translator. The poem (another great one), "Ritual de Mis Piernas" is given with five full lines left out of the translation, and no note given as to their exclusion. But this is Eshleman's business; and again, this is still the best Neruda in English to date. Sometimes he is brilliant: "compacto y turbado material" becomes "roily and compact stuff," which is nothing short of perfect.

To go off the track for a moment—speaking of another man's translations is really simple. You look at the original; you "feel" it completely; then you look at his rendering, and you say, "aha! He didn't get it." The only remedy for this is to translate yourself, or to learn the language so that you won't need the translator. I'm not sniping at Eshleman here; I'm simply trying to say that he has made what to me are mistakes, misreadings, in this work, and that at times he loses Neruda completely, makes out of him an almost inarticulate man.

The positive side of this book is quite obvious. For one thing, Eshleman has attempted all the really great poems of *Residencia*, whereas another man, let's say Belitt, takes a shot at a couple of them, and leaves the others alone. Eshleman gives us "No Hay Olvido (Sonata)," "Walking Around," "Solo la Muerte" (a fine translation), "Ritual de Mis Piernas," and the two fantastic poems of torture, "Tango del Viudo," which he gets hold of beautifully, and "Caballero Solo," without doubt, a brilliant translation. For another thing, Eshleman has understood that Neruda is not Chile's answer to Robert Penn Warren or Richard Eberhart. He has humbled himself before these great poems, and in so doing, has occasionally come up with lines, stanzas, sections, that closely approach their originals. Neruda is not flippant, he is not "humorous," he is not charming, he is not elegant. His poems, at their best, which is very often, are powerful enough to crack you open, their technique is virtually unassailable, his work is a weapon to deal with the ultimate misery that living is. I don't make a brief here for poems of this nature, but I do say that this is what Neruda, as a poet, *is*. Eshleman has grasped this, has attempted some of the most difficult-to-translate poems in Spanish, and has come off pretty well. To those who have no Spanish, this book gives a fair idea of Neruda's weight as an artist.

Kulchur, 1963

20

AN OCTOPUS/
of ice

The Complete Poems of Marianne Moore

It is instructive to note that the three elder poets that this country has taken to its heart are almost wholly ignorant of the reality of living in this country. Carl Sandburg, who wrote an amorphous verse that dealt with solved, or at least dormant, social situations which his work proffered as problem; Robert Frost, who brought a nineteenth-century Anglo-European sensibility to bear on a postcard America toward which he felt proprietary; and the subject of this note, Marianne Moore, who invented an America of "old values" from which she chose inoffensive subjects—the lovable, slightly crotchety, and eccentric old aunt.

America is maddening because it is vital—perhaps manically so—in its terminal madness, which must date from the beginning of World War I. American writers, the best of them, have busied themselves piercing to the heart of this strangely electric, though moribund activity, piercing the layers of hypocrisy and filth we are daily presented with as truth. But Miss Moore has never looked beneath the first layer, because what is there is ugly, corrupt, and filled with the kind of life and turmoil that eccentricity cannot grapple with. She has eschewed the reality of the American experience in favor of what she will *believe* is the American experience, and in the process she has sealed herself off from her secret heart. The product of such hysterical safety measures is the hysterical, safe poem. And Miss Moore's poems, in value of movement, structure, and the unrelieved doggerel of her late productions, are hysterical indeed. The early poems were rescued, as it were, by their dazzling presence as artifact. But the energy of the poetic charge, to save the poem from bathos, failed because the charge was received from a source that dried up almost immediately after the poet had begun writing: that source was a connection with the America that demanded it be reckoned with in all its rot and vigor. Miss Moore retreated inside her armor (recurring image) and dealt with what she most fervently wished, then hoped, then believed was true. These are terrible poems of the ego—locked in, divorced, puritanical, effete.

From an elegant, restrained, restricted verse of enormous glitter and craft to the greeting-card doggerel of a dear old lady—such is the progress of Marianne Moore's *Complete Poems*. It is a volume that paralyzes the reader with sadness. A poet, presented as "major," who has worked for half a century, has avoided confronting, even once, in her entire body of work, the fact that the nation is brutalized, corrupted, and perhaps hopelessly psychopathic. But the clearly inept verse of the later books is strikingly prefigured in her early work. What happened to Miss Moore is that the costuming gave out; the language failed her. And the language failed her because it lost any touch with the reality that language bears. Miss Moore retreated from life; and her language retreated with her, until it finally died, it finally became good copy, bright and slick and incapable of carrying emotion to the page, to the reader. But since the poet had no emotion save that of the most bitterly conformist, no response but that which is the expected one in this time of the planned tear, the carefully bizarre, the language fits the poem to perfection.

What it is, really, is that the verse was always rooted in itself, i.e., was verse as artifact, as protection for the "refined" sensibilities of the poet. So the poem wore itself out upon itself as the poet grew older and further removed from the world. It is hideous to listen to the claptrap concerning Miss Moore's baseball fanaticism being an instance of her interest in the "regular things." It has nothing to do with what is true. It is a luxury for silly people. If Miss Moore could not, and would not, and most certainly did not engage the real when her juices were flowing, how much less could she do so in her old age: the poem, which sustained itself, sucked its own substance for nourishment, wore itself out over the years, grinding on itself, grinding itself to death. Miss Moore cast about for subject matter outside her own human terrors and desire and meanness—outside, that is, her own humanity, much like a classy Ogden Nash. The formal structuring of the poem, set in motion to poeticize the Brooklyn Dodgers, or Yul Brynner, or some footnoted speaker of some dull cliché, fell into cuteness, the scribbling of a harmless old eccentric. But this is the final product of what began as a harmless young eccentric. (Who knows how harmless?)

The formal composition of the early poems had a value to it: it made sense, that is, aesthetically. The prosy slabs with the careful internal rhyme, the subtle end rhymes, the enjambement used with such precision that the rhymes were muted and rang in the head alone, while devoid of the nervous energy of Williams' early work and the nobility of Pound's, had their verve, their poetic rationale. In the late poems, with the language drained of charge, the "look" of the poems is the same in many instances; but the sound, the formality of the made work is lacking. To compensate for her failed language, Miss Moore used the old suits in the closet. You can check, for example, "The Steeple-Jack" against "Rescue with Yul Brynner" for an exhibit of decadence.

But there are many other such exhibits. The wretched doggerel of "Baseball and Writing"; "I May, I Might, I Must" which hardly displaces the white of the page; the already mentioned "Hometown Piece for Messers Alston and Reese." These are not simply the flagging energies of a tired poet displayed. The reason for the dreary failure of this work is that it is the perfect culmination of the Moore "machine" slowly coming to a halt—and it is indeed a machine that Miss Moore has been at work on all these years, one of glass. And although it still glitters with the look of beauty, and delicacy, and careful attention to detail, the machine is, after all, a toy. As it was from the start.

What is specifically salient about Miss Moore's poems? First, there is no sexuality. Which is incredible—i.e., that she should avoid such a basic human situation. So there are few men and women, those that exist are resplendent in their flat dimensions, clothed in the finery of the slow profundity. (Which takes the place of sex?) They are statues, or they are safely dead; they are ghostly words of wisdom, "Superior people never make long visits . . ." and "The deepest feeling always shows itself in silence; / not in silence, but restraint." Which, apart from the fact that both of these statements are patently untrue, except in Miss Moore's subworld, that is, the world where such dilettantish eccentricity passes for engagement and "trouble," are interesting in the use of "superior"—who are *they*? We know, though, who they are. They're the people who stand outside the world, annoyed at trifles, life a congeries of good manners. And "restraint" is, of course, like "continence." Thus, the whole crushing microcosm of Marianne Moore's universe, made clear in a very early poem.

What else? The animals are always pointed out as Miss Moore's private domain. Yet a look at the animal poems is enlightening because they come through, finally, as creatures out of Walt Disney. A bitterly ironic poem is the one, "Peter," with the last lines

> To tell the hen: fly over the fence, go in the wrong way
> in your perturbation—this is life;
> to do less would be nothing but dishonesty.

—which agrees with the need for the cat to maim and destroy the hen, since that is his nature. Yet the "nature" of Miss Moore's poems is such use of it as to defend her very life, her heart, against all the incursions of a *human* nature as terribly compelling. She uses the exotic animal and the exotic habits of commonplace animals (with all their animalism removed) to draw pretty conclusions about a world which the animals, and myself, do not recognize—because it does not exist except within the shining machine of words.

In "Critics and Connoisseurs," she sweetly scolds against "conscious fastidiousness" using a metaphorical swan who was guilty of this. Miss Moore deprecates the swan's actions, drawing the moral to extend to the human world. She brings an ant in, to the same effect. She does not like this kind of *person* and springs upon that attitude by using these picture postcard animals, these Walt Disney creations. (Who really did the same sort of dishonest thing in his anthropomorphic obsessions.) It is not, at this point, that one is complaining about anthropomorphism: it is that the animals are so *used*, lacking much of their juices. Miss Moore's cat, springing after the hen, will rend, slaughter, and tear the hen to bits when caught. This is also his nature, though this is the part of it that she will not see. The "Critics and Connoisseurs" works the same way. How can a poet *ask* of the humanized ant, what good the "experience of carrying a stick" is? She asks because the ant does not please her; he is metaphorically at fault in his "nature." The cat is not, so long as he doesn't engage in the ultimate rending.

A final note on this poem: She says, "Disbelief and conscious fastidiousness were / ingredients in its / disinclination to move." If Miss Moore's poems are not examples of "conscious fastidiousness," then what are they? Perhaps, at this time, she was struggling with herself, for it is in this book, published in 1935, that she includes "The Fish," her best poem, with its absolutely awed, non-cute sense of the terror and evil inherent in the creation. There was never to be another poem like it.

The poems, as suggested, refuse to admit that living people live. One recalls William Carlos Williams defending his *Paterson IV* against Miss Moore's attack: "To me the world is something which to you must seem foreign. I won't defend my world. I live in it. Those I find there have all the qualities which inform those about them who are luckier," thinking, here, I'd guess, of himself as one of "those who are luckier." But Miss Moore does not, nor did she ever, want to be informed—to her, Lesbianism is evil and foul, so it does not exist. It is not for the poet to treat. I will be careful to state here that I do not take issue with Miss Moore's right as a poet to select her materials—but when the selection *grazes* that which lives, when it selects, then, from these living things, those qualities which render them nonliving, a mere projection of Miss Moore's hazy fantasy about what the world is, this selection is pernicious and ultimately destructive of the poem.

This fear of life, it seems obvious, is not really the same as being distrustful of life, or bitter about it. Nor is it the same as *being afraid*. One can be afraid, and *in life*—Miss Moore fears the entire slate, she withdraws herself and her poem, she scolds. "In the Days of Prismatic Color," which I take to be her aesthetic, says:

> Principally throat, sophistication is as it al-
> ways has been—at the antipodes from the init-
> ial great truths.

Which leads the reader to two points: What are these poems if not "sophistication"?—and, what does Miss Moore think the "initial great truths" are? The cat who stops short of killing? The "superior people" who don't stay too long? The ant with his stick, baldly anthropomorphized to use in a metaphorical or allegorical battering? Or is "the quadrille of Old Russia" as against "a documentary / of Cossacks" the truer image of reality? It is, of course, not an obeisance to "truths" at all that she cares for; it is an instance of Miss Moore's despair at the world which does not care about her Walt Disney creatures and her fantastic politics: people do not die; ideas die. (And a lot of them are such *nice* ideas.) Or people die so that ideas (Miss Moore's) may live and find their way into poems which are ideational set-pieces about people who are unconnected to reality. Some examples of this. In "What Are Years":

> And whence
> is courage: the unanswered question,
> the resolute doubt—
> dumbly calling, deafly listening—that
> is misfortune, even death,
> encourages others
> and in its defeat, stirs
>
> the soul to be strong? He
> sees deep and is glad, who
> accedes to mortality. . . .

In "Keeping Their World Large":

> They fought the enemy, we fight
> fat living and self-pity. Shine, O shine
> unfalsifying sun, on this sick scene.

In "In Distrust of Merits":

> If these great patient
> dyings—all these agonies
> and wound-bearings and bloodshed—
> can teach us how to live, these
> dyings were not wasted.

The first example is an exhortation to courage, somehow encouraging others to die courageously: and ends, the poem, characteristically, with the image of the caged bird, singing joyfully in his captivity, having accepted his "mortality," his "eternity." Another sleight-of-hand Disney operation. The second example is the sort of thing a poet laureate writes about war: no attack upon war in general, or in specific, rather a polite one upon the folks at home, full of rottenness, while their troops sacrifice their lives for them. A schoolbook concept of warfare: "keep your chin up." The third is most pernicious because it is so hideously false, it is the "Hollywood" commanding officer's spiel to the troops before combat: "If we can stop the krauts at the valley, men, these deaths were not in vain." The poem is, even here, degenerating into good copy. The world is what it seems, not what it is, the world is *The New York Times*:

> It could not be dangerous to be living
> in a town like this, of simple people. . . .

Where the line should read, "It might well be dangerous. . . ." As even the events of 1935 proved. Did the Depression occur in Miss Moore's lifetime? Merely an unpleasantry. There *was* pie in the sky. These poems are all about it, wedge by wedge.

The poems truly take on, beginning with *Like A Bulwark* (1956), the cadence and shine of ad copy. They engage "subject" since there has been, for years, nothing left to engage, and the "subject" is the "Real Thing." Here is the beginning of Miss Moore's status as "beloved poet." Poetry, loved by everyone, loved by those who never read poetry, is produced. If one accepts the façade of America, as in 1956 Miss Moore had been doing for some thirty-five or forty years, one accepts the absolute language of that façade, and that language is the copywriter's. America, it must be obvious to even the most benighted by now, would literally cease to exist as the familiar entity it is without advertising copy: I would say that a great majority of the population would feel cheated, robbed, strangely empty and vague, without the advertisement. It is an integral part of the America Miss Moore loves and cherishes, i.e., the fake America. It is indeed an official language, violently opposed to the language of the poem, since its intent is to conceal. The concretists of today embrace the ad, and rightly so, since they have lost all pretension of caring about the use of clear language. It *is* the poem—the poem *is* the copy.

When the ad department of Ford asked Miss Moore to think up a name for their new-model car, which eventually became the renowned stiff, the Edsel, she accepted. Why was that? But, more intriguingly, why did the Ford people ask Marianne Moore? Did they deeply feel, were they deeply moved by, her poems? Why didn't they ask William Carlos Williams? Or Wallace Stevens? Or even Frost or Sandburg? Pound, the insane-jew-hating-fascist-pig-rightwing-economic crackpot—his exclusion needs no explanation. Do the Ford ad people make mistakes? Is it a mistake that Twiggy has no breasts? Is it a mistake that Sidney Poitier has a rootless American accent? My conjecture is that the Ford people made no mistake at all but hit on a poet such as Marianne Moore because her poems most closely resembled elegant copy—a lotta class. A reasonably successful businessman makes few mistakes in conducting his business, the Ford Motor Company makes fewer. The fact that Miss Moore's suggestions were too fanciful is, of course, unimportant: part of the promotion budget. James Dickey, noting this in a brief review of a Moore anthology, chuckles and chortles over the fact that her copy was not "right" for them—missing, with his usual sparkling obtuseness, the point. They were really worried over at Ford. Sure they were. It might have cost them at least $10,000 and a delay in the schedule of about a month. The ad is artifact devoted to the celebration of artifact. The last thing it wants to do is bring the world, dear God, to the consumer's mind. It selects what is fake and further fakes it. The poem without roots does the same. Both falsify language.

"Spenser's Ireland / has not altered" is remarkable in that it works clearly on the two levels of decadence I have spoken of: The quick stab and glossiness of good ad copy and the blithe dismissal of certain facts that ad copy is better off ignoring, e.g., Swift, Parnell, the IRA, the Sinn Fein, Black and Tan butchery, Yeats, Joyce, Wolfe Tone, Robert Emmett, and so on. I am amazed that the Irish Tourist Board has not asked Miss Moore for permission to quote the first three or four lines of this poem, since it functions with great clarity on that plane they function on—dear old Ireland, ah, the peat, ah, the old priests, etc., etc. But how could Miss Moore write clearly of Ireland when she cannot write clearly of her own American experience? Of her own human experience?

It is impossible to lose all touch with the world without losing touch with the language; the language will betray you at every turn if you try to break and humble it to display an abstraction which you insist on believing is true. I am not sure if the converse is true, but I think it must be. So, as Miss Moore continually faced a world which frightened her, except in its more eccentric delights, mostly bookish, so she falsified her language. Emily Dickinson most certainly did not tell us of the "world" in her poems, probably knowing less about it than Miss Moore. Then why do we still, to our profit, read her?—it is, of course, because she went down into her own tortured heart and wrote of that specific. In Miss Moore's poems, we have neither the world nor herself; her anger is clearly removed from all emotion, save that which is safely to be vented. Who Miss Moore is, these poems will not tell, unless it is by default: what they do *not* say. Or, what they say charmingly, and offhandedly, as in the tensely hysterical assault on sex and sexuality in "Marriage," surely one of the greatest attempts at sterilization in the language— all of it understanding, spinsterish language, skipping about "hearth and home"—never the bed. The language failed her as it lost its engagement with the real; and as time passed, Miss Moore added more and more supplementary material to her poems, in the form of scattered quotes from "public" sources mostly—newspapers, magazines, the writings of naturalists, etc. What is the effect of this cluttered poem, the strings of quote marks, the sounding of flat journalese in the body of the poem which builds itself around the quotes—not the opposite—the quotes used to heighten the effect of a particular line or stanza? The poem takes on the whole linguistic sense of the quotes; it creaks under the barrage of them; and, most importantly, the quotes elaborate on the idea of the poem, or elucidate it. We have the really juiceless phenomenon of the poem, rooted in sand, bolstered by secondhand quotes out of context, from sources whose sense of style is decidedly apoetic. The blind lead the blind.

I have mentioned the poem "In the Days of Prismatic Color" as striking me as Miss Moore's aesthetic, and her phrase therein, "great truths." Earlier on in the poem she says:

> complexity is not a crime, but carry
> it to the point of murkiness
> and nothing is plain.

These "great truths," however, are strangely missing in Miss Moore's work. They are not found in the formal structuring of the poems and their engagement with the world; they are, indeed, these "great truths," a series of pegs upon which the poet hangs "ideas." She *says* it, but they are not to be found anywhere in the poems. We all know what she means by "great truths," don't we? Why, the "great truths" are ... are ... the, well, the "GREAT TRUTHS"! But the poem retreats at bewildering speed, and with a display of the most fantastic sleight-of-hand, from any sense of the real, at all. This, the shoring up of the poem with grand statements about Life, and Art, and Love, and Death, and so on, while the poem in its bones refuses to confront any of these things, is another instance of irony in Miss Moore's work. For what is this dazzling footwork but her proscribed "complexity"?—"carried to the point of murkiness" where "nothing is plain"?

"Style" reveals the poem destroyed as clearly as anything in this volume: The casting about for "subject" (there is nothing left, at this date, 1956), the "look" of the early poems, the bathos of the rhyme drawn out in great pain and carelessness, the great lack of sincerity, and the everpresent quotes. The rhyme is most instructive here, the fantastic wrenching of good straight syntax to get the rhyme to fall: "have an Iberian-American champion yet" to rhyme with "alphabet"—and that latter word used gratuitously, since it is followed by the phrase, "S soundholes in a 'cello"—this is bad enough, but the rhythmic sense of the poem falls from the merely incompetent and weary to the ludicrous with "fast fast fast and faster" to rhyme with "Etche-baster."

"In the Public Garden" is notable in that it mistakes Eisenhower for a "hardest-working citizen." This was in 1958, when he was President, and in a poem read at the Boston Arts Festival. It is on a level with Frost's inaugural poem in 1960—the public poem to delight the poetry-hating audience. In the last stanza of "The Arctic Ox (or Goat)":

> If you fear that you are
> reading an advertisement
>   you are. If we can't be cordial
> to these creatures' fleece,
> I think that we deserve to freeze.

Miss Moore doesn't *really* mean that she thinks that *we* "deserve to freeze." This is the quintessence of her later manner: the "we" refers to that chic and knowing section of the public that knows she is joking. It's a delicious snobbism. The world, the "we," is made up of people who understand this code; the "we" brings a chuckle; it is a "poetic phrase" that she is indulging in. The light self-deprecation of the reference to the poem being an advertisement, with the quick admission that it is indeed so, is the machinery of archness in high gear; but unfortunately, that is *exactly* what the poem is.

For the poem "Combat Cultural" I refer the reader to Robert Duncan's remarks in his essay "Ideas on the Meaning of Form." Also, his general comments on the decline of Marianne Moore's work in the same essay.

James Dickey calls *Tell Me, Tell Me* Miss Moore's best book. In it we are presented with such poems as "Baseball and Writing," which continues the bathetic note struck in "Hometown Piece"; "In Lieu of the Lyre," which must be read to be believed; "Granite and Steel," a poem about the Brooklyn Bridge, which, curiously, neglects to quote from the finest poem on that bridge, Hart Crane's "To Brooklyn Bridge"; and "To Victor Hugo of My

Crow Pluto," which must stand as the classic attempt at a conscious doggerel that doesn't succeed in its own intent.

"W.S. Landor" is a curious poem in its praise of Landor as someone Miss Moore would like. He throws a man through the window and worries about the plants beneath. It is not Landor's act which I hit at here, nor Miss Moore's approval of this gruff, "no-nonsense" English virility, all roast beef and Yorkshire pudding and baying hounds. It is the failure shown here to distinguish this kind of anecdote as being the propaganda of masculinity. There was a guard at Auschwitz who left his chores of murdering to return to his university and take his examinations in philosophy. A brilliant student, soft-spoken, well-educated, immaculately dressed. Perhaps he loved flowers. The man thrown through the window is a literary abstraction, like the swan, the ant, etc. The language in a vacuum.

"Rescue with Yul Brynner" carries on the spirit of "Style." It is Miss Moore crying in the movies.

In *Hitherto Uncollected* no further aberrations are revealed.

So, in reading through this body of work, these poems of an entire lifetime, one sees the clearest graph of decline imaginable in the work of a "major" contemporary poet. What I have tried to show in these notes, however, is that this decline did not come about through a sudden failure of power on the poet's part; but that the later, really bad verse, was absolutely prefigured in the earliest poems. The poet failed as her language failed, and her language failed because she shut out the real.

> It is with certain women as with waves of the sea. Springing with all their youth, they leap over a rock too high for them to run back. The pool they form will lie there henceforth, stagnant, shut in, beautiful under lightning because of the salt crystals forming in it, slowly substituting for its life.
>
> René Char

The Park, 1968

21

Ross Feld's Plums

There is a dry intelligence that informs the often exotic figures of these quite extraordinary *Plum Poems* and that consistently prevents them from being gorgeous only. It is a great pleasure indeed to read a young lyric poet who insists on structuring his work so that it stringently removes itself from the intellectual fads that clutter so much contemporary verse. By this I mean to say that Mr. Feld writes fiction; i.e., the poem is its own reward.

One insists more strongly of late on art, not on a product that is the result of sophistication and social alertness, but on art: the clearly realized and exquisitely formed artifact that will move not a fraction of an inch to meet anyone. I find it here, again and again, in lines, fragments, whole poems— in the entire fabric and texture of the book, in fact.

Good artists do not appear with any great regularity, despite the propaganda to the contrary, which posits the bizarre image of whole troops of artists appearing every few years, like graduates from a college of aesthetics. I submit that Mr. Feld is an artist, and that his work will be ignored or attacked, his audience minuscule for many years, and his objectives, more often than not, totally misunderstood: he will become, in all probability, a "poet's poet." One often wonders what other kinds there are.

Plum Poems, 1972

22

Emerald on the Beach

Selected Poems. By John Wieners

The poems in this book are drawn from John Wieners' previous collections, starting with *The Hotel Wentley Poems* and ending with the remarkably beautiful *Nerves*, published in 1970. It is a reasonably good book for those readers who don't at all know Wieners, but it has the curious deficiency of making the work of these dozen years appear as a graph of subtle yet progressive stasis. The opposite is the fact, yet from this selection one would never know that *Ace of Pentacles* and *Nerves* are in every way more accomplished and mature than the *Wentley* collection. The problem lies in the selecting, of which more later.

Wieners has taken his world of drugs, despair, seamy and loveless sex, and myriad defeats and made from it a powerful and singular poetry, a part of which is constituted of lyrics as beautiful as any written by an American poet in this century. He draws on everything for his poetic vocabulary—slang, popular song, bar- and party-talk, fragments of other verse, etc. At the core of the poems is a fine-drawn and fixed hopelessness in which beauty, love, nature, and art itself are in no way expected to right wrongs or ameliorate anything. In an odd way, Wieners is a religious poet, not, certainly, as Herbert is, but with similarities to Baudelaire. None of your "free and loving" acceptance of the earth's good here: guilt is real, and God is neither inside one nor a pal.

The poem, for such writers as Wieners, is not a way of improving one's life or fortunes, but is a kind of supplication to God, an offering given, since there is nothing else to give. Taking Wieners this way, it is hard to conceive of a poet more out of the current swim. We live, it is no secret, in an age in which the contemporary poem is thought of, with increasing frequency, as a sort of slate on which any doodle may be scratched: the poem as placebo, as key to wisdom, as testament, confession, holy mystery, as tool to open any can of metaphysical soup. Or, the poem as intermediary between "life" and "art." In this thinking, the poem is rarely thought of as a finished product, a result, but as a conductor of ideas more important (of course) than the poor thing that conducts them. "Life is more important than art" is the banal motto on the banners of the true believers who exhaust you with their verbal electricity. These poems, replete with love of nature and mystical baloney, ooze and spread, odorous slabs of Liederkranz. Nowhere can they be grasped, fixed, made to hold still so that one may determine of them their failure or success. Of course, they are not *meant* to fail or succeed, "uptight" conceptions indeed, if I know my kitsch. Things melt into each other, words slop and slide together, those cute and "vivid" images that Lovers of Poesie delight in extracting from the general morass glimmer at you from the pages and pages of slogging lines in which nothing is real but the "integrity of one's statement," etc., etc. Mystical baloney, to be sure, and sliced thick. Or sex as truth. The poet is delighted, in his effete and precious way, with the wonders of everyday life: a charming vase, a daisy (a real daisy!), a fantastic orgasm, his woman's full breasts, and on and on, good, good! yum-yum! As if the world were put here to amuse the intelligent and aware.

Wieners, on the other hand, is that most disconcerting of sports. His poems succeed or fail, written as they are out of an artistic sensibility. If his poem has saved his life, he doesn't tell you so in line after line. Nor are the poems flashed around like tailor's shears, cutting dandy suits in which to clothe his sensitive nature. At the risk of boring you to tears, let me say that Wieners grasps the materials of his life and refines them into art, which latter is long famed for being aloof from the artist's intent. If the idea does not carry itself over into the construction, too bad. As they say, just another long foul. Strike two! The poem explains nothing but its words: your new wife, your garden in the rain, your gallant doom—none of it matters in the least if the ear be tin or the poem a classroom blackboard. Some hick whose name I have forgotten recently wrote that "metaphor is real." That's the kind of magic you buy at the A&P. Five will get you ten that this same lout of the muses thinks that *Finnegans Wake* is "artificial." This is all funnier than W.C. Fields. The next step in this endless seminar is that "everything" is art, and that "everyone" is an artist. Meantime, Wieners, for one, gets on with his forms. His words glint against each other.

All the *Wentley* poems are in this book, wondrously charged early work that came, in the late fifties, sharply to the attention. At the time they seemed good, merely good, dazzled as we all were by that budding excitement of discovering that not all poems had to be written in the manner of Roethke or Auden. Now we can see that they have more than held their own against writings contemporaneous with them. But more importantly, Wieners has refined the language of these early poems into something gem-like, trusting it, all the way, to carry and structure his emotion. When he falters or seizes upon some aberrant manipulation of his form, he fails utterly:

> If thou in me the full flush of love see
> Know it comes from the rose that magnifies
> To breathe in some corner of that sure sky,
> A coarser blossom than eternity
> Likewise perishing and lost from earth
> To bloom anew in realms beyond pain
> Where fleshly vision cruel time disdain.

In these lines from "Mermaid's Song," the stilted and clumsy rhyme forces the poet into inverted sentences, tortured syntax and a heavy, uncharacter-istic use of abstract nouns to carry his meaning, a meaning which is never clearly etched. In "Ally," a poem that is almost there, we find enormous ambiguities, none of which I take to be consciously made, but which are, on the contrary, the fruits of hurried and inexact syntax:

> My father's black ashtray
> hollowed out of 1930 foes
> of woe and death
>
>   • • •
>
>   it stands here still
> to fill the sad stuffed cigarettes
> of Philip Morris, Ltd.

Is the word "foes" meant to stand for "cigarettes"? I think so, yet how is the ashtray hollowed out of the cigarettes? And at the end of the poem, is it the ashtray that fills the cigarettes? How can that be? I don't want to be precious and insist that poems must have the logic of the philosopher or scientist, since that is exactly the logic that art has no use for. But here I speak of the bones of the poem, the syntax itself. Wieners is not a surrealist, he is not distorting language for a particular aesthetic end. This poem, quite simply, fails. When the syntax is questioned, it has no reply.

But these and other failures are, as I have said, there to be seen. Each poem holds itself, a closed system. One may say that Wieners' poems yearn toward perfection; they are not shards of a continuing process, but are lyrics. I mean, they are *unashamed* lyrics, ingeniously made scarecrows in the fields of corn. The reader can pick out specific flaws in every Wieners failure; they are functions of language. When he is working well, he can give us "With Meaning," a poem that builds with the careful intensity of a sonata, and ends with a snap like a door being locked.

Rise, shining martyrs
over the multitudes
for the season of migration
between earth and heaven

Rise shining martyrs
cut down in fire
and darkness,
speeding past light
straight through imagination's park.

and this poem closes—

Yes rise shining martyrs

out of your graves, tell us
what to do, read your poems
under springtime moonlight.
Rise and salvage our century.

There are no tricks in "With Meaning," none at all. The poem, like all of Wieners' poems, unravels before the eye, and as it moves to the poet's imagination, his sense of time, his manipulation of images, so it completes itself as an entity. One has the sense, almost always, of the poet feeling his way through his poem: as his intuition is right, so will his poem be right. When his intuition fails, his poem fails with it.

As I said at the beginning of this review, the one problem with this book, and it is major in that one expects a "selected poems" to contain the poet's best work, is in the selections themselves. I have no idea who was responsible for this selection; but if it was the editor, then he has no idea of Wieners' strengths. If it was the poet himself, the editor was remiss in not urging him to consider inclusion of those poems from *Ace of Pentacles* and *Nerves* that are necessary to an understanding of the poet's great gifts and accomplishment. I would say that a selection of Wieners' work, to be at all representative of post-*Wentley* writings, would have to include at least "My Mother," "Dream," "Two Years Later," "Looking For Women," and "Forthcoming."

Finally, to support my opinion that Wieners, at the top of his form, is among the finest American poets of this century, this daring and perfect poem from *Ace of Pentacles*.

Long Nook

There she took her lover to sea
and laid herself in the sand.
Go up and undress in the dark.

He is fast, was down the dune
with silk around his waist.
Her scarf was small.

She opened her clothes to the moon.
Her underarms were shaved.
The wind was a wall between them.

Waves break over the tide,
hands tied to her side with silk,
their mind was lost in the night.

The green light at Provincetown
became an emerald on the beach,
and like stars fell on Alabama.

There is not a line in this miraculous poem not charged with risk. Yet the poem sings as if it were fated to be so constructed. It has the nobility of the inevitable that only the best art can claim.

Parnassus, 1973

23

George Oppen: Smallness of Cause

In a way, poets possess within themselves infinitely more answers than ordinary life has questions to put to them; and this provides them with that perpetually latent, superabundant, and, as it were, irritable richness which at the slightest provocation brings forth treasures and even worlds.

This greatness of effect combined with this smallness of cause is quite simply what marks the essential poetic temperament.

Paul Valéry

It is the child who is the branch
We fall from, where would be bramble,
Brush, bramble in the young Winter
With its blowing snow she must have thought
Was ours to give to her.

Valéry's "smallness of cause" is discoverable in the title of the poem from which the above is taken: "From a Photograph." This calm and quiet stanza proffers a condensed conceit that holds the child, in the standard figure of the first line, as the offshoot of the parents, but suddenly, in the first three words of the second line, turns the child into the stable element from which the *parents* separate.

The curious metaphor is then "proved" in the final two lines, rife, as they are, with the unspoken regret of the parents in the face of a world over which they have no control despite the child's trust. The child, in her innocence, is "the branch" they fall from in helplessness.

The poet implies: We see the past in the crystal of the photograph. *Now* we know! Too late. The parents can exercise their wisdom only in the context of the photograph; they can enlighten the child as to their helplessness—*then*, in the lost and irreparable past. But were they, by some miracle, able to return to that past, they would again be as impotent as they were when the world of the photograph *was* the present.

"She must have thought/Was ours to give to her." She must have indeed. We knew better and can tell her—now—that we knew better. But now it no longer matters since she knows better, too.

It is an exquisite, and, more to the point, almost "depthless" metaphor, mysterious and yet so clear that this attempt at explication is doomed to murkiness, even though I have avoided complicating matters by touching on the words "brush" and "bramble" as possible signs for a childless past, signs that make the metaphor even more complex.

This fragment of a small poem "brings forth treasures and even worlds" and is justly representative of Mr. Oppen's finest work.

Paideuma, 1981

24

A Glance at West's West

> At this time Tod knew very little about them except that they had come to California to die.
>
> *The Day of the Locust*

Thus West on the zombie *émigrés* from the American heartland who had gone to Southern California, Los Angeles, Hollywood, to soak up the Golden Life: the sunshine, the oranges, the ambience of stardom! And, as he so precisely noted, found, after a very short time, that they had saved and dreamed for nothing. Cheated.

He writes that the violence in them was great enough to destroy civilization. He was speaking of the late thirties: that violence was siphoned out of them, temporarily, in the Second World War. The undirected fury became xenophobia and the Depression ended in mountains of overtime pay.

So these stuporous people, once the insulted and injured, now snug in postwar homes built on Boeing and Republic and Kaiser money, turned their hatred toward the left, where it was meant to function most comfortably anyway.

Remember when West was thought of as a satirist and *The Day of the Locust* as a "Hollywood novel"? The book notes the beginning of a process: the collapse of Western culture in its most glittering outpost and the emergence of the state itself as a model of commodity fetishism. Ronald Reagan smiles from out the pages of West's novel; West invented him as Kafka invented information gathering as a profession. Mr. Reagan is an ideal governor, the absolute embodiment of a shoddy ideal. There is no sincere stupidity that doesn't create, eventually, its own rationale, conduct, operating procedures, its own critical formulae whereby it may be, in all seriousness, discussed: witness the advertising business. Witness the best-seller list. Areas of idiocy within which various degrees of the spurious are compared.

If California is a madhouse, and it seems to be, and if West presupposed it in that 1939 madhouse of his Hollywood, which he did, then California has its man in Ronald Reagan and may speak of him as somebody to be taken seriously: he *is* the Governor. That he may be whatever certain people might want him to be has, now, no place in the discussion of his "worth." Political analysts discuss the possibilities of his administration as they would those of a Bob Hope administration. If the stupid persists, it develops its philosophers, who do not question the philosophy but hash over its fine points. In the body politic, stupidity triumphant functions as a graph of societal corruption and breakdown. I was at a party the other night, and a Washington businessman told my wife that Dean Rusk is, in private life, a gentle, sensitive man. He did not see how weird that is.

So this Westian California, saved from *lumpen* destruction by the "intervention" of the Nazis and Japanese—somebody other than themselves to despise—has, indeed, treasures, its man, an actor: somebody who is not what he seems to be when he is at his most sincere.

These Westian dispossessed sent their sons to war and made their claim to prosperity with the suddenly available war-economy cash. Postwar California grew fatter, its anger internalized. The sons of the now-happy "locusts" joined the police force, in a perfection of sour irony.

We've had nobody quite like West. Other "Hollywood novels" address the problem of the pure heart caught in the glamour of the film world. It is all romance—the hero sullied by corruption or defeat. But West saw what made the madhouse tick, and, more pointedly, what made it the barometer of a decaying nation. It was "the people" themselves: at first furious toward some curious nothing that had cheated them of their dream; then, with a small fragment of the dream, furious toward those who held it in contempt. The second generation of West's mob speaks of Reds, and pornography, and beatniks, and peaceniks. The hatred has a target and it is not the Wehrmacht. The hatred also has a rationale: protecting that Mexican patio in Anaheim from the new dispossessed. The minds are lulled by Frank Sinatra, and an occasional demon like Mario Savio reinforces their righteousness.

In the middle of the novel, we read: "Maybe they were only the pick of America's madmen and not at all typical of the rest of the land." We now know that they weren't "the pick," but the gauge, the barometer, the avant-garde. They have elected their governor and deserve him; and if all goes as indicated and according to pattern, Mr. Reagan, or someone very like him, will be our president, and *we* deserve him.

You will understand that none of this has anything to do with what used to be called politics. There are no politics anymore. There are only sociological "sets," impacted, and controlled by ownership of data, so that all "political differences" here are but flimsy choreographies that display carefully controlled and selectively revealed half-truths, or perfect lies. It is, it seems to me, the final victory of a debased democracy to propose candidates who were conceived in celluloid and who speak with the voice of the sound track.

Guerrilla, 1967

25

John Hawkes' Oranges

The Blood Oranges

I see *The Blood Oranges* as one of the best novels published in this country in a decade. It is a virtuoso performance that never flags, and one has to go all the way back to *The Good Soldier* to find anything comparable to it. Written, as is Ford's novel, through the screen of the first person, it tells a story, through the narrator's, Cyril's, eyes, of sexual license, sweet carnal abandon, and adultery raised to the level of the sublime. Because Cyril has been one of the four people involved in this idyllic sexual adventurism— along with his wife, Fiona, and another married couple, Hugh and Catherine—his telling of the tale, his opinions of the other people involved, his musings, philosophizings, and justifications, must all be taken warily; just as Ford's John Dowell does not tell us the truth except through the very quality of the language he uses to relate the story of the good soldier, so Cyril allows us to see not only *his* truth, but *the* truth.

Some of the reviews I have seen of this novel have been astonishing in that they have mistaken Cyril's voice for Hawkes'. Is it possible that after all these years there are still people who think that the voice of the narrator is the author's voice? It seems incredible that there are such people, and that they write these opinions, surely, one gathers, in all seriousness. One of these worthies was incensed with Hawkes because Cyril cannot see how "awful" he is. The fact that he cannot see this is one of the points of the novel.

The story of *The Blood Oranges* is simple, the plot stark. It is the quality of Cyril's voice that carries the book. He is bemused, cool, arrogant, flowery, self-satisfied, superior; he is also, when it suits the tale, falsely humble and penitent. Throughout the free and adulterous married life he has lived with Fiona, Cyril has constructed the erotic tableaux in which they have been involved. He has moved the pieces, and involved himself and his wife in unending, leisured, and totally free sexuality. In Hugh, he meets a man who will not accept his terms, and so Hugh is given us (by Cyril) as a "poor soul," an unfortunately sick figure. He is, in the parlance of the day, "up tight."

Hugh is filled with guilt and remorse over his adulterous conduct with Fiona, and over his wife's equally adulterous conduct with Cyril. Yet Hawkes is not so simple as to make Hugh, despite Cyril's opinions of him, a hero. Hugh is a photographer who has spent his life taking pictures of naked girls, whom he bribes and bullies; he is torn with lusts which his morality will not let him satisfy. He cannot stomach Cyril but is wild for Fiona.

This ménage ends in tragedy and death—neither of which concerns Cyril, except insofar as it marks the end of an idyllic season that has been spoiled by Hugh's stupidity . . . or so Cyril says. It is the tale, as against the way that Cyril tells it, his comments on certain occurrences as against the fact of them, his opinions of things that the reader can see plainly for himself, that give us the truth about this brief affair. It does not matter whether Cyril is lying cynically about his feelings, or whether he has constructed this *persona* to guard himself against despair and horror, just as it does not matter with John Dowell. Hawkes' genius gets the whole story told, and it is a story that is complex, ambiguous, and replete with blind alleys. As is Dowell's in *The Good Soldier*, Cyril's voice is so reasonable, so civilized, so candid that one almost forgets that he has been the prime factor in the tragedy the novel encloses. It is a magnificent performance by one of our few major novelists.

A last word. As if to alert the reader to what he is up to in his novel, Hawkes uses as an epigraph a quote from *The Good Soldier*: "Is there then any terrestrial paradise where, amidst the whispering of the olive-leaves, people can be with whom they like and have what they like and take their ease in shadows and in coolness?" Ford's answer to that question was "no." Hawkes, on the other hand, says "yes, there is" but adds that it is only for a little time and that such ease must be paid for in misery and blood.

Modern Occasions, 1972

26

Lost Lives

JR. By William Gaddis

The value placed upon money (not what it pro-
cures for you, but *it*) is pathologic. It is the great
American malady. . . . The possession of learning,
of genius in the arts or sciences—*nothing* seems to
weigh in the U.S. in comparison with money. . . .
If one wrote something for public consumption on
these lines people would sneer, genuinely bored.
"Oh yes. The 'almighty dollar' you mean!"—Of
course it *is* what I should mean. But it is one of
those things which, if only they can survive *identification* and *denunciation*, can go on forever and
brazenly endure.

Wyndham Lewis, Letters

For now long after Wilde had withdrawn to join
the compost smoldering in Europe with Pater's rec-
ipe for success in life, the tale how for art's sake
he'd faced Leadville's bullies to a standoff continued to amuse here where invention was eliminat-
ing the very possibility of failure as a condition for
success precisely in the arts where one's best is
never good enough and who, now the song would
play on without losing a note, could resist the
temptation to shoot the pianist?

from Jack Gibbs' uncompleted manuscript, in JR

William Gaddis' new novel is about money—its power, its pervasiveness,
its curious progression toward the unreal as its quantity increases; it is also

and inseparably about the waste of talent, substance, love, and ultimately lives, and the base misuse and destruction of art and intelligence. The literally hundreds of materials used by Mr. Gaddis to deploy and elaborate his themes take their shape as accreted layers of data and innumerable threads, twisted and tangled. It is a magnificent work that is at once savagely comic and drenched in bitter pathos. While it is not tragic, it surely exists at the edge of despair. By a painstaking marshaling of detail, the major characters are given us finally as exhausted, beaten, and desolate.

It serves no purpose here, in a brief review, to paraphrase the densely crafted plot of *JR*. Suffice it to say that everybody and everything in the novel is interconnected in what might justly be called a perfect if insane logic of possibility. *JR* does not work on the level of a meager naturalism but supposes a world that exists of and for itself and in which all the characters are rigidly predestined to play out their roles. It is a claustrophobic world that works, within itself, like a syllogism. The author insists on a closed system: that this system plunges, with maniacal precision, toward denouement *within* that greater system that we may label the "real world" makes it no less a creation of supreme effectiveness and fictional truth.

JR, a sixth-grade pupil at a gadget-ridden, computerized, and flagrantly intellectually bankrupt public school on Long Island, sits at the center of the novel, a boy who is the epitome of greed, the quintessential product of twentieth-century culture run to seed, plastic, and decay; at the same time, he is vulnerable, alone, touching—a castoff of his society and of his broken family within it. From this center, he sets in motion a chain reaction of financial wheeling-dealing that touches the seats of power where the decisions that affect the structure of the world—its politics, culture, social priorities—are formulated. He is, in his precocious strivings toward acquisition for its own sake—for the sake of attaining whatever, God help him, he may take to be the good life—a perfectly formed miniature of the macrocosm that he imitates. This latter world is given us most clearly in the financial workings of the Diamond Cable Corporation, an industrial giant that controls a good share of the world and many of its leaders, all of whom are bought and sold like shares of stock.

Caught in this vortex are Jack Gibbs, a despairing, cynical, and tortured drunk who cannot finish the book (on the "social history of mechanization and the arts, the destructive element") he has been working on for years— or, more precisely, avoiding working on—and Edward Bast, a young and awkward composer who is a marvel of naïveté, who feels that his art is all that he is here for, and who works like a demented robot. These three are the major figures in the book; dependent from and peripheral to them are perhaps two dozen more, all of whom are locked into the madness that JR's schemes awaken and fuel.

Mr. Gaddis has entwined these characters' lives in such subtle and elaborately complex ways that "answers" or suggestions of possible answers as to their motivations and relationships are not so much given as they are strewn across the novel's pages. The curious and devastatingly poignant links between Bast and Gibbs are spotted throughout the book in an almost casual way; JR may be seen, finally, as a kind of new-model Gibbs or Bast; Gibbs is a gigantically doomed figure—surely the protagonist of the book, lost from the start—and Bast is his counterpoint. The complexities are endless and ironic and shattering. Minor characters function in odd, neurotic, yet precise ways, elements of data in this enormous investigation of avarice and waste and their casualties.

Painters are cheated of their money, used and exploited as producers of saleable goods; writers are blocked, thwarted, duped, or twisted into shiny and agreeable hacks; lovers are sacrificed to fates that function as cosmic jokes; a school is perverted, drained, and finally sold; groves of ancient trees are paved over in a "deal" and in another a house is moved; marriages are smashed and soldiers sent to their slaughter carrying toy guns; and all of this (and dozens of more instances of perversion and corruption) is not only inevitable, it is logical, legal, and normal. The cause of this socially acceptable devastation is the quest for profits. On its simplest and most obvious level, *JR* is a compendium of those things that have been done, over the past half-century, to the people of the world by their governments and those whom governments truly serve. It is also, as I hope I have suggested, an investigation of the artist in a society that not only has no need for him but that despises him, and a mordantly limned picture of the "common man"— armed with his manipulated opinions and his jest of a "voice" in public affairs.

I should of course say something about the compositional techniques of the novel. It is completely written, but for brief transitions, in dialogue. Mr. Gaddis' ear is the perfect one of all first-rate novelists, by which I mean his speech as here recorded is beautifully crafted so as to appear to be real speech. His characters speak in cadences as precisely stylized as those of, say, Hemingway or Henry Green. It is not the product of the tape recorder that we are given, but the carefully selected and shaped materials that reveal each character as definitely as physical description. The patterns and tics of each character's speech are so brilliantly molded, so subtly and yet totally different one from the other, that the reader, after his first introduction to a character, has no difficulty in identifying that character in subsequent passages. It is a remarkable achievement and, I think, a stroke of genius on Gaddis' part to have structured his novel this way. Not only do we stay in absolute touch with what is being said by everybody, but we begin to hear not *only* what is said, but what is *meant*. The "time" of the novel is of course rigorously restricted to the actual time it takes the characters to say what they have to say. Perhaps most importantly, this method of composition allows us to see the surfaces of things—what is really there, what people really appear to be to each other and to eavesdroppers (like the reader). This jettisoning of tawdry and banal "psychological" probing and the "hidden motivations" of characters allows Mr. Gaddis a clean surface, blessedly free of bunkum masquerading as the profound. What we know is what we hear.

JR strikes me as one of the very few distinguished and *written* American novels published in the last decade; indeed, it makes most other novels of this period seem watery or pretentious or both. Its comedy is that of all excellent comic artists—it conceals the ultimately absurd hopes and pretensions of life. It is a brilliant work—a great novel.

Partisan Review, 1976

27

Larry Woiwode:
Beyond the
Bedroom Wall

Beyond the Bedroom Wall displays the talent of its author. In an odd way, its problems are rooted in this fact. Through some six hundred pages that deal episodically with the Neumiller family over three generations, the reader is presented with an almost dogged display of fine writing. It is the kind of writing that can be found in almost every issue of those large monthly magazines that still pretend an interest in "serious" fiction, a professional genre writing, the constant delight of editors and reviewers since it is at once neither demanding nor trashy. There's nothing wrong with this—it is very high-class entertainment, as skillfully made as any successful film of the last ten years. It tells the reader what he already knows, a knowledge posited by the entire history of modern fiction; the stimuli, as it were, are carefully placed to elicit the proper responses, just as Woody Allen's work is funny because Perelman invented it.

I am not suggesting that this novel is a failure; it is far from that. And I do not derogate Mr. Woiwode because he is not involved in what is variously called "superfiction," "metafiction," "surfiction," etc., which are academic words tagged on to sundry minor experiments. Nor has Mr. Woiwode made a novel that creaks along in the dear old, and regularly lamented (since it only exists as a tour de force) "traditional" mode. He has written, as I've said, episodically, eschewing psychological motivation, tension, character development, climax, denouement, and so forth. His credentials, as they say, are impeccable. But there is something wrong with the book. It is too shiny and complacent, it is too safe, and it is conscious of pleasing.

The novel has its excellent points, surely. Certainly the first-rate sense of place—in this case the Midwest—is one. Mr. Woiwode has an acute feel for locale and for the combination of camaraderie and loneliness that small towns throw up like gas stations. He's very good with children—the Neumiller offspring are excellently given, each sketched in a new pose from chapter to chapter as they grow up, so that we see them as discrete entities, not boring instances of development. And his children are neither cute nor monstrous. Tim, as the son who is "left out," might in fact stand as a perfect paradigm of how fictionally to handle a strange child without making him into a wind-up toy like the dopey little girl in *The Bad Seed*, for example. A minor point, but children draw many a dishonest writer on to his deserved destruction. It's much easier to fake adults.

Woiwode often shifts from the third person into the first and this should work to change the pace and mood of the work. Sadly, though, every time a character thinks in the first person he becomes startlingly articulate, literary, and often pretty flowery. These instances draw Woiwode into his most egregious writing flaw, i.e., the urge toward profundity. For some reason, he finds it almost impossible to handle scenes that deal with profundity of emotion or the "mystery of life" without sliding into a thick, clotted rhetoric that serves only to muddy and cheapen the very emotions he wants to reveal. I'm tempted to say that Mr. Woiwode thinks of this writing as poetic, whereas it is but another assault upon that embattled art. When he describes what people *do* in the grip of deep feeling, he is fine, as witness the first chapter, "Burial." But when he wants to tell the reader what people *feel*, his prose becomes, for all practical purposes, inarticulate. It's almost as if these emotional sets generate "thoughts that lie too deep for tears," and the language that attempts to carry them collapses into gunk. This is the opposite of the way poetic language functions, in which the writing becomes clearer as the emotion is focused more sharply.

The people who inhabit the novel are well drawn, although some of them are too well drawn, that is, they are characters with a capital "C." There is a drunken hired man out of central casting, Greenwich Village denizens carting around language and paraphernalia that even a plumber like Tom Wolfe could recognize as spelling "stoned hippie," a third-rate Lower East Side poet who comes across like John Carradine, and who is quite predictably—although I was rooting for Woiwode—bittersweetly shattered. These are all instances of lapses of attention, failures of energy.

The weakest writing in the book occurs after the children are grown and gone from home. It occurs to me that Mr. Woiwode may be lost when he's out of his territory. Certainly, his New York scenes are hopeless, surrendering his absolute sense of place for stock pieces that could be written into scenes for Broadway plays—"Strange and Frenetic New York." Some countermen in a Ukrainian restaurant on Avenue A are turned into noble figures, strong men who can cope with life, etc. It is sentimentalizing that nothing can rescue. Woiwode is too good a writer to fall into these traps, but he consistently handles Charles, the son who goes to New York, in this way while he is in New York. He changes from a thoroughly interesting child into a foil against which trite generalizations can be played.

In a very real way, *Beyond the Bedroom Wall* has the same kind of fictional rationale as do *Look Homeward, Angel* and *Of Time and the River*. It's a fond and penetrating look at a lost life, a way of laying ghosts. And like Wolfe, Woiwode cannot resist the temptation to make his people into giants— taciturn, brave, deep, wise, beautiful, effective, strong. Their very plainness is tortured into heroism. To handle plain people plainly, and at the same time to make them reveal the truth about themselves and their community, is quite possibly the hardest thing that a writer can do. There they stand: dull, boring, ordinary—yet unique and absolute. How to make them interesting? But is that even the question? I don't think so. The question may be: How does one carry the plainness into fiction so that the character does not become a Character, does not become a falsification? Flaubert did it, and so, in our own literature, did Williams, two writers uncanny in their ability to find the glint of truth in the most banal situations. We see, through their ordinary characters, an entire world without distortion of either world or characters. Woiwode's characters, insofar as they are gigantic, are unreliable. They are, so to speak, historical without being history.

Despite these faults, it is a good book, one among a paltry few each year. For this reason alone, it is notable. As I have said, its author is talented; but I feel, ungenerously, that Woiwode has not demanded enough of his talents in this novel. Nowhere does he chop and fight against his material. There is no section, no chapter, no paragraph that strikes as being written uphill, written against what came most readily to hand. The novel takes the path of least resistance throughout, and one gets the sense that the author, in composing the book, discovered nothing that he did not already know. The whole is a kind of explication of given materials and ideas, a vast set piece. The work lives in that area in which the author is comfortable. The novel lacks what can be called a poetic impulse—though it is filled with "poetry." It is talented. It is professional. It is, God knows, "well written." But it is not enough.

Partisan Review, 1976

28

Never on Sunday

A Month of Sundays. By John Updike

The surface of Mr. Updike's writing twitches and quivers incessantly, never more so than in this new novel about a faintly hedonist minister "with doubts." By some process of intellection that is foreign to me, this prose tic has been critically taken to be a sublime style; the disparaging word, as it were, is rare to come by apropos Mr. Updike's work. When it is discovered, it manifests itself as no more than a slight reservation. I don't know why this should be so. Mr. Updike has all the grievous faults of an Oscar Wilde updated to include contemporary paraphernalia, speech, etc.; but none of these things can disguise the purple blush that suffuses the work. It is, if I may use such a word, unachieved; i.e., its fancy images are not in touch with the world but emblazon it. The writing is what is in some quarters known as "vivid."

"We played in each other like children in puddles," Mr. Updike writes. Why not "mud" instead of puddles? Or "dogs" instead of children? Or anything at all for that matter? When the aim is "vivid" writing, it seems that anything goes as long as the surface dances.

The work buckles and falls apart time after time under the weight of this concatenation of images, often linked together by comparisons that work to conceal the reality they are supposedly revealing: ". . . newsletters and quarterlies that pour through a minister's letter slot like urine from a cow's vulva."

Mr. Updike has many more tricks in his book, one of them the disfiguring and falsifying one of anthropomorphizing anything that threatens to escape the net of his ego: "The moon peered crookedly over his shoulder, curious enough to tilt its head" and "The blue night barked as I opened the door."

It might however be argued, fairly enough, that this is not Mr. Updike's voice, since the novel purports to be a diary/journal kept by the Reverend Thomas Marshfield, the narrator. In fact, the flap copy, taking note of this, bubbles that the minister's confessions are rendered in a "wonderfully over-wrought style." This might legitimize the flaws of the novel except for the fact that Marshfield's style as given in *A Month of Sundays* is the author's in other books. The only one I have to hand is *Pigeon Feathers*, but haphazard rummaging through it turns up—in the third person—the same "wonder-fully overwrought style": "The walls of the college buildings, crusty and impregnable, swept past like an armada of great gray sails." Which, in its way, is almost as shiny and meaningless as this fragment of Wilde's: "It seemed to me that all my life had been narrowed to one perfect point of rose-coloured joy. She trembled all over, and shook like a white narcissus." Both specimens work to remove us from the matter under observation; the com-parisons muddy the things compared; the adjectives function so as to give us the appearance of specificity, lest we see the rabbit being put into the hat. These are triumphs of that sensibility that cannot leave off worrying the world into its own design. I cannot accept the Reverend Marshfield's style as being his own—Mr. Updike's other works of fiction display the same style with endemic consistency.

There are a couple of things to say about this novel. While it is not "about" sex, sex is the engine that drives it. However, it is neither pornographic nor filled with the grim and humorless details of the post-Sadean technologist. It does not stand in breathless awe of sex-as-mystery as invented and pat-ented by Lawrence. It is—what can I say?—amused. It is witty and bored and knowing. There is nothing of the comic in the novel—Mr. Updike cannot make anyone laugh. The comic writer accepts reality as intelligible in itself, not as a poor drab thing that awaits his gilding. Comic things are inherently comic; and we laugh when the comic intelligence reveals their essence, when it recognizes them. Wittiness does not recognize, it explains. It gives us an "insight" into its subject, whereas it seems to me that the comic grasps the entire outside of its subject. I go on about this because I don't understand why a writer would choose to use this kind of wryly amused and sophisticated cleverness to deal with a subject that does not respond to it—that, in fact, resists it tenaciously except on the level of bedroom farce—which is rarely farcical and never sexual. I suspect that this mode allows Mr. Updike's romantic sensibility full play. With it, he can most certainly eat his world. But he can't have it too.

Then we have the characters. Mr. Updike is of that school that holds that characters are the sum of their parts; i.e., add layer upon layer of description touching upon modes of dress, manners, speech, habitations, possessions, mores, etc., and presto! we know who the character is and how he will act in a given circumstance; we know, that is, his reality. Conversely, if we know what he says and thinks, we know what he will wear, his tastes, and so on. The author partakes, in other words, of the tried and true novelistic signals in ordering his characters' activities and lives. An odd sophistry of causality inheres in such constructions. Jane, Marshfield's wife, is prim, proper, intelligent, educated, athletic. It routinely follows that she is sexually unsatisfying to Marshfield; she is civilized when she is confronted by his lover, and so on. His lover is slightly shabby, a trifle vulgar, rather embarrassingly emotional, and divorced. She, of course, lives in a raw, new housing development; she is crass when she meets Jane, etc. The reader almost expects Mr. Updike to make her chew gum and subscribe to the *Reader's Digest.* Marshfield's assistant is young, soupy-minded, liberal, "against the war." His attitude toward, for instance, young people with drug problems? You guessed it. And on and on. The signals flash, the attitudes stiffen, the characters "walk off the pages." This is the kind of characterization one expects from Neil Simon, an effortless sliding into the path of least resistance. It has little to do with the making of serious fiction.

Yet all these things that I touch upon are reckoned by Mr. Updike's admirers—and they are many—as strengths, not weaknesses, as wonders of truth, style, audacity, vision, even as indications of greatness. But each page of this book throws up a wall behind which it is well-nigh impossible to discover the manifold realities of the world that the author chooses to deal with. We are given this world as seen by Mr. Updike, as interpreted by him. We are given wit and talent and we are given invention. But we are not given literature.

Oddly (and sadly) enough, this kind of fiction is often thought to be poetic, though it has nothing to do with poetry unless one conceives of the poem as a bauble. On the other hand, Hugh Kenner has termed this sort of writing "a surface scummed by iridescent prose." That strikes me as both just and exact.

Partisan Review, 1976

29

Blue Gass

In one of his poems, William Bronk writes:

> One thinks how
> in certain pictures, envied landscapes are seen
> (through a window maybe) far behind the serene
> sitter's face, the serene pose, as though
> in some impossible mirror, face to back,
> human serenity gazed at a green world
> which gazed at this face.

—affording me a rubric for William Gass' new book. Gass' world is, of course, blue, not green, and one cannot say that he gazes at it serenely. But he sees this blue in the manner in which Bronk's poem sees: there exist, as they say, layers. Gass writes: "blue the color, 'blue' the word, and Blue the Platonic Idea." *On Being Blue* is a luminous work, a tour de force on blue, that word (and color) reverberant with what is called experience. One might call it a symbolist work if one is careful to insist upon a symbolism that made a poetry devoid of symbols. Or, more accurately, a symbolism whose words symbolize words. And so here blue equals blue by identity.

There are the words and Gass loves them. Is it redundant to note that a writer loves words? Not in our time, when celebrated authors employ the language like so many battered suitcases in which to haul putrefacting ideas: to the bank, one could say, were the laurel made of sour grapes not the guerdon for speaking plainly. The superscription of Mr. Gass' title is "A Philosophical Inquiry," yet I see in this somber phrase the glimmer of a smile. Each time the book moves into or toward the philosophical, it beats back into its words—it exists precisely *there*. William Carlos Williams, in a rule-of-thumb aesthetic that governs a great structure of sophistication and elegance, says: "No ideas but in things," and, perversely, proves his theorem by concentrating on words existent in a field of energy they themselves create. Did he not also say, "What does it matter what the line 'says'?" Gass knows precisely what he means.

That fiction of Gass' that I have read seems to fight its materials, its very location, as this book does not—yet *On Being Blue* is as much a work of fiction as is *Omensetter's Luck*. He is happy here, whereas in his fiction his words, functioning in the context of a peopled narrative, take on a curious opacity. The people in *On Being Blue* exist in flashes and glints, blue glints, as a woman preparing salad at a sink, the naked girl in a sad photograph seen in the writer's adolescence. Gass is absolutely aware of the problems posed by the composition of fiction: to tell the truth in terms of the language and not in terms of the meanderings, psychological or otherwise, of characters. He says: "We want to know. At once. Everything. And if it's going to be boring, we want the truth replaced by lies. Most novelists are bought. They will oblige." The indictment is almost gentle. Almost. Gass will not oblige, and his fiction is a struggle to allow his language release from "what happens." The difficulty has always existed for writers and has not become easier of solution because mimesis is no longer our home. Theories do not haul the freight. *On Being Blue*, free from the demands of fiction, is fiction.

The book floats in an ambience of sexuality, "blueness," yet it is not about sex. It does not even deal with sex except in terms of how language nails it (or does not) to the page. Gass points out how, in the description of the sexual act, the writer's language often betrays him. "Lawrence is the saddest example," he writes; perhaps, too, implying that Lawrence's other descriptions are successful in direct relation to their distance from that which they describe; i.e., they become more luminous as they are more artificial. And, of course, we remember Lawrence, intent on the truth, recording, almost grimly, and totally unaware that as his language became more the luggage into which he crammed those amorous groans the further he got from the clarity of the actual. He forgot that the imagination is not a gadget for turning out replicas. Everything happens on the page. A man can no more will himself into art, despite his good intentions, than he can throw a curve ball. "The poetry," said Yeats, "is not the pity."

In his book Gass waits on his words. He shows himself a virtuoso of the language given him. To my mind, he is occasionally blurry, by which I mean he reads between the lines, as in a gloss on a scene from *The Portrait of a Lady*, or in "you often have to tug the reader's sleeve before he'll hear a bladder making Joyce's *Chamber Music*," a remark based on a shaky legend that the great artificer did little to discourage. (He may have invented it himself.) I object also to "the words which in our language are the worst off are the ones which the worst off use," a clever phrase, but one which seems to confuse the speech of the formally miseducated (or uneducated) with that of those whose language issues from an oral and illiterate *paideuma*.

But this is to rake up a few flaws in an admirable work, one which treats a difficult subject: how language is at once a label and a specific, autonomous thing, and how the writer must engage this medium, all that he has. Poetry is not made of ideas, but of words, Mallarmé told a disciple.

On Being Blue celebrates both language and that which it represents and carefully draws our attention to that difficult middle ground on which the writer finds himself in lifelong struggle to join the two without sullying or smearing the clarities of either.

Bookletter, 1976

30

García Márquez's Monster

The Autumn of the Patriarch. By Gabriel García Márquez

The Autumn of the Patriarch is a densely written novel about the life of a gargoyle dictator of what used to be called a banana republic in the Caribbean. He is the perfect beast; and although Gabriel García Márquez has presented him to us as a prototypical fascist, his sadism, megalomania, paranoia, and slushy sentimentality mark him as a monstrous composite of the twentieth-century totalitarian leader. He is legendary, omnipotent, and "immortal," in that his people believe that he has died and been resurrected at least once during his life of not less than 107 and not more than 232 years. The novel opens with his real death and proceeds, in nonchronological fashion, to survey the details of his rule.

It is a good book, an accurate albeit slightly surrealistic—one might say eccentric—portrayal of the grotesque. I say "slightly," because those of us who have lived through the past four decades of this century have come to know that the most bizarre and subhuman acts of world leaders are viewed as a kind of norm: they are accepted as achieved probabilities. We have been, in Whittaker Chambers' phrase, "hit by the freight train of history." García Márquez's nameless brute is certainly no sicker than the Stalin who said, upon hearing a huge audience spontaneously applaud Anna Akhmatova as she entered an auditorium, "Who is behind this demonstration?" It is important to note, however, that García Márquez's dictator is, in essence, a collage of the Latin American. There is in him little or none of the demonic (Hitler), the righteously persecuted (Stalin), or the icily ascetic (Franco). What comes to mind as we read are memories of such despots as Trujillo, Batista, Perón, and Papa Doc. The patriarch's urge toward cruelty and slaughter is spectacularly exotic, and he never ceases to think of himself as "one of the boys" who has been somehow seduced by fate into a chafing bureaucratic role: he murders, not by means of efficiency, but in defense of his own personal power. He, in his own flesh, is the nation. He is also the nation's persona, or nationalism itself.

One of the most valuable aspects of this work is García Márquez's relentless assault upon what might be thought of as the "romance of murder." The patriarch is often shown as an embattled defender of the old ways, an old-fashioned man who cannot understand or countenance the efficient liquidation of enemies of the state (the section dealing with his misery over the ascendance of a psychopathic and aristocratic chief of the secret police is most to the point). The author is clearly demonstrating to us that the patriarch's methods of cruelty and murder, though "hot-blooded," end in the same agonies and deaths that colder methods achieve. The author will not allow the reader the luxury of conceiving of murder as righteous and forgivable. This may seem a small point; but one has only to recall, for instance, middle-class America's frighteningly romantic notion of the nobility of the Mafia to understand that there has been afoot for many years a neurotic conception of the murderer as knight-errant. We have agonized for a half-century over "good" political purges and "bad" ones. García Márquez puts all this insanity in sharp perspective. He will not permit us to think of murder as various in quality; it is one of his novel's excellent points.

The book partakes of the surreal, but it does so little more extravagantly than does the work of Céline or Hubert Selby. All three writers extrapolate horrors from the mundane weave of everyday life and show us, by and large, nothing but these horrors. Although they are clearly and naturally presented, their accumulative power forces us to shift our focus and perceive them as the whole world of their protagonists. It is more a selective realism than it is surreal. By sheer mass of selected details, García Márquez proffers us a universe that is monstrous because of what is excluded from the presentation. There *are* wholly surrealistic touches in the novel, most notably the episode describing the patriarch's sale of the sea—which is carted away—to the United States in settlement of a huge debt, but these I see as unnecessary strokes that flaw the book.

The prose is simple to follow, its surface and structure familiar to anyone who has read even a little of the work of the classic moderns. It reads, as do many contemporary Latin American novels, as a kind of pastiche of the methods of the international avant-garde of some forty years ago. And like much of the work done in that mode, the speaker—often the patriarch, but occasionally different observers—indulges in pronominal shifts in point of view and in pages-long, run-on sentences.

If there is a complexity to the novel, it is a horizontal one: it demands we pay attention to and remember the hundreds of minor details that go to make up its rich impasto surface. The pleasure it affords the intellect is in watching a bravura performance unroll—it has no subtlety, nothing "unsaid," nor does it mean to have. Although I have not had the opportunity to examine the original text, I suspect that Gregory Rabassa's translation, if it is on the same level as his translations of, for instance, Cortázar, Goytisolo, and Vargas Llosa, is of his usual excellence. Certainly it reads brilliantly, with neither awkwardnesses nor solecisms that are not clearly intended.

Bookletter, 1976

31

David Antin
Talking

Talking at the Boundaries

Ever since he began publishing in the mid-sixties, David Antin has been a remarkably interesting and intelligent poet. He was, early on, peripherally associated with the poets who were attempting a revivification of the art through the employment of what was then called the Deep Image—Robert Kelly and Jerome Rothenberg foremost among them—but attention to his work revealed that his association with them was more a matter of friendship and geography than it was a matter of aesthetics. Mr. Antin was not then interested, nor is he now, in what one calls (loosely, God knows) "the imagination." That is, invention and the making of "images" or replicas assume no place in his poetic. His concern has always been with allowing his language to seek its own form and allowing that form to stand as his content. "How can we know the dancer from the dance?" Yeats asks.

This new book of "talk poems" is an inevitable outgrowth of Mr. Antin's work of the past decade. The poems herein were all "talked" to audiences, without benefit of text, hot off the griddle, and constitute a return to oral poetry, and, in a very real sense, a new way of seeing the lyric. They are long, sinuous pieces, turning and twisting about a central theme or themes, and approaching that center by means of all the intellectual devices that the poet can lay his hands on. The voice that speaks these poems is incisive, articulate, witty, and learned. The works herein—there are eight of them—stand as the products of a unifying and synthesizing intelligence, of an ability to see, in the air, the invisible outlines of an unachieved form. The poems are the attempts to achieve that form.

It goes without saying that the kind of intelligence that succeeds in making a form that is its own explanation is a poetic one, despite Mr. Antin's confessed discomfort with thinking of himself as a poet. As he says in a preface to his first piece, "if robert lowell is a poet i don't want to be a poet if robert frost was a poet i don't want to be a poet if socrates was a poet ill consider it." In one of his pieces he talks about the making of pots in oral societies and points out that the art is in the making of the pot, not in the pot that is made, the latter being the outcome of the art. The reader may approach this book with that idea as gloss.

The New York Times Book Review, 1976

32

Le Style de Queneau

Exercises in Style, originally published in France in 1947, and in this wonderful, now reissued translation by Barbara Wright in 1958, comprises ninety-nine ways of telling the same story (which is not a "story" at all). Underneath this surface lies a profound investigation into the nature of fiction, an investigation which should make even the most committed devotees of the Novel of Ideas dismount, at least for a moment, from their hobby-horses. The investigation is presented as a series of unasked questions, none of which is answered. The whole is carried off with the brio and dazzling intelligence for which Raymond Queneau is justly famous.

A narrator on a Paris bus sees a young man with a long neck, and wearing a felt hat, quarrel with another passenger, whom he accuses of jostling him. Seeing an empty seat, the young man sits down. Two hours later, the narrator again sees the young man in the street with a friend who is advising him to have another button sewn on his overcoat. That is the story. We then read it ninety-eight more times, each retelling deploying a different style, from word games and permutations, through slang, jargon, and cant, to narrational attitudes toward the subject matter, modes of formal rhetoric, and other linguistic tactics. It is an enormous pleasure, a book devoid of pomposity and fake wisdom, and if one's attention but skates over its surface, the delight the work gives may be reward enough.

However, as I have noted, Queneau is amusing himself while he tacitly attacks cherished convictions as to the way fiction works; it is a benign assault, precisely because it is comic and "light." But the questions raised are very serious indeed, and even the recognition of them, sans an attempt to come up with their answers, will, I suspect, bring up short anyone who thinks that fiction is an imitation of reality.

For instance, the story as outlined above is supposedly the real story, the theme, so to speak, on which Queneau plays his variations. Fine. But who says so? Not Queneau. His first telling of the story is titled "Notation." His sixteenth telling is titled "Narrative." Is "Notation" *realer* than "Narrative"? In the first exercise we read that "The chap in question gets annoyed with one of the men standing next to him. He accuses him of jostling him every time anyone goes past." In the sixteenth exercise, we are given: "This individual suddenly addressed the man standing next to him, accusing him of purposely treading on his toes every time any passengers got on or off." The data have changed. How can we now tell what the real story is? What reality is this fiction reproducing? If some omniscient "Queneau" is writing these two exercises, telling us what he saw, why has he decided to adjust his vision? Perhaps the first exercise is a lie. Perhaps both are lies. Did any of it happen? If it is all a lie, or if one or the other is a lie, does fiction tender us any "truth" at all? Maybe all facts are inventions. Is fiction, which supposedly has a responsibility to its audience, supposed to do this? Perhaps fiction should be experienced as one experiences a tree: there it is.

If this minor contradiction (and there are dozens more throughout the text) calls into doubt the putative didactic and mimetic function of the fiction writer, how are we to approach, say, *Oliver Twist*? Dickens might be as much at odds with the reality of Victorian London as Queneau is with the reality of a Parisian bus ride. Does fiction's value lie only in itself?

In the third exercise, "Litotes," we read (and I give the exercise entire):

> Some of us were traveling together. A young man, who didn't look very intelligent, spoke to the man next to him for a few moments, then he went and sat down. Two hours later I met him again; he was with a friend and was talking about clothes.

This, let us say, happened. All right. It is here rendered as classic understatement. But the technique of litotes works only if we know what is being understated—or does it? Suppose that we read it divorced from what we know, or think, the story to be. Is it self-sufficient? It isn't much different from: "Someone must have been telling lies about Joseph K., for without having done anything wrong he was arrested one fine morning"—the celebrated opening of *The Trial*. Or from: "None of them knew the color of the sky"—the first sentence of Crane's "The Open Boat," a sentence that is not considered mysterious or obscure, even though it is absolutely empty of information—is, in fact, a textbook illustration of litotes. We are beginning to see that fiction drained of data functions as well as fiction packed with it.

Each contradiction in the book raises new questions: What is a narrator? Is there a difference between a first-person narrator and a third-person narrator? Does a narrative point of view falsify or intensify the "real"? Can a false point of view be truer to the "factual" than an honest one? If a narrator is lying, what happens to his subject matter? What if he lies only part of the time?

Exercises in Style lays to rest (or should) the quaint idea that fiction is composed of two equal parts: form and content. It also calls seriously into question the generally accepted contemporary dictum that "form is never more than an extension of content." What it posits, in a great, bravura performance, is the joyous heresy that will not go away, despite the recrudescence of such aesthetic nonsense as Moral Responsibility, Great Themes, and Vast Issues as the business of fiction, and that heresy simply states: form determines content.

Book World, 1981

33

Travels with Calvino

If on a winter's night a traveler, Calvino's version (and antiversion) of the *nouveau roman*, fits the conditions for "proper art" proposed by Dedalus/ Joyce: "The mind is arrested and raised above desire and loathing." It is a wonderful piece of work, labyrinthine and convoluted, informed by a dead-pan humor and pastiches, imitations, and parodies of an entire battery of modern and postmodern literary techniques.

It begins with an *almost* conventional storyteller's address to the reader: "You are about to begin reading Italo Calvino's new novel, *If on a winter's night a traveler*. Relax. Concentrate. Dispel every other thought." We immediately see that "Italo Calvino" is somebody other than the author, and as we read, discover that "you" is not the usual foil, the time-honored figure to whom the narrator tells, in the first or third person, his story. "You" is the second-person protagonist of the novel; and he is, above all other things, a reader. What he does, or wants to do, in chapters that detail his adventures, is read. The chapters dealing with "you" alternate with the chapters that he is reading; but through error, carelessness, chance, design, conspiracy, these chapters (ten of them) are not from the same book; they are the first chapters of ten different books, and each breaks off at the point of crisis or suspense: they are cliff-hangers.

What is Calvino up to? I think that he is doing what the practitioners of the contemporary novel have been doing for at least a quarter-century, putting into practice an idea succinctly stated—in 1923!—by the formalist critic, Victor Shklovsky: "The ideas in a literary work do not constitute its content but rather its material, and in their combinations and interrelations with other aspects of the work they create its form." The "content" of Calvino's novel is precisely the material from which he makes the form that we hold in our hands as this book. This novel's splinterings, ambiguities, contradictions, distorted mirror images, thematic variations, off-key fugues are as absolutely representative of objective reality as the linear, plotted, sequential narrative of the conventional novel, the latter as much an invention, and as totally artificial as the *nouveau roman*, and with the equivalent relation to objective reality: none.

We have learned, over the years, to read the signs that a Dickens or a Conrad use, but they are only signs, manifestations of invented techniques. The books in which they are deployed use "ideas" as "material" just as Calvino does (or Beckett, or Robbe-Grillet). That we insist that Dickens' "ideas" constitute his "content" is *our* problem and critical failing. His novels are as strange and as artificial as the one under review. Calvino's novel more bluntly insists that the world of the book equals the world of the book. If, as Mallarmé says, "everything in the world exists to end in a book," then "everything" must stand for *material*, to be used by the writer to make forms that are those of literature, not reality.

Calvino's strategies are so numerous that I can do no more than point out a few of them: The first-person narrators of the ten chapters from the ten different novels are different, yet they all have curiously similar affinities and problems; the protagonist-Reader, "you," has adventures that seem, at times, to be blurred reflections of the adventures of the ten narrators; a writer, Silas Flannery, who has (perhaps) written one (or two, or none) of the chapters that "you" reads, keeps a diary in which he writes: "I have had the idea of writing a novel composed only of beginnings of novels. The protagonist could be a Reader who is continually interrupted," and so we read a novel by "Italo Calvino" in which a novelist considers writing the novel in which he already exists; the Reader meets six other readers to whom he tells his difficulties in continuing the novels he has begun. To the ten titles he adds another, suggested by the conversation, a "relic of some childish reading," that he feels should be included in the list, then gives the list to one of the other readers, who reads aloud:

> If on a winter's night a traveler, outside the town of Malbork, leaning from the steep slope without fear of wind or vertigo, looks down in the gathering shadow in a network of lines that enlace, in a network of lines that intersect, on the carpet of leaves illuminated by the moon around an empty grave—What story down there awaits its end?—he asks, anxious to hear the story.

He thinks that this is the first paragraph of the novel that "you" would like to continue but cannot find. "You" protests that these are but titles, to which the other replies: "Oh, the traveler always appeared only in the first pages and then was never mentioned again—he had fulfilled his function." This is precisely what happens to the traveler in "Calvino's" first pages, except that the traveler is not "Calvino's" traveler, but a character in a novel that a character in a novel has been reading.

This is a brilliant work of great imaginative power and artistic authority. With it, Calvino has, in Shklovsky's phrase, "ripped things from their ordinary sequence of associations."

Book World, 1981

34

Paul Bowles: The Clash of Cultures

In William Carlos Williams' "A Beginning on the Short Story (Notes)," he says, writing of Paul Bowles' first novel, *The Sheltering Sky*:

> How . . . is Bowles going to get the girl undressed. He is going to *act* to do it. By setting the imagination to work. WORK. The artist is now a woman, a particular woman. He is therefore bound by her conditions and so he works at it . . .
>
> The woman is going to be undressed *willingly*—within a time limitation of a train schedule. She will *want* to be undressed even while she fights against it—by running out.
>
> So he gets her soaked to the skin. But on a train? in Africa. How? Read it. Lesson No. 1.

Williams' characteristically trenchant observation of one of Bowles' techniques is one that holds true for all the novels and short stories that Bowles has published since *The Sheltering Sky*: he is an author who works to avoid cliché by confronting his materials, not by sidling past them with the help of the codified tics and patterns of "fine writing." His work is unsettling, but rarely because of the raw materials, the content, of his stories. Rather, it is the acutely conscious attempt to deal with these materials honestly that enables him to transcend the content that, in other hands, might be the stuff of sensation or didacticism.

The language of Bowles' fiction is reticent and formal, but often brutal in its flat candor. No wonder Williams admired him. Over his work there lies a barely visible "haze" of anxiety or terror. His characters, once embarked upon the adventures that he invents for them, carry them through to the end; there is no point in a Bowles story at which one can say, with any certainty, *there* is where the story takes its turn. His stories do not take "turns," but follow strait and undeviating paths, the beginnings of which are anterior to their first words. We "come in" on them, as it were.

It is as if Bowles has made a compact with his readers, one that assumes that he and they know that people are weak, vacillating, self-serving, envious, and often base, as well as being, more often than not, irrational because of fixed and unexamined beliefs in country, class, religion, culture, and so on. Granting the existence of this compact, the stories may be seen as inevitable, their characters not so much caught in a web of problems as playing out, so to speak, their hands. In a curious way, the stories may be seen as modern variations on the Jonsonian use of medieval "humours."

Bowles' *Collected Stories 1939–1976* was published in 1979, and gathered together thirty-nine stories written over those years. *Midnight Mass* consists of twelve stories written since 1976. I don't think any of the twelve have the authority of "A Distant Episode," "The Delicate Prey," or "Pages from Cold Point," but the title story, "Midnight Mass," "The Little House," and the long "Here to Learn" are not much inferior to them. For those not familiar with Bowles, it should be said that he is most at home in his work in a North African setting, usually Moroccan, and that most of his stories have to do with Arabs or with Arabs and their dealings with Americans or Europeans. I would say that much of Bowles' power and clarity, his freshness and eschewal of the banal has come about because he uses this material without resorting to condescension, awed delight, or sociological analysis: the specific world of Morocco is *there*.

Nowhere in Bowles do we find any hint of the exotic. His Arabs don't think of themselves as such, but as people who live the lives that have been given them. The brilliance of Bowles' work is rooted in the fact that his prose takes his non-Western world for granted, and this matter-of-fact attitude is tacitly held in subtle opposition to what might be called the reader's expectations. We bring our great bag of *idées fixes* to Bowles' Morocco, and he calmly proceeds to empty it in front of us. Furthermore, Bowles' Western characters are often seen to be carrying that same bag in the stories in which they appear: their reward for this cultural error is usually disaster.

It should be noted that those stories that deploy only Western characters are handled in the same way by Bowles, so that the reader has the eerie feeling that he is reading about people that he *should* be able to recognize, but does not. The author's attitudes toward Western culture and Western people are very hard on the ideas of the marketplace. This technical ability has grown, as I have suggested, from Bowles' refusal to follow the fictional path of least resistance. He does what the good artist everywhere does: solves the problems he has created for himself with the same tools used to create the problems. He is responsible to his work and not to the dim flickerings of "taste." These are distinguished stories indeed.

Book World, 1981

35

La Guaracha

Macho Camacho's Beat. Translated by Gregory Rabassa

This novel, which functions brilliantly on linguistic, structural, and socio-political levels, is defined by an extravagant and mordant sense of the comic. Like all excellent comic writing, the laughter is generated by language, not situation. At the heart of Luis Rafael Sánchez's book are rage and despair, without which comedy never rises above the level of bobhopeism or the animated cartoon. His humor is, in Brian O'Nolan's phrase, "the handmaid of sorrow and fear."

Permeating the island of Puerto Rico in the middle of the Nixon administration is the runaway hit recording, "Life Is a Phenomenal Thing," a *guaracha* by Macho Camacho and his band. The record is on every jukebox, played on every radio station countless times a day, and sung in the streets by people of every class and stratum of society. It is woven through Sánchez's novel as leitmotif and chorus; it is, clearly, a manifestation of the apparent "spirit" of modern-day Puerto Rico.

Macho Camacho's Beat is an evocation of the island's true spirit, given us through an accumulation of information concerning four major characters. As the lie of the *guaracha* meshes with the truth of the island, a mood of profound irony envelops the novel as we see that the colonial culture of contemporary Puerto Rico is as false and debased as the *guaracha* that so bitterly represents it: The irony deepens as we become aware that the *guaracha* is accepted by the islanders themselves as symbolic of their *true*, lost culture, as if Italian-Americans were to believe that the fat, happy mamas who ceaselessly stir "real" spaghetti sauce on commercials for one or another brand of processed garbage are images of themselves.

Senator Vicente Reinosa, a wealthy, self-satisfied, philandering, and corrupt politician, a perfect creature of American commercial interests, is caught in a gigantic San Juan traffic jam while on his way to see his black, uneducated, and ignorant mistress, on whose crackerbox of a house he pays the rent. His wife, Graciela, neurotic and stupid, a kind of vulgarized Emma Bovary, is, at the same moment, visiting her psychiatrist, a man of spectacular cynicism, the perfect panacea for his clients and their ludicrous maladies. Mired in the same traffic jam, in the Ferrari that he quite literally adores, is the senator's son, Benny, a dull, pampered parafascist whose thought processes make those of Leopold Bloom seem absolutely Aristotelian. In brief chapters, these four—husband, mistress, wife, son—are written of over and again. Each time that they are returned to, Sánchez adds new data or enriches old; and by this steady accretion of detail, the four are used to reveal the essence of their perverted society, created and fostered by external business interests. These chapters are divided into sections by short paragraphs that speak of the omnipresent *guaracha* in the depraved language of publicity hacks.

Nothing "really" happens in this novel, and although there is a loose narrative connecting the main characters, there is no plot to interfere with Sánchez's purpose, which is to investigate, with all the resources of language that are at his command, a society that is but a dream of merchandising, a lobotomized market for overpriced goods and ideas of the Good Life, hypnotized by wealth and a sterile American culture grafted onto an even more sterile, loony idea of European "glamour."

Sánchez's linguistic resources are multiplex, and he uses them with profligate genius: the book is short, but densely written, and its language occurs in clusters of verbal energy. The texture of the prose is composed of direct and indirect dialogue, authorial (and "Authorial") intrusion, sudden shifts from the third to the first person (and vice versa), and an odd, insistent imperative voice that might be the author's, that of an unnamed observer, or that of "Puerto Rican-ness" itself. Sánchez's vocabulary is of a piece with his design—he uses, in isolation and in incandescent combinations, the language of degenerate politics, crippled rhetoric, advertising, pop culture, academe, smarmy and imbecilic "youth," cheap patriotism, business, vapid psychology, the best seller, the vulgar poor, the stupid middle class, and the idiotic rich. Out of it all he has made a novel that totally exploits its materials and that operates as do all true works of literary art: it exists only in terms of its medium, its ocean of words. Devoid of cant and sentimentality, it is a literary event.

One of the techniques by which writers illuminate the filth of decaying societies is to use fragments of the decay as the raw stuff of their work. Flaubert did it, as did Joyce and Lewis. In our time, it has been done by, among others, Burroughs, Pinget, Gaddis, and Goytisolo. With this novel, Luis Rafael Sánchez joins this company of salutary assassins.

Book World, 1981

36

The Ending
Is Wanting

Eternal Curse on the Reader of These Pages is, like Manuel Puig's *Kiss of the Spider Woman*, developed almost entirely as a splintered colloquy between two unlikely companions. It is also, like the earlier novel, a structural failure, and for much the same reason: the conclusion, disastrously, comments on and "explains" an otherwise richly ambivalent and mysterious text. It is as if Puig lost his nerve and decided, for whatever reason, to serve that famous "general audience," an audience that is already grandly served by what Blanchot has called "the nonliterary book," the book that has, "before it is read by anyone . . . been read by everyone." Puig's natural readership, the readers of literary books, could comfortably fit into Madison Square Garden; but in this book he seems to be reaching out to snare the same people who think of, say, John Gardner as pretty complex. It's too bad, because Puig *has* something, most obviously a wonderful sense that the essential elements of life, life's serious "things," are precisely the elements of soap opera, sit-coms, and B-movies. Both *Kiss of the Spider Woman* and this new novel *almost* set these two planes one atop the other, so that they look like one plane. But both novels fail, and the failure is one of form; or, to be clearer, the novels fail because Puig holds his content to be somehow more than just materials—to be a set of ideas.

This novel's two characters are by turns (and turns!) dull, envious, narrow, crude, cruel, misinformed, and politically boring and ingenuous—and at times, disingenuous. Larry, the younger man, an American, even speaks of revolutionary "struggle"—here in the land of flabby unions, pots, and looms: the author's ironic sense of dopiness here is brilliant.

We are almost immediately aware that Puig is aware of the fact that he is writing an ambiguous comedy in which the deepest feelings about sex, love, family, marriage, patriotism, loneliness, and on and on, are proved to be also the "deepest feelings" of those who turn these things into the corrupt products of the market and national politics, those products that keep us dozing in the face of their familiar, pleasant, and undisturbing selves. All the dialogue is vapid, its "themes" but a weird reflection of things long ago debased. Puig has set himself a tough problem: to criticize cultural enervation in the same language that has helped bring that enervation to pass. So we read on.

Puig is not at all interested though in his putative content: he "tells" us this throughout the novel, and in many ways. Larry, the American loser, is hired, perhaps, to be a companion to an old Argentine, Mr. Ramirez, another loser. Larry is a bum, or perhaps not, a failed academic, a mealymouthed radical, a hopeless husband and son, and a career opportunist. But he may also be a liar. Mr. Ramirez was, maybe, a true radical, a heroic revolutionary of the left, a failed husband and father, and also a liar—again, maybe. They contradict each other; they contradict themselves. Mr. Ramirez insists that Larry tell him stories about his family and marriage, so that Mr. Ramirez can "become" Larry, can have a life other than what his life was—whatever it was. They intersect each other, are swallowed by each other, and *are*, at many points, each other.

To further enrich this hash, they have convoluted talks in the most hopelessly bad dialogue this side of comic books, the pulp magazines of my youth, and B-movies, in which one or the other of them plays the roles of victim, hero, betrayer, etc. It is delicious. Larry's life is taken over selectively by Mr. Ramirez, and, in part, the converse is true. Whole swatches of dialogue are repeated verbatim in different contexts, serving to change the "meaning" of the words—words that are already almost completely drained of meaning, so that language becomes a shadow of a shadow. It is very interesting work.

Even more interesting is that one slowly comes to suspect that Larry may not exist at all, but is an invention of Mr. Ramirez's, someone onto whom he can project his own misery and sadness, through whose talk Ramirez's ruined life can become that of another man, a fantasy American to take the heat of Ramirez's bad conscience. On the other hand, Mr. Ramirez may be Larry's invention: we have no true evidence for anything, since the text, which can be, as in all fiction, verified only by itself, gives us none. Even the places in the book are carefully restricted to names, words—nothing is described.

But then: The last eight pages of the novel are made up of a series of letters that serve to "explain" it, to tell us that Larry is indeed real (and worse, that he is the lout we were not sure he was); that Ramirez is noble and good, though mentally ill (we were not sure of any of these things either); and that the book has a "subject" after all, something like "appearances are deceiving." The effect is catastrophic, and the textual strength, the *risk* of the novel, disintegrates. The complex deployment of what Barthes calls the "middle voice" (in this case one should perhaps say "voices"), through which Puig permitted himself no authorial intrusion, is subverted at the very end of the novel, damaging its wholeness irremediably. This is terribly depressing, at least to me, since it is clear that Puig is a writer of luminous talents.

Book World, 1981

37

John Gardner:
Rhinestone
in the Rough

John Gardner is of the puppeteer school of novelists. He moves his characters in ways vaguely imitative of "real" people, puts stagy, pseudoauthentic dialogue in their mouths, and dresses them in costumes direct from the Wardrobe Department. The reader is to suppose that he is looking at Life. One can almost hear the numbing rhetoric about how if it was good enough for Dickens, for Tolstoy, and so on *ad nauseam*. That it was not good enough for Nashe, or Cervantes, or Sterne, or Austen, or James is quite apparent, but Mr. Gardner works in the aberrant mode of realism or naturalism, that upstart of imaginative writing, and to such writers this *arriviste* mode is the only mode.

He is the darling of reviewers, some of whom occasionally complain mildly of the "toneless" quality of his prose: they mean "styleless" but have difficulties with that word because of their enormous problems in recognizing style. His work is taken seriously because his mirror-up-to-life routines reflect the images that his ill-read audience takes to be important: Look! There we are! Relentlessly descriptive of the fragmented quotidian (on which he imposes "order," *à la* Robert Frost), he is understandable and quite wonderful to readers to whom Jane Austen and Henry James are radical and difficult (they don't *say* anything). That these latter writers are these things to such readers is because of their departure from the mimetic, a departure that dates back at least to *Le Morte d'Arthur*.

In his "On Style or Writing," Rémy de Gourmont notes that "there are two kinds of writers: writers who can write and those who cannot write." In the latter camp may be placed those writers with a contempt for, or aversion to style, the writers of "ideas," of substance, of the famous *content*, that odd ingredient that exists like the man on the stair: one meets it but it isn't there. Mr. Gardner, with a great stack of wooden books that he has sedulously inflicted on the public over the years, is one of those writers who cannot write, one for whom, or so the published evidence seems to show, style appears to be analogous to the effete, the frivolous, the "literary." He is a writer who goes about his business doggedly pretending that Flaubert never existed, or, if he did, that he was a "realist," a kind of Gallic Tolstoy. He gouges his paralyzing books out of *ideas*. It seems that he wants to tell us . . . the Truth!

October Light, a recent Gardner novel, seems to me an excellent subject for a cursory examination of the author in bloom. It may, or so I propose, stand as the quintessential Gardner approach to fiction. A look at this work may make it possible to locate and isolate the virus that informs the canon. This canon has, depressingly, taken its place as the focus of a new trend in American fiction: the "think" novel for the reader ready to graduate from Harold Robbins, a genre much like the painting of Andrew Wyeth or the music of Aaron Copland. Art without Tears. *October Light*, then, may be read as a guide to the author's *œuvre*. It is amazing in its witlessness, using the language with a carelessness hardly ever found outside the idiocies of the consumer goods perpetrated by the hack robots grinding out Good Reads. It is rich in solecism and cliché, crammed with characters who Walk Off the Page and with dialogue that reads like the speech we hear daily, unchanged and unselected, without design, dialogue that is, in Valéry's phrase, utilitarian.

We are given an old, crusty, bigoted Yankee farmer, James Page. He chases his old, somewhat sensitive and refined sister, Sally Page Abbot, into her bedroom after smashing her television set. There ensues a war of wills when Sally refuses to come out of her bedroom. Neighbors, relatives, and friends are summoned from Central Casting to help, but they fail.

The Past is dredged up in all its Mystery.

We discover certain Skeletons in the Closet.

At the close, both James and Sally have Strange Experiences and Insights into Truth and Reality.

Sally finally emerges, Wiser and Better. As is James.

Both have been Cleansed in the Purifying Fires of Self-Examination.

Music up and Credits. All this is seen, as you surely will have guessed, through a haze of soap bubbles floating iridescently on blasts of hot air rising, ever rising, from the churning narrative. One can imagine Dickens (to cite a misnamed realist) doing this at twelve.

But, enter Literary Experiment. Sally, while in her room, reads a tattered copy of a trashy paperback novel, *The Smugglers of Lost Souls' Rock*, which is presented to us in counterpoint to the Real novel. It does not work as counterpoint (or gloss), but since nothing else in this book works, its inclusion is a perfection of ineptitude. There seem, on occasion, to be tenuous connections or slippery correspondences between the Real novel and the Trashy one, but Mr. Gardner cannot make them work as commentary, correlative, or irony. The niceties of technique of that wild, avant-garde movement, Symbolism, are ignored, lost in the same limbo in which dwells Flaubert. Mr. Gardner sits stunned before his own materials.

Consider a small catalogue of exhibits drawn from *October Light*. I assure the reader that these fragments are absolutely representative and have many counterparts throughout this work. From the Trashy paperback:

Mr. Nit struggled to find words, bit his lips together, and squinted.

—and from the Real novel in which this Trash resides:

He said nothing, biting his lips together and not meeting her eyes.

• • •

She bit her lips together, watching him pour the whiskey. . . .

What are we to make of this? What is Mr. Gardner doing? Why is he doing it? Does he know or care what he is doing? Possibilities present themselves: (1) Trashy novels are as good as good novels, (2) Trashy novels are no worse than good novels, (3) Mr. Gardner's Trashy novel is on a level with his Good novel, (4) All writing is to be considered as sets of data to which style is inconsequential, (5) *The Smugglers of Lost Souls' Rock* is the Real novel, and *October Light* its prophet. The last is interesting to consider, since it implies that Mr. Gardner thinks either that writing which is patently rubbish is not so or that he has no measure by which to gauge his own writing, since it is demonstrable that the writing in "both" novels is equally wretched. Can this all be a joke? Is the author giving us *two* parodies, one of the world of garbage fiction and one of the world of Gardner fiction? This idea is not defensible, however, in the light of Mr. Gardner's other novels, all of which flounder as hopelessly as *October Light*. We are stuck, it would seem, with the fact that Mr. Gardner is one of those "writers who cannot write," a Robert Bly of fiction.

The curiously machined mental processes of the hack are at work in the above fragments. When arriving at a problem of description, the true hack turns briskly into the celebrated Path of Least Resistance, and, rather than *looking* at what is before his eyes, the veteran laborer rummages in his bag of scraps and finds, ready to hand, a phrase, a simile, an analogy, an image, from which every ounce of energy has long since been siphoned. The reader will surely recall the famous corpse: "He looked at him as if seeing him for the first time," a construct that I have come across in at least fifty novels. Of course, Homer nods. But this particular Homer is comatose. The above quotations reveal a mind working in smooth grooves of banality, a brain worthy of claiming kinship with that of Monsieur Bouvard. The wonderful foolishness of those bitten-together lips! And given us, not once, but three times! It is delicious. I asked myself how else those lips might be bitten: separately? one after the other? And it will be recognized that in the world of mimesis, it is *de rigueur* to deal with more than one aspect of a "closely observed" face, hence, the effortless move to the eyes, the process of seeing. Conventional practice, or, how it really is in *life*.

More wonders: In the Trashy novel, we read this idiotic degradation of the simile:

> The lines of the houses were as clean and precise as the hands of clocks, and the streets moved over the hills like well-planned arguments.

Those "lines" might well be "as clean and precise" as the blades of knives; those "streets" very comfortably move "over the hills" like perfectly delivered lectures. (Or, the reader may insert his own comparisons.) This is known as Vivid Description, or, The Return of the Blob. But it may be protested that this excerpt is from the Trashy novel. What of the Real novel?

> ... in the middle of the valley, the village sat like a village of toy houses, a Christmas village waiting for fake snow and lights.

—a triumph of cliché from the Warehouse of Hackneyed Phrases, to be found on the same floor as the cartons filled with the Clouds that Sail Across the Sky like Great Ships.

We might look closely at the following, again, from the Real novel:

> She stared at the wall for a time, thinking nothing, at first with an expression of sadness and compassion, then with a sterner expression. Her jaw became firmer, her eyes more fierce.

Disregarding the graceless, installation-manual prose of the whole, what is the *matter* with it? Why is it so blurred? We find the answer in the useless comparative "sterner." The prose is saying that an expression "sterner" than the expressions of "sadness" and "compassion" appears on the face described, but are "sadness" and "compassion" ever "stern"? Then, the poison at work, Mr. Gardner blusters into two more useless comparatives, "firmer" and "more fierce." Her jaw is "firmer," her eyes "fiercer" than they were— when? When she had "an expression of sadness and compassion" on her face, a time when, apparently, her jaw was only *firm*, her eyes but *fierce*. The prose, because of this endemic carelessness, simply decays. The grammar, the syntax, have no bones, and the sentences they should support collapse.

This inattention leads to unconscious howlers, as in (from the Real novel):

> He had a curious, boyish habit, with which she never interfered, of chewing little pieces of the newspaper while he read it.

—a glorious sentence: I see this man assaulting the paper, nibbling on a corner of the editorial page, gnawing the box scores. We assume, of course, that the author *means* something else, but he does not tell us what he means. His language obfuscates as does that of the advertising copywriter.

There are also displayed, throughout *October Light*, flashy similes worthy of fiction-workshop students with poor instructors. I give three as *exempla*. The first uses the Crippled-Analogue Shuffle:

> She remembered when his hair, snow-white, had been as brown as shoe polish.

(precise, in a world devoid of all other colors of shoe polish). The second employs the Garbled-Comparison Hop:

> By the whitewashed post six feet away, the cats sat watching, soft and tame-looking as pillows on a couch. . . .

(excellent if one thinks of pillows as possessing the qualities of living creatures).

The third is the tried-and-true, local-color, Down-Home Two-Step:

> His faith in laconic truth cracked and gave way like the wall of a haybarn. . . .

(that, past the bucolic ornamentation of that collapsing barn—which functions like our clock-hands and well-planned arguments—leaves us with the problem of meaning as to "laconic truth." Brief truth? Pithy truth? A truth sparing of words? The truth known by our friend whose mouth is full of newspaper? Whatever, "laconic truth" is certainly a no-nonsense truth, it is a part of country wisdom.)

The preceding are all from the Real novel, as is the last, and my hands-down favorite fragment, clearly an example of *furor scribendi*:

DeWitt . . . moved to the head of the stairs . . . a wide, shy grin on his red-headed, freckled face. . . .

Cursed as he is with this monstrous deformity, DeWitt had *better* grin.

There is no point in going on with this. My point has, I hope, been made. Where there is no style there is no fiction, or, as Williams remarked of the sonnet, "Who cares what the line 'says'?"

In an astonishing interview with Mr. Gardner, published soon after the appearance of *October Light*, the author is quoted as saying: "Writing is not in its best phase right now. I think I'm lucky—I'm one of the best there is."

He is incorrect in his assertion.

He goes on to say: "I have to write all the time because I write very slowly and I throw away an awful lot."

He does not throw away enough.

Blast 3, 1984

38

"For my day had passed."

Ralph Cusack's *Cadenza* is a chain of stories that slide into each other over a period of arbitrary fictional time, as well as space; they neither end nor begin and are variously ordered and combined as discrete instances of memory moving into fantasy moving into dream moving into actuality (the "present"). This actuality (the "present"), however, may be the actuality of memory or fantasy or dream: they too exist in their own "present." So we have no firm grasp at all on time, or perhaps one should say that in *Cadenza* the past is the present. It may be that there is no time at all in this work, that the work is but an utterance, always in the process of being uttered, at the timeless edge, the invisible line between life and death.

It is always about to slip into comedy, not satire or wit, but the anarchic comedy that exists in the sort of arrogant mind that knows that the world is irremediably insane. Fair, perhaps, but no less insane for all that. The world is comic *because* it is insane, its insanity a bulwark against all amelioration. And it is funnily, impossibly sad, because any attempt at amelioration ultimately takes its place in the general slough of madness. In *Cadenza*, this anarchic comedy is never indulged in, despite Cusack's clearly revealed comic spirit. It is a funny book but it does not destroy with laughter, the latter always poised at the brink of becoming, but most usually asserting itself as what might be called a wry smile. This delicate equilibrium between the comic and the rueful, this knowledge of the author that the world is not funny *enough*, constitute the power of this brilliant work.

But *Cadenza* is not, assuredly, tragic; it manipulates the emotions "played

to" by tragedy indifferently, even carelessly: we are not permitted that delicious spuriousness. Nor is it lugubrious and solemn, though its materials
are most easily treated in such wise.

There is in this work the sense of the forever-lost past, and this past informs the entire work. In the contemplation of this past and its impossibly
chaotic configurations, the work is settled, grounded. From this place in
which it rests, it proclaims that there is perhaps *no time*: Or, the past is the
present. It *is* the present. We see that this past, of necessity dead, has the
precise value of the present, since they are the same thing. That is, they are
both dead. Comedy does not have the penetrant abilities to get this said.
Which is why Cusack cannot give his comic gifts their liberty.

Death and dead events, the dead past in the narrator's skull, *are* the present and present events, are then, "life." It is all of a piece. As we live we
die, and there is no "present" worth our contemplation. Our narrator, drunk
and alone in a train compartment, makes love to the sweetheart of his youth.
He doesn't *think* about this. He makes love. As he does it passes into memory, it disappears as surely as it disappeared at an earlier point on his life's
graph—and what is more absurd than those points on the graph that are the
measure of lost time? He will make love to this girl again, surely. And it will
be as real as . . . real. *Cadenza* is a book of ending, of the terminal. It is a
book of death.

Adrift, 1983

39

Ross Macdonald:
Some Remarks on the
Limitations of Form

It is surely not an original observation to note that *The Blue Hammer*, Ross Macdonald's last novel, is an oblique, a kind of subtle completion of that which was adumbrated in the first Lew Archer novel, *The Moving Target*, though the later book is at once more complex, less rhetorically gaudy, and reliant on metonymy rather than metaphor for its scaffolding. *The Blue Hammer* works, that is, vertically rather than horizontally—the missing Chantry painting is not analogous to anything, nor does it function as a symbol; on the contrary, it is a sign, a correlative, for the evil, waste, and betrayal that the novel uncovers, or, perhaps more precisely, that the past gives up. Macdonald goes so far as to give us a clue to his recuperative intentions by referring, in *The Blue Hammer*, to the death, in *The Moving Target*, of the thug, Puddler, at Archer's hands. This passing fragment of information is absolutely irrelevant to the solution of the mystery and is placed into the text so as to call attention to itself and to its author's conception of his evolving work.

We do a disservice to Macdonald's writings by considering them as outside the quite rigid and artificial structure of the detective novel. Ross Macdonald nowhere surpassed or transcended the limitations of the form in which he chose to work. He worked brilliantly *within* the rigors of this form. That is his strength and valor as a writer.

The detective novel is as thoroughly locked into its form as is the sonnet or the ode, and it is comprehensible or intelligible only in the context of its history. Macdonald can be clearly "seen" as a descendant of Hammett and Chandler, and they are understandable only insofar as they exist within the tradition of the ratiocinative story as defined by Poe. While it may be possible to transcend this form, such transcendence merely takes the detective novel *out of itself*, so that it is no longer the detective novel but something else altogether; as, for instance, one might say that the theater, as a form, has been transcended by the motion picture. Certainly it has—by no longer being theater. Macdonald trusted his form and was held by it because of what, from *The Galton Case* on, he surely saw were its depthless possibilities and inexhaustible permutations. In an interview, he says: "My books are somewhat limited by the kind of structure and subject matter that is inherent in the contemporary detective novel. I seem to work best within such limitations." I read the phrase "somewhat limited" as a kind of modest irony: it is the "limited" quality of his books that makes them perfect models of a particular kind of fiction, a fiction for which many American critics regularly apologize, or, worse, attempt to make more "serious" by denying that it is this particular kind of fiction—the detective story. Macdonald has often been praised for being better than the genre within which he worked. But it is self-evident that his brilliance as a writer is firmly located in his purity of design: his "ideas" are as unremarkable as those of newspaper editorials—or Christianity.

The French, however, have never taken the detective story lightly, and it is instructive that the *nouveaux romanciers*, most notably Michel Butor and Alain Robbe-Grillet, have used variations on the form as the basis of many of their works, variations that range from the detective as murderer, as in Robbe-Grillet's *The Erasers*, to the layered complexities of present as instant past, as in Butor's *Passing Time*. Of Butor's work, John Sturrock, in *The French New Novel*, writes: "The real detective is now the reader; the narrator assembles the relevant evidence but he is denied the power to conceptualize it."

I don't mean to suggest that Macdonald has done anything of this kind in his novels, although it is apparent that Archer is slowly transformed, from book to book, from the detective who has "the power to conceptualize" to a man who acts as a kind of catalyst by means of which the evidence inevitably and relentlessly conceptualizes *itself*. He does not so much dig for information as he is led ineluctably to it. The leader of the Society of Mutual Love, in *The Blue Hammer*, says: " 'You seem to be a man engaged in an endless battle, an endless search. Has it ever occurred to you that the search may be for yourself? And that the way to find yourself is to be still and silent. . . ?'" And Archer thinks: "They were questions I had asked myself, though never in just those terms." In this final work, Archer, although he asks questions and pokes, prods, and worries recalcitrant and lying characters in his search for truth, is, in a curious but salient way, falling into silence. He talks as much as he did twenty years earlier, but the talk is somehow *given* him by the unfolding corruption that "wants" to be revealed. Murder will out. Archer has been changed from a mere seeker to the midwife who will deliver the original sins that exist at the core of the case.

Ross Macdonald has said: "I once made a case for the theory . . . that much of the modern development of the detective story stems from Baudelaire, his 'dandyism' and his vision of the city as inferno." He might well have gone on to say that the dandy, a pure product of the Décadence, survives, in a basic mode, as the fictional private detective. Baudelaire, in "The Dandy," writes:

> It [dandyism] is the burning need to create an originality for oneself, a need contained within the exterior limits of convention. It is a kind of cult of oneself which may survive the search for happiness to be found in someone else, in woman, for example; which may even survive everything that is called illusion. It is the pleasure of astonishing and the proud satisfaction of never being astonished.

And further: "The characteristic of beauty in the dandy consists especially in the cold attitude which comes from the unbreakable resolution not to be moved; you might call it a latent flame which you guess exists, which might but which will not spread its light." These definitions fit, of course, Lew Archer—and Marlowe, Spade, and the Op as well.

The pertinence of Macdonald's remark becomes more pointed when one recalls that Baudelaire wrote with great perception on Poe, and that one of the aspects of Poe's work that was most admired by Baudelaire was its artificiality; i.e., to Baudelaire, Poe labored to conceal all that might seem spontaneous in his writing, so that all of it appeared to be the product of a "cold" intellectualism, far removed from the *bête noire* of the Décadence, the automatic writing of inspiration. In contemporary terms, there are few manifestations of fiction more contrived than the detective novel—Macdonald's being no exception. The beauty of this genre lies in its crystalline balances; there is no way that it can "go where it wants to go." It is a perfect expression of dandyism with a dandy as its hero.

It may also be relevant to Macdonald's acute remark on Baudelaire to note that an important facet of the writing of the Décadence was its fascination with time- and space-exoticism (to distance itself from despised naturalism). In Macdonald's novels, it can be argued that these motifs survive as the looming and secret past and the curious culture of Southern California.

I have said that Macdonald trusted his form. I should add too that nowhere does he mock it, even as he began to rely less and less on Hammett and Chandler. The analogies and comparisons used in his early work are taken from the essential vocabulary of glossy similes and straight-faced ironic locutions that inform the entire genre. Some of these, if not all of them, are from a common fund of tropes and imagery available to all detective-story writers, so that they would be at home, so to speak, in the elegant work of Chandler as well as in the clumsy writing of Spillane. In *The Moving Target*, for instance, we find such flashy comparatives as: "The light blue haze in the lower canyon was like a thin smoke from slowly burning money"; "She made the blood run round in my veins like horses on a track"; "Universal City wore its stucco façades like yellowing paper collars"; "Mrs. Estabrook looked up at us with eyes like dark searchlights"; and, in ironic mood, these constructions: "Her hand grasped his left knee. He let it stay there"; "I wanted to respond to her melancholy look, but I didn't know what to do with my face"; "I made myself uncomfortable on a hard-backed chair against the wall." There are dozens more, all of them givens of the genre. They are the sort of thing that Victor Shklovsky, in "Art as Technique," is thinking of when he writes:

> The more you understand an age, the more convinced you become that the images a given poet used and which you thought his own were taken almost unchanged from another poet. The works of poets are classified or grouped according to the new techniques that poets discover and share, and according to their arrangement and development of the resources of language; poets are much more concerned with arranging images than with creating them.

The conventional phrases noted above are the "images" that Macdonald had to hand during his early career. The novels from *The Galton Case* on, however, reveal "new techniques," and it is the discovery and use of these techniques that make Ross Macdonald without peer in the highly artificial and difficult form in which he worked, a form that constantly begs to collapse into the banal.

By the time we arrive at *The Blue Hammer*, we are in the presence of a prose that is flatter, less ornate, and lacking in the bright analogies and ironies of the earlier books. This novel has removed itself from the surface conventions of the genre and relies almost wholly on the understructure of complex form for its effects. As I have suggested, the book functions vertically, doing away with the simple metaphors of *The Moving Target* in favor of the dissociative techniques of metonymy. The associative comparative (this is like this and therefore . . .) has been discarded.

While it is fruitless to speculate on that which is unwritten, it is possible that Macdonald might have finally reached a point in his fiction at which the uncovered truths about his shattered and doomed people would show them to be criminal only in the *moral* sense; that is, he may have come to a fiction in which there were no criminals, only victims. He seems to me to have been heading there. His ultimate victim could well have been Lew Archer.

The line linking *The Moving Target* to *The Blue Hammer* can be described as a graph of maturation. This graph reveals that Macdonald neither derided nor cheapened the detective story and the linguistic paraphernalia germane to it. He was, early on, surely aware that it was no more than paraphernalia; and he used it, I should guess, because his mentors had shown him that the metaphor is a method whereby the detective story—with its grid of connections—can be most efficaciously constructed. And the structural metaphor can be repeated, *in parvo*, in the quick, bright analogies of the surface. In his early work, Macdonald thought metaphorically, and his novels are made like those of his teachers. He surrendered to the form and also eschewed the fetish of originality in favor of a position as a wholly serious writer working in a tradition that he honored.

When he came to his own necessity and began to see that his given materials were not things that stood for other things but were, instead, the blinds and masks for the hidden truths that Archer would have, almost unwillingly, thrust upon him, he changed his flashing and associative method for the plainer one that permitted the world and Archer their confusion. Archer ages and becomes wiser, but it is a wisdom rooted in the knowledge that the solution to specific mysteries cannot approach the mystery of his own being. He is still essentially the dandy, but his aloofness and control have begun to crack in the face of a world that is just about out of control. He has reached the point at which analogies are simply lies in the presence of such a reality.

Yet Macdonald occasionally still gestured toward his teachers, and even in *The Blue Hammer*, a novel whose overwhelming ambience is that of a penetrant greyness, we read such sudden glintings of the "older style" as: "Like a flashing ornament suspended from an infinitely high ceiling, the red-tailed hawk swung over the Biemeyer house," and "The shadows under the trees were as thick and dark as old blood." Those are *hommages* to Hammett and Chandler, no longer necessary to Macdonald, but laid into the text consciously and lovingly.

As with all committed writers, form, for Ross Macdonald, was not something to chafe against, but to transmute and develop within its own container. Through his early deference to a rigorous and conventionalized form his later, unconventional art flourished.

Inward Journey, 1984

40

Moderns

The Moderns: An Anthology of New Writing in America.
Edited by LeRoi Jones

LeRoi Jones, who has edited this volume, and who has contributed some of
his own fiction to it as well as a useful introduction, has been wise in his
decision not to make this book a "showcase" anthology, but one which presents the work of fourteen consistently interesting prose writers as index to
what has been happening in American fiction since about 1945—postwar
American fiction. It is, in these terms, a valuable volume, and one which
should receive the widest possible publicity. These men have little or no
rapport with the other literary fiction which is readily available today; they
exist in a world which seems, at first glance, to have nothing to do with the
world (suggested as true) in which Seymour Glass moves, in which Rabbit
Angstrom postures, in which Baldwin's Negroes and Mailer's "hipsters" get
drunk, laid, and bitter. To any reader of *The New Yorker* these fourteen
writers will seem to have concerns which are, if not irrelevant, at least vulgar; likewise, their styles will seem gross, precious, ineffectual, or inarticulate.

What, of course, separates the fiction of these fourteen from the fiction
of *The New Yorker* is an entire land, the United States, to be precise. Things
happen in this country which are couched in terms of the utmost brutality,
not only emotional brutality, but economic brutality, police brutality, the
sheer brutality of events. If one is a writer, one looks at this madness, this
waste and dross, and tries to put it into a prose which somehow fits prag-
matic truth. The meanderings of Updike seem absurd inside the walls of the
Tombs; or, try to tell a couple of tough Puerto Rican kids on Avenue D that
you're a sensitive plant. Mary loves John; or John will lose his job if he

227

doesn't write this distasteful ad copy; or Mary is screwing the neighbor; this all becomes ludicrous. The "terrors" of being twice-divorced and graying in one's East Seventies apartment seem waspish, if one holds them against what is happening to the souls and hearts of men who are unemployed, wasted, and graying in a furnished room in San Antonio.

What I mean is, the realities of our time are given (or at least, touched on) almost in full in *The Moderns*—they have little to do with being a poor little rich boy, or a potential "artist" trapped by job and family. The trouble with the proficient and polished prose "fiction" of our time, and I use the quotes because it is that, "fiction"—people moving from A to B to C, and then doing something, *a*, which is a climax, which leads to *b*, THE END; or, one reads fiction every day—if one reads the large-circulation magazines—which has as its concerns those things which were wrapped, tied, boxed, and given to the world for all time by Chekhov, de Maupassant, Joyce, Anderson, Hemingway . . . I was going to say, the trouble with this "fiction" is that it works in terms of those things which are the realities of the *official* malaise of our time. Who is so square as *not* to put down the FBI? Or flabby liberals, or segregation? Every diligent reader of the above-named popular, contemporary writers knows what face to put on when one of these buttons is pushed; what is difficult is to know what face to put on when, say, Creeley presses a button—his *own* button. Then our staunch *literati* fall back on their stock of glowing clichés.

O.K. This is a long-winded way of saying that the America these people deal with is an America which the middle class doesn't see and wouldn't get if it did. It makes no matter that it is a fragmented America, some of it terrifying, some brutal, some merely banal. Dawson's businessman in "The Invisible Glass" would not be recognized in the pages of *Slick*, or *Jive*, or *The Urban Chicster*; this is a guy whose *life* is on the line, I mean his *life*; it's not a story about, "oh dear, we don't love each other anymore, what to do, what to do. He turned heavily in bed." A nice warm feeling spreads over the reader, as he says, "how true." Dawson's man is in, as they say, deep trouble, *agenbite*. The book runs into, or will run into, a doubly complex hostility because not only are these men writing of ignored and/or unsavory pockets of American life, they are writing of these pockets without attempting to clue the reader in. If you don't know, lady, then . . . and etc. Which may be arrogance in a sightseeing guide, but which is necessity in a writer.

On top of this, there are hundreds (I know, to my misfortune, at least dozens) of "literate and intelligent people" who have what can only be called a non-American sensibility. People who find, say, Irwin Shaw meaningful. Or who think that the English "angry young men" are saying something useful. It's incredible to me that writers like Osborne, Wain, and Braine can have a vogue in the U.S. of A. Everything they bitch about was totally taken care of by such minor lights as Steinbeck, Fast, and Farrell years ago . . . not to mention great writers like Dreiser and Norris. It's as if these Englishmen woke up one morning and discovered that a few people have most of the money and power, and the rest have what's left; and they began to write indignantly and excitedly about this phenomenon. I've really grown bored with the old drivel about the lack of sophistication in American writing; when the limeys can get away with that sort of "protest" novel without a hiss, all I can say is "pass." The killer is that the writing in *The Moderns* will no doubt be considered "unsophisticated." That's because it doesn't move in the trappings and syntax of Evelyn Waugh or J. D. Salinger. What a bunch of saps we are, our readers are. The gradations in the official literary mind run roughly like this: the gentle writers, who really "explore" the tenderness of life, childhood, etc. are distilled in a Salinger, from whom we move to the harsh astringencies of the world-weary, like Mary McCarthy and Irwin Shaw; then we get to the real tough cookies, Mailer and Baldwin. Argghhh! Remember Plato's cave? These writers are the shadow-naming expoits, and the writers in *The Moderns* are the slobs from up in the sunlight who can't tell an ass from an elbow.

I have my preferences in this volume, but I would rather just talk about the work as an attempted delineation of the scene, here and now. Jones breaks his writers down, in his preface, into the two camps of urban and nonurban, which is o.k., but they really are so much more refined when you get into them, that I'll let that division be.

There's so much that is good in here. Many of the writers include work I have read, and many have work that is new to me, although I have become acquainted with them through other pieces in anthologies, magazines, manuscripts, etc. I might as well start from the top with Eastlake, who disappoints terribly with "The First Bomb." It's a setup, disparate people traveling together, their talk touches on those things which reveal them (but which don't, really). A compressed *Wayward Bus*. The other story, "Little Joe," is a honey, and if you think Salinger can write about kids, take a look at this dialogue, and then go buy *The Bronc People*. The *writing* brilliance of this is that it is *not* the way kids talk; it is an invented *patois* which is used as a tool to make you see these children and see the world they function in: a world within a world. How refreshing it is to come across somebody who doesn't think that a kid is a little adult. Eastlake's improbable language insists on that fact; the story also broods with the likely future of the "hero." A grim one, Little Joe is a schizoid, and things don't turn out warm and cuddly. This man is a good writer, solid constructions, a "classic" short story, which proves, too, that one can function *within* the old forms (as do Rumaker, Selby, Woolf).

I can't say enough about Edward Dorn, beautiful, beautiful, the almost

unbelievable combination of anger and compassion which works in his poetry to such great advantage shows here in three of the best stories I've ever
read; "Beauty" should be anthologized immediately in those "Best Stories"
series so that it will get the audience it deserves. This guy is going to be one
of the great American writers of our time, which statement is, I'm aware,
embarrassingly pompous.

Woolf has two wild stories that tear up some of the clichés of our life and
then burn them—both done with gentle, mocking humor, but not at all
what I'd call "good-natured." "Work in Flight Grounded" is, possibly, the
last word on the hokey insanity which is commercial air travel. The Babbitts
who never heard of Sinclair Lewis (O'Hara has it that Lewis didn't know he
was writing satire, but woke up one morning to find himself being called a
satirist and played it straight—he's got a point), and if you've ever sojourned
in a Midwestern town, you'll think that the book is on the banned list, are
spitted beautifully on Woolf's sharp prose. He's a funny man, but the laughter is a defense against the madhouse that this country is on the edge of
becoming. If you can possibly conceive of someone writing a humorously
macabre account of Lee Oswald's murder by Jack Ruby, but writing it in such
a way that it is not bitter, and not an elaborate "sick" joke, but a quiet scream
against the shabbiness of the American Way, then you've got a prose which
is close to Woolf's.

I'd never seen anything of Paul Metcalf's before, but "The Doll" is a
strange and Kafka-like story, or like the work of the Italian writer, Tommaso
Landolfi. It's not surrealism, in which all the *forms* and objects are recognizable, but are put into varying abnormal combinations—it's a nutty situation to begin with; but once granted, everything moves to its own tune, its
own logic. The feeling is like the fantastically bizarre seasickness chapter in
Céline's *Mort à Credit*. "Indian Game" disappointed me because I had heard
so much of the book from which it was taken, *Will West.* I like the movement
and technique, poems alternating with prose, but the upshot of the story, a
murder, just doesn't come off, for me; a heavy symbolism, a cause and effect
reality, which is not up to the imagination of the style.

John Rechy has three "travelogues" which I think very good, except that
I've had it when it comes to the hip author giving me the Word. The alternation between excellent and incisive observation, and a blushing kind of
naïveté also mars this work. But when he gets into *what* is seen, he's very
fine, and valuable. Also, a lovely *précis* of a typical Mexican movie is a
vehicle for some clean prose. I've not yet read *City of Night*, but it's been
put down by every swish who has a half-done faggot novel in the drawer. On
the basis of these three pieces, I'd say that Rechy has the vitality and energy
of a potentially important writer if he can get over his own need to tell the
reader of his amazement at "life." Michael Rumaker has an old piece, "Eight

Dreams," which originally appeared in *Measure*, and it acts as a bridge between his old (and "famous") stories like "The Pipe," "The Desert," "The Truck," etc., and the two new stories shown here, "The Teddy Bear," and "The Puppy." They are "deceptively simple" stories; the style is, as Mitchell Goodman has pointed out, much like Sherwood Anderson's. They also have the bare line of WCW's prose, and their concerns are much like Williams'. An anecdote about the initial breakthrough to a remote and disturbed man in a mental hospital, and an anecdote about a man (the same one?) in a cabin; he's woodshedding—from life itself. His brutal killing of a borzoi puppy serves as an entrance for him back into the world of health. These stories are very good, very strong, and it seems a pity that Rumaker has for so long been thought of as a writer whose subjects are violence and death. He wants to go another way now—O.K., then let him. The stories are quiet, sad, but in them there is hope for the protagonist(s). Flaubert has shown us how disarming such clear writing can be in "A Simple Heart." And how lasting.

The six stories by Robert Creeley are perfect; "Mr. Blue" has, of course, become a modern prose classic, and it's amazing to realize that it was written almost ten years ago. The verities of poetry, the careful placing of words in a line, their syntax, the *use* of punctuation, none of these things have been so closely attended to by any fiction writer of our time. For a small test of sincerity, set Creeley's "The Grace" against Updike's "Wife-Wooing," and see what I mean when I say that the eminently respected and successful writers of our time have simply copped out. Of the group of stories, I had never read "The Book," and it stands as a precise remark on the desperation and despair of a smashed marriage.

Years ago, when I published *Neon*, Fielding Dawson sent me an early version of "Captain America," which I rejected, and through that we got to know each other. The version presented here is the finished one, and shows Dawson's involvement with the anonymous shuttlings of the vaguely talented person in a milieu which has, as artistic apex, a self-conscious "Bohemian" clique. It's hopelessly sad. These places, these towns exist, these people dabble in the arts and make some mark on the aesthetic life of East Bohunk. Sometimes you see them in New York, the language barrier is fantastic, you don't know what in hell they're talking about when they tell you that they just last year had a one-man show in the Zippo Gallery in Joliet, or they read in the Hepcat Coffee House in downtown Memphis. "Bloodstar" has always been a favorite story of mine; it's a delicate and oblique treatment of Lesbianism, somewhat exotic perhaps, but the force of the last paragraph is inescapable. "Early in the Morning" is a tour de force which remains that no matter how you look at it. I've already noted "The Invisible Glass," which is the only example of Dawson's "new manner," and it's a more subtle and probing handling of the same vaguely "cultured" world in which Webster Groves (or Captain America, if you will) moves, only these people are not artistic and are more well-off. What Dawson has saved from his old stories, and what has always been his strength as a writer, is the use (as counterpoint to the internal action) of seemingly fragmented external action and/or dialogue. His weak stories are those in which he has forced the bizarre qualities of such apparently meaningless "happenings" to carry the load completely. He's also got away from the Chandleresque use of adjective, which is all to the good.

Hubert Selby is represented by two stories, which hardly show him at his best, which is very good. One, "A Penny for Your Thoughts," is a story done off the top of the head, and while it has as controlling idea Selby's preoccupation with unhappiness as a result of the loss of control, it fails to demonstrate the shattering power of "The Queen Is Dead" and "Strike," two great stories which will be included in his soon-to-be-published (one hopes!) *Last Exit to Brooklyn.* "Another Day Another Dollar" is one of the stories from that volume included here, and it is a clinical detailing of a stomping given to a soldier by a bunch of hoods in Brooklyn. It is a strong and honest story, and moves swiftly forward in its terrible action. The difficulty in writing of Selby's stories is that all those which are part of the not-yet-published volume are *parts* of that volume, in the truest sense, that is, the book is not a *collection* of stories—it is more like an exhaustive analysis of a Brooklyn subworld, each story adding to the total presentation. It's very difficult to remove such a small part as "Another Day Another Dollar" and say anything about it. I hope that readers will find the whole book available by the time this review sees print.

Kerouac has his old nostalgic piece, "Seattle Burlesque" here, and I've always liked it, it's Kerouac at his enthusiastic best, drunk on detail. I can't say anything about "CITYCitycity" because I haven't been able to read it yet; it just throws me. "Manhattan Sketches" is Kerouac-with-notebook in the Apple, remarks on passersby, window displays, catalogues of food in cafeterias, etc. It's O.K., but far from the Kerouac of, say, "October in the Railroad Earth," which is still, for me, his best short piece.

Burroughs is cooking on his mechanism burner here, with the cybernetics oven also turned on; it's good Burroughs, if you like Burroughs. He bugs me with his attention to technique-as-end involvements. Adroit, but . . . even the wild, the manic and grotesque humor of *Naked Lunch* is here only glimpsed.

LeRoi Jones has two excerpts from his book, *The System of Dante's Hell:* "Hypocrite(s)" and "Thieves," both of which are fiercely honest, obsessively precise catalogues of events and people from out of the narrator's childhood and young manhood. The style is loose and "informal," but perfectly fitted to the kind of easy shuttle from place to event to person here set down. The whole book should prove one of the more interesting works of fiction of the last few years. "The Screamers" is a beautiful and masterful sketch of a Negro R & B dance in Newark, ca. Illinois and Gene Ammons days, what, maybe '49 or '50? What's so beautiful here is that it is a story about *Negroes* (attention J. Baldwin and Ralph Ellison et al.). I've been to a lot of local Brooklyn dances in my day, with the same sort of youths attending, but they were white; the dances were *not* like this one, although the probability of violence often became real. Jones is probably the best writer on the kind of urban Negro I am contemporary with—or, to make that clearer, his Negroes are black. The cats in this story are what my dear old buddies used to call jigaboos; that Jones has refused to invest them with some spurious white-artistic-intellectual "heart" is to his credit; he's an honest man. How can I say this? If you called one of these cats a spook, or a jig, he wouldn't say something like, "but I've got a B.A. from Columbia," nor would he say, "that's a nasty and foul name." He'd probably let you have it. It's only in the last ten years or so that the genteel and "literate" (there's that word again) reading public has been shot full of the idea that a Negro is some sort of potential white man . . . while the lower classes, e.g., *the poor*, know that this is rubbish, and simply a lie; the lie has been compounded and spread by the popular Negro *writers*, which seems to me a shameful thing. As if a Negro has to be an "educated, intelligent, and well-spoken individual" to have his *rights*. LeRoi Jones is a man who has made into literature what most other Negro writers have made into a white man's fondly cherished chimera. Or, if I may be allowed a parallel: an Irish bartender I know told me that the Irish writer whom he utterly loathes is Frank O'Connor because his stories are designed for an English public; he makes up stage Irishmen in a stage Ireland for an English audience, who think it all just too delightful—"quaint" old Ireland.

Diane DiPrima has three tiny stories which are interesting for their acerbity, but their "points" are obvious and rather too assiduously thrust upon one. They have twists of irony laid carefully in via a Hemingway-like diction, but they aren't phony; too carefully "prepared" perhaps. "Southwest" has the tone and movement of Jones' sections of *Dante*; but the interests are hazy and surreal, although the writing develops a power not shown in the short pieces. It's maybe too determinedly literary for me; I'm a mark for a story in which *things* happen to *people*.

The last writer in the book is Russell Edson, with pieces from a long work, *Gulping's Recital*. There is a heavy reliance here on the kind of fatalistic attitude of nihilism and sterility one may extract from the world Beckett presents. The writing is clever and accomplished, and the piece called "The Soldier" moves with a grim intensity which reminds me of the scene in which Molloy painfully circles his house on his one crutch.

That's the book; and as I said earlier, it's a carefully selected representation of what has been happening in the last fifteen years or so, here in the United States. I expect its reception to be hostile, snide, and barbed; George Simon will have a field day with it, reassuring the readers of *The Hudson Review* that it's all the product of ignorant and illiterate minds. But to the curious student of contemporary America, its life as well as its letters, *The Moderns* is an excellent Baedeker.

Kulchur, 1964

41

Ten Pamphlets

State of the Union. By Aimé Césaire
Lachrymae Mateo. By Clayton Eshleman
Sing-Song. By Paul Blackburn
Crystals. By Frank Samperi
Definitions. By David Antin
The Galilee Hitch-Hiker. By Richard Brautigan
Voyages. By Robin Magowan
Living with Chris. By Ted Berrigan. Drawn by Joe Brainard
Identikit. By Jim Brodey
Aloud. By Bill Dodd

From what I understand, *State of the Union* is the first collection of Aimé Césaire's poems to appear in English. This small book, jointly translated from the French by Clayton Eshleman (who is the general editor of the Caterpillar series) and Denis Kelly, selects poems published by Césaire between 1947 and 1960. I haven't the French before me to check against, but the collection has a unanimity of tone and language that convinces. Césaire is a kind of modern "surrealist" (if that term has any currency), and the brutal anger against colonialism and exploitation displayed in many of these poems finds a language which is curiously more effective than bald propaganda.

> When they grab my leg
> I hurl back a jungle of lianas
> Let them lynch me
> I vanish into a row of figs.

And:

> It's not pigment powder
> not myrrh
> a pensive fragrance or delectation
> but flower of blood on flower of skin.

The last lines of the title poem ask a question we're all of us white men going to have to answer, and soon:

> in the 180th year of these states
> but what in the heart unfeeling clock
> nothing zero what not a drop of blood
> left in the putrid white
> antiseptic heart?

It's simply not enough to set "Love" against that bitter query. There are some poems that seemed intolerably thick to me in sense of language, but I don't know if that's Césaire or not; and one poem has the line "LIFT UP YOUR HANDS," which seems, given the context, as if it should read "HANDS UP!" But it is a remarkably rich and cogent collection, with great energy and vitality.

Some years ago, I recall reviewing Mr. Eshleman's first book, *Mexico & North*, in a disparaging way. I remember it being one of those books which could neither be praised nor damned: the poems were "well written" and worked, but totally lacking in juice. Well, something has happened to Mr. Eshleman since that time, for this little book of three poems has a great deal of strength and authority. I believe these poems, and Eshleman here has a voice and position of singularity:

> vaginal flap
> headgear, ballturret of the jet
> that is by mercy
> arrested in flight

The difference between this really elegant line and the work in the first book is in a reliance on the poem to seek its own shape, whereas *Mexico & North* was forever *telling* me something, i.e., laying on me a narrative point of view, with Care—lest I not respond. These poems stick themselves up at you, take them or leave them.

As everyone who reads poetry knows, Paul Blackburn can do just about anything he wants in the poem. He changes his diction, voice, cadence; the lines are, many times, projected by a wiseguy accomplice of Blackburn's who may, at any minute, become the poet. What is constant, however, is a wry, flat statement of the world: ah God, what a hopeless place it is, after all. The poem "Do That Medieval Thing Again, Baby":

> Love is a weakness, a
> sickness, a fear & a terror, and—
> I love I can do that
> and risk
> that evil thing
> wherein our own heart go forth from us

sets a basic theme upon which Blackburn plays his changes. The last poem of the six in this pamphlet has a great staggering sweetness of hopeful futility, like, what's the use?—nevertheless!

> I'll be all the warmth and music of words I can
> to women and to men

Frank Samperi has been, for some years, deeply influenced by Zukofsky. His first book, *Song Book*, was a running down of Zukofsky's music, a patient and meticulous application of technique. This book contains a short essay of philosophical bent, followed by a clutch of poems. The essay is fragmented, almost like notes, and deals with, loosely, ways of knowing. It is interesting insofar as Samperi comes out of such thought into his brief and crystalline verse. But the poems are still heavily engaged with Zukofsky; from the prose of the essay, I looked for a "denser" poem, but find here this:

> here's
> a
> cherry
> spray
>
> for
> each
> of
> you
>
> —could
> n't
> find
> any

birds;
they've
flown
to

woods

I cannot see why Samperi should persist in this. It seems to me as self-de-
structive as crafting the end-stop couplet, or the endemic stubbornness of
the Audenesque poem which keeps cropping up in the academic quarterlies.
I would suggest that Zukofsky has had great success in the control of such
short-lined verse because of the application of a unique and bone-dry intelligence; i.e., his songs are songs because the intelligence plays within the
movement of the lines. Would anyone ever consider Zukofsky to be a singer
such as Campion or Herrick? There is little attempt at simplicity in Zukofsky's work; his music is difficult and rings as much because of his placement
of ideas as it does because of his ear. This work of Samperi's strikes me as
exercise. Certainly sure, certainly talented, but essentially a use of a music
which cannot be profitably separated from its intellectual motivation. I
would like to see Samperi break open his poem, fall into carelessness, if it
should come to that, and work from that into what he must surely be, as
himself. Not these delicate projections, essentially precious. If they were set
to music they would still, I feel, lack strength.

David Antin makes his poems out of materials from Wittgenstein, insur-
ance handbooks, intelligence of nerve gases, and other "found" materials.
I rather like what he is doing here; some of the verse becomes remarkably
effective in its ordering, destruction, reordering, juxtaposition. Part III of
the poem "Black Plague," based on a selection from Wittgenstein, is a
perfect example of his methodology. I see here, though, such a deliberate
structuring of the poem; the lines are set down in heavy configuration of
declaration, many of them flat sentences which rely for their poetic power
on the changes, made almost as declensions, which Mr. Antin works. It
would be curious to see what he might do if he fought this material instead
of using it wholesale—de Kooning as against Lichtenstein. But I cannot
recall seeing this kind of poem written better or with more dexterity and
skill.

Richard Brautigan, the remarkable comic novelist, who is the author of
A Confederate General from Big Sur and *Trout Fishing in America*, has here
a book reprinted from the original White Rabbit edition of 1958. It has nine
short poems which take their shape from quotations from Baudelaire, and
from the kind of residue in the reader's mind concerning his recollection of
Baudelaire's life—or what we take his life to have been, relying on his

poems. Sometimes they work and sometimes they don't. The perfect poem is the second one, "The American Hotel."

> Baudelaire and the wino
> were drinking Petri Muscatel.
> "One must always be drunk," said Baudelaire.
> "I live in the American Hotel," said the wino. "And I can
>   remember dinosaurs."
> "Be you drunken ceaselessly," said Baudelaire.

—which is really a kind of comic genius. It might be useful to note that these poems have a sense of "camp" about them, clearly manifested, and much more intriguing than what is now going down as wit. (I saw some offal the other day, *Pop Poems* or the like, which must have been written by a plumber.) But they are very subtle and literary, and function dryly.

Robin Magowan's *Voyages* is wordy and somehow musty, poems go on and on, long after the reader is finished with them. There is a great deal of physical description of place, occurrence, action, which sits there on the page and which one expects to somehow function—then the poem ends, and we see that *that* exactly *is* the poem. Sometimes there's a strange twist, an energy is displayed in some fast and purple cadences, but then the poem gets back to its plod. Here are some lines which emerge in a poem called "The Elysians" that are as good as anything in the book.

> Suddenly we stop stamp three times knocking
> We are entering
> One with the stalks, the blue
> Leaping dead, whose tongues
> Are a bright liquorice of poppies
> Breasts that tinkle bells, fins,
> Trees, sunken sky over which we mount, drawn
> As on a last tide of sunlight, the horses
> Behind us, blood red . . .

—and then the poem reverts to an undistinguished clutter of describing. There are a lot of pretty, studied similes, many of them worked in with the phrase "as on" or "as in." They dull the poem and give it a weird archaic feel, almost as if Magowan is translating from a nineteenth-century text.

Not much to say about *Living with Chris*, because it's a picture-poem; a few lines of verse to a page, each page also containing a drawing, comic-strip genre, by Joe Brainard. Berrigan is a second-generation "New York school" poet, author of *The Sonnets*, a notable book, and this is a puff. Whatever value it has is inseparable from its presentation. It cannot be reviewed.

In his Notes to Identikit Jim Brodey says: "Daily the work grew more com-plicated until finally in some version I became so immersed in what was happening in words that I began to literally be torn loose from my own mind when writing and wrote with no thoughts or patterns or 'sense' of what I was doing." The poem is constructed from workbooks kept over ten months and Brodey also tells us that each section of this poem "was to have been followed ... with a long Coda, setting down how I felt or thought or dreamed or saw the work contained within the individual section." But these "Codas" were never included.

I wish that they had been included. Brodey is into a kind of automatic surrealistic writing here, which makes no pattern that I can see. The work does not cohere. Does Brodey want it to? Does he care? I don't want to get into that old rut about the poet's "need to communicate" because it's really so much trash. But is the poetic language vitiated when its very architecture, its syntax, is really totally garbled? Burroughs, who certainly works poeti-cally, has specifically disarranged his materials in order to splinter meaning and response, to "cut word lines" and come into control of language beyond the "media" possession of it. But Burroughs is intelligible in the sense of language's formal desire to be so. Brodey constantly throws me, I am opened up, but to what purpose? My own, comes one easy answer, *not* the poet's. If Brodey wants that, he succeeds; i.e., he loses all hold on his poem and it becomes everyone's province. Each man his own poet, except here we are out of the stuffy and moribund "interpretation" bag, and into "feeling." There are plenty of interesting elements in *Identikit*, a very exotic sense of rhythm and placement of noun; but I have to think of them finally as just that, elements, from which Brodey can make poems. These are investigative notes out of which the poet must create poems.

Bill Dodd's *Aloud* is a collection of poems read aloud, composed, that is, on the tape recorder and then transcribed. Dodd feels that the *writing* of the poem, that physical act, spoils his sense of the poem's truth. He says, in "A Note on Oral Composition":

> Activity of sound
> voice diffused by the eye's considerations and the strength and
> or weakness of back, arm, hands cramped.

O.K., I'm not going to carp with anybody's method of composition, but it would seem to me that if the poet feels his sound, his voice, is sullied by the fact that he has to get it out of him and onto paper, then he is not sure of that voice; and certainly the use of another machine, a tape-recorder, will not make him surer. In transcribing, one must arbitrarily cut the line. If one follows the breathing patterns, fine. But one follows the breathing patterns when engaged in writing as well. The alternative to transcription is the rereading of the poem, aloud, during which line corrections are made. There's another interesting note of Dodd's. He says, "Too visual, my sense, to begin with, that long misled me." It might be that the sense which most intrudes itself on the poet is that sense which should be, not avoided, but exploited. The poems are clear enough, a little loose and rambling for me, which might be because of the ease of tape-recorder availability. In a long poem called "Mt. Shasta," he spoils a description of his emotional state upon first seeing the mountain by ending it with

> ah, this is the
> nature that I speak about, this is where it's at.

That casual colloquialism damages his seriousness of intent irrevocably. But there *is*, on the whole, that seriousness to Dodd. He speaks with a great deal of feeling about nature, about his own terrible loneliness, about the conflict between the beauties of rural America and the soul-murdering populace therein. For the recognition of that fact alone, I would commend Dodd to you: because if the poet is maimed in the cities, and wasted in the sticks, then where is he? Bill Dodd is an honest man, afflicted at this time, I think, by a somewhat affected "naturalism."

Poetry, 1968

42

Black Mountaineering

The Black Mountain Review, 1–8
Numbers. By Robert Indiana and Robert Creeley
The First Decade: Selected Poems, 1940–1950,
Derivations: Selected Poems, 1950–1956,
Roots and Branches. By Robert Duncan
Olson/Melville: A Study in Affinity. By Ann Charters
Causal Mythology,
Maximus Poems IV, V, VI. By Charles Olson.

It is difficult to remember the isolation a writer such as I felt in the fifties. The sense, the absolute insistence upon the fact that one had no peers that were of use or interest seemed depressingly clear. There were magazines, of course: they made the young writer even more depressed. Not only was there no hope of being represented in their pages, but that writer whose learning had come from the tradition of Williams and Pound knew that his work, scattered and inchoate, had no relation to the narrowly conceived policies of these respected journals. There were attempts to provide showcases for the "new writers"—I think of Discovery and New World Writing—but it turned out that these publications were edited by men who accepted the given of that time and were simply looking for more of the same, albeit by different names. Then there were the "experimental" little magazines that would publish anything—anything at all. Meanwhile, one worked in a kind of numb solitude, unpublished and unread, and, more to the point, without access to those works that could have acted as direction and buttress to one's own false starts and scribblings. How fantastic it was, then, to see the Black Mountain Review: a journal that not only presented the work of men who shared one's concerns, but that established a ground on which the American writer could stand. It was, or so it seemed, against the grain. Now, of course, we see that it was in the grain, and much of the work that was treated with such exaggerated respect between 1945 and 1960 has revealed itself to be aberrant, nontraditional, and essentially frivolous in its concerns. I mean to say that the viability and energy of that work done by Pound, Williams, Zukofsky, Oppen, H.D., Dahlberg, et al., *surfaced* in the *Black Mountain Review* in the verse and prose of a generation of writers that had been "officially" looked for by the entire literary establishment. Of course, when they showed up, nobody in that establishment knew they had arrived. It wasn't many years ago that Olson was called "an aging beatnik." Duncan is still referred to as an "experimental" poet, and so on and on. But the recognition of that ground was instantaneous to those who, like myself, had thought of their own conceptions of the poem as freakish. There it was, this magazine, clearly new, clearly arrogant, with a first issue that contained Olson's brilliant essay on Robert Duncan, "Against Wisdom As Such," and an attack on Theodore Roethke, thought of by many people as a major American poet.

A ground to walk on, a force, an encouragement for all young writers who felt themselves to be disenfranchised. So that it was a gathering place for all of them, whether they were published in it or not. It was indeed a subversive magazine, partly because its thrust into letters was positive; that is, the sense, the entire tone of the magazine posited the value of its own concerns; it was not a journal that devoted itself to a derogation of that work against which it was set; rather, it gave you Olson, it gave you Duncan, it gave you Burroughs, it gave you Rumaker and Selby. There was the example before you of its beliefs. It proved, along with *Origin*, which was neither as catholic nor as intelligent, the proposition that with the end of the war the dominance of an effete, academic, and European-oriented literature was also ended.

It is beautiful to me that the magazine has been so justified; that is, that those writers who appeared in its pages should show, now, as teachers of the young. That so many of them have been proved masters is obvious; what is more important is that those who have disappeared, or failed, left this residue, contributed a poem, a review, whatever, still valuable in trying to understand exactly where and how the unaffiliated made a stand. This is, of course, a tribute to the intelligence of the editor, Robert Creeley, a man who somehow got this fantastic engine going, and who edited each issue into a complete statement of *the fact*. As Creeley has said elsewhere, the writers of that time needed the dignity of their own statement—and this magazine provided it. The dignity of *their* own statement, not the dignity of *one's* own statement in some hostile context, that is, Duncan in, let's say, *The Hudson Review* of that time. Creeley clumped together the most disparate literary intelligences of the time, clear in the knowledge that they formed a true configuration of the new letters.

From which consideration, we should take up Mr. Creeley, and this small luxury edition of ten poems, done in conjunction with Robert Indiana, who contributes ten number-serigraphs. The poems all appear in Creeley's new collection, *Pieces*; and they are brilliant: it is Creeley at the very top of his form. It is perhaps impolitic to say so, but there has been a great deal of muttering—much of it contented muttering—about the "bankruptcy" of Creeley's verse since the publication of his book *Words*. Such a poem as he writes has become suspect, perhaps, in this time of the longer and more loosely constructed poem. But I see *Words* as an interim book, a resting, if that can be the case for a poet, before the reassertion of that glittering strength I have come to think of as Creeley's own particular gift to the American poem. *Numbers* is certainly no book on which to base a judgment of the poet's current productions, but there is enough here to show that *Words* was a collection of confrontations with those elements of the poem that fell, so it seemed, so simply to Creeley in his earlier work. What kind of continuance from *The Whip*, *A Form of Women*, and *For Love*? None—but a hard, a very hard coming to grips with the fundamentals of this art that seems never to yield simply. The poems in *Words* that were praised were those we had come to think of as the kind of poems that Creeley would write—those that were rejected or ignored were those that revealed this descent into the bases of the language given him—to *see* how, after all, it *worked*. Now, with *Numbers*, the poem has subtly changed its movement, it is less constricted stanzaically, it is more elliptical; it is that poem we admired in *The Whip* settled, dear God, more irrevocably into its own statement of the poet's intelligence. I love the man's work because of the honesty of its own darkness, my failing perhaps. That there *is* guilt, and a certain lost innocence, and that it is personal, in one's own life. So Creeley finds these exact words:

> When they were
> first made, all the
> earth must have
> been their reflected
> bodies, for a moment—
> a flood of seeming
> bent for a moment back
> to the water's glimmering—
> how lovely they came.

It becomes even clearer to me that Creeley has been the bridge from Williams to us. How to say this? He has made that work accessible to us; he has made it usable. It is Creeley who has made the forms and structures of

Williams' poems available to us in terms of our own necessities and desires. The problem, in those early days, was to carry the acute perceptions and linguistic inventions of Dr. Williams into a postwar America. The sensibility that informed those poems—faced with Charlie Parker. What to do? How to do it? There were the many imitations of Williams, a borrowing of that sensibility, nothing worked. Creeley's early poems took all the vitality of that work and translated it into a language that his contemporaries could read. His "ducks in the pond, ice cream and beer" in an old, lost poem are the images (and Spicer will teach you that they *are* images) of an America rootless, caught up finally to the America Williams saw and recorded in those despised poems he wrote—for hardly anyone—for thirty years. Did we think he was kidding when he said "By the road to the contagious hospital"?—and then Creeley said, "What should the young / man say, because he is buying / Modess?" Images of America, not in ideas but in the absolutes of real things. This is a bitter country and its bitterness persists beyond one's momentary content.

So, *Numbers* shows the poet at his work, so that anyone interested can understand. But read *Pieces* and see how these ten poems function therein. The serigraphs by Robert Indiana are decorative and unnecessary. The note by Dieter Honisch has such malarkey as "they represent an American generation that has done away with the self-coding that was in vogue in the fifties, and they take a new approach toward reality. They celebrate life— love, eating, drinking, friendship—in a simple language. An easy, folksonglike mood typifies their works which are crammed with life." None of this is the fact.

Reading Robert Duncan's three books—two new and one reissued—we have the opportunity to chart the development of a master. It is strange that, as I have mentioned, this mastery has been so often treated as "experiment." Duncan himself says, "I am not an experimentalist or an inventor, but a derivative poet," on the back cover of *Roots and Branches*; yet the flap of *Derivations* says, "This second volume covers his most experimental and prolific period." And there have been many critics and reviewers who, faced with what is clearly the work of a richly gifted man, admit this work with the qualification that it is experimental. This is a subtly derogatory word and may be taken to be a euphemism for that work which cannot be called "serious." Let me go into this a little bit. Had Duncan focused his poetics on poems like "The Venice Poem" and "An Essay at War"—that is, continued to write in this luminous vein, a brilliant and single vision, I submit that he would have been accorded all the honors the literary establishment could afford. Perhaps not all the honors, but a meaty bone or two. But he went from these remarkable poems to a total confrontation with the poem as an instrument whereby the poet is relieved: he stands outside of himself.

The Stein imitations and *Writing Writing* develop the problem, if you will, of reality as itself and reality as it is created in the poem: they make a specific statement so that the poem is constructed as a province apart, and wherein the imagination revealed in the structure of the poem is real. The imagination is real. Williams said that "only the imagination is real," which statement does not mean, it seems to me, that the imagination can extend itself beyond the ongoing language given the poet to work with. That is, simile as "artistic" ornament is still a form of verbal garbage whereby the poem is dirtied, no matter the poet's insistence on the simile as a figure that carries his imaginative thought. If the imagination is to be real in the poem, that is, if the words themselves are real, and not counters for reality—well, then the poet has his work cut out for him. "Losing ourselves in the otherness of what is written," Duncan says. Because, contemporary propaganda notwithstanding, the poem is not a tool but a manifestation of the poet's imagination that is absolutely real; and as it is composed, it becomes an "otherness." It is no longer ours, but it is an artifact. Unfortunately for metaphysics, politics, and religion, it *is* an artifact, it is itself, an otherness. "And vast as the language is, it is no end but a resistance through which a poem might move. . . ." The poet knows that fearful pleasure when he gives the language its head and sees the poem embody the foreign elements, the unknowns, of his imagination. "I attempt the discontinuities of poetry. To interrupt all sure course of my inspiration." So that the imagination courses forth to find itself structured into art.

The Stein imitations, which have been justly celebrated, are not only remarkably successful as a tour de force, they complement the poems of *Writing Writing* and of *Letters* (also included, in full, in *Derivations*) in their insistence on the word within the poem as final poetic reality. In *Letters*, the poet says, "As we start the sentence we notice that birds are flying thru it; phrases are disturbd where these wings and calls flock; wings are a wind, featherd, a beating of the air in passage or a word, the word 'word,' hovers, sailing before dropping down the empty shafts of sense toward. . . ." The explanation of the poem is the poem, it sets up its resonances in its own structure, it arranges its correspondences. It is worth noting that the teaching of Jack Spicer seems, in the poems of *Derivations*, to be most clear.

I see in the exquisite beauty of Duncan's work the configuration of the true poet who has wrought it. A man who at first fought doggedly with that work so that it would make sense of, and bring some order to his life; but the development of this work admits a graph of surrender to the fact that the writing of poems brings order to and makes sense of—only the poem. As the poet himself writes in a note on *The First Decade*, quoting his own "The Venice Poem":

> Never in living
> but here, here,
> all felt things are
> permitted to speak.

Confronted by this sublime intransigence, what else can a rhymester do but call this work experimental? Duncan is in service and bondage to The Art of Poetry, so that his very career is an affront to those who conceive of this art as a "part of" their lives. We look for Duncan in his poems, where else? "The poet's intelligence is made manifest in his poem," Williams says: this truth must be driven home, it seems clear. If the poem is stale and false, thus the poet's intelligence. Exeunt hundreds of scribblers, fading away with "But I meant to say" on their lips.

In *Roots and Branches*, Duncan writes:

> —the poet's voice, a whole beauty of the man Olson,
>   lifting us up into
>
> where the disturbance is, where the words
>   awaken
> sensory chains between being and being,

stating, here, that "disturbance" is a quality of the poem necessary to its success. The poem, as it exists between poet and reader, as it is alive in both the writing and the reading, is, in fact, a disturbance, one that awakens us, or irritates us into attention. It disturbs and allows us release from our tired and tried ways of seeing, so that the language itself is a way of seeing, is sight itself. I think that for Duncan there is no understanding or recognition of the real unless it can be so seen in the language of the poem. This book, *Roots and Branches*, along with the one published previously to it, *The Opening of the Field*, display the great power of the poet, a full use of those materials tested in fire in the poems written between 1949 and 1956. The poems show a strength and beauty which place them among the major literature of this time.

> Who left the notes accusing himself
> of being me? In the morning
> I was relieved of what knowledge?
>
> lifted by angels that are
> rays of the actual sun
> out of the solitary.

Yet these leavings, these
shreds behind day light,
of women's bodies, dismemberd lives,

renderd hideous, where they were
attackt, these hackt
remnants, partly devourd. I cannot say

clear what I so feard
and could not go back to see. These
back of furniture in deserted rooms

decaying, these too? O are these too?
returnd to the day's light?
the sun's rays?

The last poem of *Letters* contains this:

Every nation has as spectacles of the victory of its language those victims the
song claims, men who turnd their attentions and paid the exactions the language demands. For all who enter that kingdom hear a glamor and see a ruin—
out of themselves. And leave the language reshaped to embody their ordinary
words as poetic speech.

Ann Charters' book is valuable to those readers who have but a slight
acquaintance with Olson's work, and none at all with the commentary on
it by such men as Edward Dorn, Robert Duncan, and Robert Creeley. But
it is one of those books that rise and fall in interest, the heights being excerpts from the work of the subject himself, and the depths, sadly, being the
critic's own commentary. But I see Mrs. Charters struggling with this com-
plicated man and deciding to make one facet of his work crystalline; it is a
primer, really, but it should get the reader away from it as fast as possible to
the work itself. I don't want to draw up a catalogue of things that Mrs.
Charters presents, but it is worth noting that certain of Olson's conceptions
are traceable to the scholastic philosophers' conception of *quidditas*, the
"whatness" of things. Mrs. Charters is wide-eyed about this, as if it is a
strange idea. She says that Olson's "concerns are those of a philosopher,"
which is not true. She speaks of Olson's methodology as one that juxtaposes
facts and parts to "create a multi-layered texture as complex in its intuited
interactions as the experience of life itself," which, while so, is a structural
device employed by much classical modern literature. She will say: "Olson's
similes, like Melville's, are Homeric—hyperbole, larger than life." There is
nothing larger than life for Olson, nor Melville, nor Homer. And, "Olson

is a visionary, and the characteristic of a visionary is that he sharply limits what he sees. In the last two sections of *Call Me Ishmael*, Olson focuses only on the tragic aspects of Melville's life." Melville *had* a tragic life. And there is more. But, as I said, Mrs. Charters points out those works of Olson's that are important not only to an understanding of his view of Melville; they are important also to an understanding of Olson. The most valuable part of the book is the postscript, which is a lecture given by Olson at Black Mountain in 1956. From that lecture, let me take a rubric, if you will, for a few notes on *Maximus IV, V, VI*.

"One can define an act of art as a vector which, having become private and thus acquired vision, ploughs the vision back by way of primordial things. Only thus can it have consequence." And, later, he says, "the objective immortality of actual occasions requires the primordial permanence of form, whereby the creative advance ever re-establishes itself endowed with initial creation of the history of one's self." Now let me jump over to *Causal Mythology*, a lecture given at Berkeley in 1965. "The Earth, then, is conceivably a knowable, a seizable, a single, and *your* thing." And, "As I said, I have arrived at a point where I really have no more than to feed on myself." And in "Billy the Kid," an essay which appears in *Human Universe*, this: "What strikes one about the history of sd States both as it has been converted into story and as there are those who are always looking for it to reappear as art—what has hit me is, that it does stay, unrelieved. And thus loses what it was before it damn well was history, what urgency or laziness or misery it was to those who said and did what they did. Any transposition which doesn't have in it an expenditure at least the equal of what was spent, diminishes what was spent. And this is loss, loss in the present, which is the only place where history has context." So, presented with these brief quotes, we get a sense of the plan of Olson's *Maximus*. A remedy whereby the past may be "relieved"; the poet must push and tear, thus, at Gloucester, as *polis*, so that it give up to him its unrelieved past:

1. Gloucester is not in Europe, it is not of that historical past, and the poet is in Gloucester—it is his city.

2. Its shaping force and reason for being is ocean (*Okeanos*) and the fruits thereof. And the dangers. The sense of the sea: people who are born and raised on the coast have a totally different sense of the world than those who are born inland—believe it. See, throughout *Maximus*, Olson's clear writing on storms through which men sail. Here, read "3rd letter on Georges, unwritten."

3. The materials of Gloucester's history are freed by the intercession of the poet, who orders, *not* by his ego, but by the sense of himself in this city, part of its continuing process, history here, not as a sense of time past, but

as present to us as time in space: "the objective immortality of actual occasions," that is, the past is *here*, "in the present, the only place where history has context."

Thus, Olson telling you for himself, in "Letter 27":

> An American
> is a complex of occasions,
> themselves a geometry
> of spatial nature.
>
> I have this sense,
> that I am one
> with my skin
>
> Plus this—plus this:
> that forever in the geography
> which leans in
> on me I compell
> backwards I compell Gloucester
> to yield, to
> change
>   Polis
> is this

—stating the three concerns of this major undertaking.

So we see that the simple allusions to *The Cantos* and *Paterson* are not precise; are, in fact, incorrect. Pound insists on time to yield to him, he walks through time, he goes back into it; Williams takes Paterson as a repository of American corruption, the breaking down of the sweet gifts of nature by the Puritan ethic, linked with the commercial, but finds his hope in art. (But in *Paterson Five*, however, goes out of Paterson to find it.) Olson has attempted in this poem to replace the ego as the force which drives into history with the poetic intelligence as receptacle, into which history flows and is carried by the vector of art into the present. So Olson's care for Herodotus as against Thucydides. The former acting on history, finding out, his self *in* it; and the latter, the camera or tape recorder, "just the facts, ma'am," which are *just* the facts, that is, what is *not* recorded also *happened*. And stays unrelieved. Which the poet relieves by the word, an entity, the absolute key; that is, if it cannot be said, it is not. Olson writes, "one can't do anything right without the right words to go with it."

Now let me end this by, perhaps, getting myself in trouble. Olson holds the most delicate balance; the poem teeters, always, that is: I see Olson as a lyric poet, in both senses of that term. But a lyric poet who selected the long poem in which to make his most important statement. But on the one hand, his "lyrics," his songs, are a falling backward, as another poet once termed it; and in those pieces of *Maximus* I see Olson's ego come clear, wrench itself loose from that denial of ego so otherwise apparent here. On the other hand, we hear the lyrical voice, the man himself speaking, not *into* history, but as a part of historical incident, reacting to the incidents also around him. What I am trying to get at here is that Olson, along with the other achievements of his career, has given us a new sense of the lyric; that is, that it is possible for a man to say "I" in his poem and have that "I" considered as part of the space and time of history: the "I" carries the event into the present and is a strangely natural "I": it is a rock, or it can range about freely as the seas. But I also love the contradictory—if it be so—song we are given as gift. We are dealing here with a very remarkable artist, and with a sensibility that makes the process of the poem inestimably richer.

Poetry, 1970

43

Empty, Empty
Promises, Promises

> For a month and a half Joyce remained in the
> correspondence department. . . . He had to write
> between two hundred and two hundred and fifty
> letters a day. . . . The effect was to wear out his
> trousers. He had two large patches on them, and
> to conceal these he had to keep on his tailcoat even
> during the August heat.
>
> Richard Ellmann, *James Joyce*

This picture of the young James Joyce in 1906, working as a clerk in a Roman bank, might as well serve as a rubric for this piece, which will deal with capitalism: "Does capitalism do anything beautiful for us? Can it create anything of lasting value in the arts? Can it do beautiful things?" Joyce, in his ragged patched pants, sweating in Rome, surrounded by money—what is that but the true Joycean touch, right out of *Finnegans Wake*? It could be, in fact, another stroke in his portrait of Shem the Penman. It has the elements of darkly comic Irish humor: the ne'er-do-well artist with brain afire. In a minute he'll get drunk, sing a dirty song, and fall on his face.

The reader will see that my conception of capitalism has to do only with its effect on the single, the unique, human being. Or let me put it this way: I'll give you the Seagram Building if you'll bring back Baudelaire and give him a hundred dollars a week. Capitalism in its relationship to the arts is like love: it has no meaning worth our attention once it moves out of that area in which real people with real faces, bodies, and names live. Abstract ideas are at the root of wars, famine, and destruction. Think of the sins of nationalism. Did you ever eat a nationalism? Capitalism is the same smeary sort of thing. It cannot really *do* anything for Tom, Dick, or Harry. It is a kind of idea into which power can crawl. One can then expect it to do things; one can insist that it produces a William Calley, as one can insist that Marxism produced Stalin. If you believe this, you believe in "historical inevitability." I can't hear you as you ride away on your hobby-horse.

A configuration to ponder: the Metropolitan Museum and the Marlborough Galleries. What is going on here? Millions being traded back and forth, men who probably have a great deal of trouble sewing on a button or sweeping a floor raking in sawbucks by the pound. It's all business. And right over here, ladies and gents, some numbskull of a painter ("Who *asked* him to be a painter?" a voice grumbles) who can't make the rent for a studio big enough for him to paint and house his family in. "Tell it to the Marines," do I hear you say? Okay. If this equation doesn't say capitalism plus art equals many rich dealers and one broke painter, what does it say?

Don't get me wrong. I don't think that government, whatever that is, should "subsidize" the artist. Government tends to think in terms of things being useful, and with art, they are lost in the stars. "We'll put that dam right over here, Charlie, right? Then the valley will be green, the floods, etc., everything wonderful, right! Now, this poem—what about this damn thing? Get it out to the People! Right! A little culture, a little beauty! Brighten the corner where you are! By God, it's as good as a regular-guy priest and Bob Hope rolled into one if we play our cards right!" The idea is that art is a hammer or saw that is used to build culture and hope and high thoughts in the minds and hearts of the unwashed. Well, I say to hell with it. Art is no missionary casting about for souls to save, nor an entertainer traveling far and wide to laugh it up. If you want it, you have to go and get it—it's distressingly still. It's also useless. You say your marriage is breaking up, you have a bleeding ulcer, your son is a heroin addict? Here's a Van Gogh—take a good look at it. Right! Now, read these poems by this guy, what's-his-name. Rimbaud. Now, how do you feel? Your marriage is worse than ever? Your stomach is burning through your belt buckle? Your son ran away from Synanon? Van Gogh and poor Arthur didn't do anything for you, is that it? It's no surprise—one always suspected that artists couldn't pull their weight.

Art has no use. Art is beautiful. Art is beholden to no man. Art is also made by artists. Ah, there's the rub. These latter eat, sleep, need warmth in winter, clothes, etc. Patches on their pants, all the rest. Whatever the

noble plumber needs, so does the noble poet. "Capitalism" doesn't do anything for this obscure human being except allow him to work at a job that
will pay the rent and buy his chuck steak. It does for the artist what it does
for any man. As far as its doing "beautiful things," it may do them by default,
or accidentally. If Chase Manhattan wants some art on its officers' walls,
then the painter who made this art gets some money. (There is a chance he
might even be a good painter.) Chase Manhattan gets some money to the
artist. This is known as Capitalism in Action. But who can care about the
fact of the pictures on the bank's walls? Chase Manhattan should have pictures of currency on its walls, or far-seeing past directors, eyes fixed on the
Eternal Truths, or even group photos like those great images of corn one sees
in saloons in places like Brooklyn—you know the kind I mean (or do you?
Hello! Are there any people out there who were born and raised in New
York? Hello? Hello?): GALLAGHER'S 12TH ANNUAL CLAMBAKE,
RYE BEACH. In the pictures are longshoremen, cops, firemen, truck driv-
ers, mailmen and assorted clerkish losers from the "financial district" smiling
drunkenly through the boilermaker haze and sunlight, their wives gallantly
supporting them. Well, there's no art there, brother, nor should there be,
just as there should be none on the walls of Chase Manhattan's offices. I
mean to say that a Clyfford Still would be just as ridiculous on Chase Manhattan's wall as on Gallagher's. If you don't believe me, ask Still.

I see myself in those offices, pictures worth a half-million dollars glittering
beneath their ten thousand dollars' worth of special lighting. I have a hole
in my hat, no job, sixty bucks in the bank, and my only collateral, as my
dear mother used to say, is my right arm with the blood dripping. I'm looking
for a loan to pay the rent. Then I say "I'm a writer," the magic words that
propel me into the street—courteously, of course. Once there, I can look at
the Seagram Building, brought to you by Capitalism, Inc. Somehow, capitalism has failed me, and I produce this same art Chase Manhattan reveres
in one of its many forms. But their taste! Their sensibility! Their love and
care! Can it be that capitalism and art go hand in hand only if one of the
hands is not made of flesh and blood?

In any event, I'm an artist, for better or worse. I've had many jobs, hard
and easy, reasonably boring and crushingly so. In this way I have survived
through capitalism's largesse, i.e., paychecks. That is the something beautiful that capitalism has done for me. If I were a painting, I'd be worth more,
but let that go. As for the Seagram Building, I can take it or leave it. People
work there, moving papers around. They watch the clock, flirt, cringe, complain. Ho-hum. It's got nothing to do with me. I have nothing against this
building but have here used it analogously in homage to Joyce's famous cow,
made by a man hacking in fury at a block of wood. Stephen Dedalus asked
if it was a work of art. He didn't answer his question, but I know the answer.

Or, to end on a, for me, uncharacteristically Zen note: *Question:* Is the Seagram Building an example of capitalism doing something beautiful for us? *Answer:* Buy James Joyce a pair of pants.

The New York Times, 1973

44

Dan Rice

I first saw Dan Rice's paintings in the winter of 1957–58 in his loft in New York. This was about two years after his inclusion in the group show, "Four American Painters," at the Poindexter Gallery. Thinking back on this initial exposure to Rice's work, it seems to me almost incredible that his vision of the picture and his conception of what painting should be have never varied. His attitude has been constant over the past twenty years; certainly, his talents have matured and his skills have sharpened, but the lyrical impulse of his work has stayed the same.

It is odd for me, as a writer, to try to say something about Rice's work that will have some meaning in terms of painting. I am brought up short by this fact because of the words, "lyrical impulse," that I have written above. Is there such a thing in the painter's world? I have no clear idea, but surely Rice paints lyrically if the word has any meaning in the plastic arts. This impulse is the province of the poet—I will go so far as to say that true poetry is lyrical and can be nothing else. At that moment when the poet's voice is transmuted into the voice that exists within the poem, that voice that we take to be the poet's voice, the poem has settled into its lyric mode; it is a sudden "hearing" that occurs in the poet's mind and that finds its being in the words of the poem. The poem is aloof, objective, and still; and yet it is the creation of a solitary and personal voice that has invented a solitary and personal voice.

I "read" Rice's paintings that way. The man is not revealed in the pictures; the man as a painter is. The lyrical mode can occur in both Keats' sonnets and *The Divine Comedy*, in figurative painting and abstraction. It is, as Pound said, "the quality of the affection" that matters. In many of Rice's pictures we seem to discover landscapes; that is because they are there. In others are the faces of women. These too are there. These images exist almost despite themselves; they are "spoken" by the painter, they exist in and for the paint that has formed them, beyond idea, as a good poem is beyond idea. It was Braque who said that a painting is finished when the idea in it has been obliterated. In Rice's paintings, we find idea changed, almost as we look, into pure image. The idea is obliterated by painting it into the picture; only then does it become an instance of the lyrical.

As far as Rice's skills go, I am ignorant of the niceties of formal design and technique. Suffice it to say that Rice deals with paint as an absolute medium. For a painter of his age, one of the second generation of abstract expressionists, the last ten years have been difficult, hysterical as they have been in their mass-media, public-relations mentality and their confusion of art history with criticism. I cannot think of another important movement in art assaulted so vigorously and discredited—as being exhausted—so swiftly as abstract expressionism. This was, it seems to me, an enormous mistake, based on some unexamined idea about the banality and lack of originality in the work of those painters who came after the giants of the New York School. Combined with a manipulated market and a lust for the novel, the movement was quite forcibly submerged.

Yet it seems to me a hard fact that only the surface of the possibilities of abstract expressionism was touched by the "founders" of the New York School. Certainly, Rice works in color as does no one else. Kline, in his last color paintings, was exploring a method of using color in the way that Rice does, but Rice had started earlier. Color in these pictures is used structurally; the images are literally built out of color. I mention this only to demonstrate that the early expressionists raised, as it were, many questions in their work. Far from being a bankrupt movement, expressionism was, so to speak, just getting interesting in the sense that it began to grapple with subtleties, when it was declared passé. Color-field painting, while it has its various brilliancies, is a kind of side-stepping of the problems that Kline engaged toward the end of his life and that Rice has spent his artistic career trying to resolve.

These pictures are truly made. Beautifully brushed, they have rhythm, balance, and harmony. They are, while beautiful, not pretty—an indication of Rice's strength in handling color in an almost sculptural way. This strength, this control, strike the viewer as the product of an extremely fine artistic intelligence. Baudelaire once asked if Ingres' draftsmanship was absolutely intelligent, a question that today would probably be considered philistine. This was the same Baudelaire who dismissed the chic—which meant then exactly what it means now—in painting as a memory of the hand and not the mind. Rice's paintings are not only sublimely made, they are, to my mind, absolutely intelligent and utterly remote from the chic.

Catalogue Note, 1976

45

Mort Lucks

Mort Lucks, who exhibited in many group- and one-man shows at the Tanager Gallery from the mid-fifties to the early sixties, will be remembered by gallery-goers of that period for his dryly brilliant abstractions. His work has not been seen by the general public since the mid-sixties, but it is clear from this show of new paintings, done over the past year and a half, that his vision and talents have deepened and matured since that time, and that he is currently working at, as they say, the top of his form.

Degas remarked that it is essential for the painter never to bargain with nature, and that there is real courage in attacking nature frontally in her great planes and lines. This may be read as a truism, yet how many artists *do* attack nature "frontally"? Lucks does, and in these paintings has selected for his attack flowers, generic or archetypal fauna, and simple aquatic organisms. Some of the pictures concentrate on one of these subjects, others on combinations of them; all treat these forms as the quintessential structures that they are, by which I mean to say that the paintings resist, even refuse, to permit literary analogies to be made, e.g., *flower equals pretty*. That is because this artist knows that flowers are *not* pretty but are, in fact, awesome in their formal design. He has looked at his flowers and his other images as if they were invented yesterday and has executed paintings that reveal this formal design without concession to either the sentimental or the received idea.

Some of his images are seen as if the viewer himself were the same size as the subject; that is, we see *inside* the subject, or we see but a fraction of its whole, enlarged so that the resultant form is pure abstraction. But I hasten to add that these paintings are in no wise instances of the realistic given a patina of the abstract; they are not forced into abstraction. Their power lies in the fact that Lucks sees his models as the bewilderingly sublime forms that they in truth are. He paints what he sees; that his eye may be pressed directly against his model makes for a negation of that model's presence in its surrounding space. We may say that the form exists outside of any space that is not enclosed by it. It becomes, then, unfamiliar, removed from the space that would "tell" us what it is as mimetic form.

Lucks' artistic strategies in these paintings comprise a compendium of possibilities for the rendering of forms. There is, for instance, one painting with a background field of high-keyed green, whose lines and planes lead the eye up to, as it were, the lip of a flower; yet as we look, we have the compelling sense that the eye is being taken *down* and into the cup of the flower. The picture has certain affinities with Vorticist painting, but is in no way imitative of it. These effects are possible because the artist has, by his insistence on a perspective that denies the flower's surrounding space, denied *us* our bearings: we are in the flower's world. Other paintings, those that employ marine imagery, deploy shapes that literally float up and off the picture surface; we might be looking down into water, or up through it, or across it, the eye submerged. Recognitiion and meaning are not pertinent in seeing these pictures; indeed, we are not meant to recognize anything. Nature, these paintings say, is beautiful, not pretty, and not beautiful because it has been infused with narrative meaning. These forms have their specific *quidditas*, they are isolate and formal and perfect, they are themselves. Lucks has compelled us to see them as such.

Lucks' palette in these pictures is bright and hard, yet strangely subtle as well. Some of his colors are high-keyed off shades, some dark and austere, some pure and luminous. On the one hand, his palette captures the great range of colors that nature shows us, that its phenomena possess; on the other, there is often no attempt at absolute reproduction of nature's colors. The color is occasionally exotic and arbitrary and serves quite strikingly to remind us that we are not to take these paintings as nature studies, but as delineations of the mysterious actual.

It was, of course, Mallarmé who insisted on the language and not the idea as the medium for poetry, in his "I say: a flower! and, out of oblivion, there arises, musically, that flower absent from all bouquets." Lucks' flowers and all his other forms are, like Mallarmé's, his own, the product of his frontal attack upon nature. These new paintings, conceived with a clear intelligence and executed with great authority, show Mort Lucks to be one of our best artists.

Arts, 1978

46

A Note on William Anthony

A number of years ago . . . I taught drawing at
a commercial art school. My students wanted to
learn how to draw accurately. . . . To help them I
did exaggerations of the mistakes which beginners
make: heads too large, torsos like sand bags, skinny
necks, legs resembling carrots, elbows and knees
that looked as though they'd suffered from some
sort of tourniquet treatment. I put all these mistakes together to form a classically idiotic figure.
Then this satiric how-not-to took on an insane life
of its own in *my* work.

William Anthony

The public purpose of William Anthony's drawings would seem to be explicit: the presentation of satiric or parodic images. His methods are clear,
as may be seen in his drawings of the "right" and "wrong" ways to render the
female figure and the human hand. So far so good. But there is something
beyond this satire, this parody, this relentless metamorphosis of the seen
world into one made up of equal parts puerility and vapidity. The drawings
are "funny," often hilarious; but the laughter of the spectator is somehow
tempered by a realization that this claustrophobic world is, in essence, a
ghastly one.

It would seem most useful in this introductory note to attempt a brief
examination of Anthony's private purpose. I see it, as I have suggested, as

something that goes beyond what appears to be rather gentle fun-poking. It is, at its core, a devastating revelation of the grotesque that exists at the heart of mass-man. What seems rather lightly given may be seen, on reflection, to be a rather acute posing of certain questions as to our cultural and social fix. A salient exhibition of this may be noted in Anthony's parodies of the work of pop artists; they are notable in that they all but imperceptibly manage not only to call into question the culture that can produce the artifact that stands as primary model but also, and more importantly, the art celebrated for its meticulous duplication of that model. Anthony's soup can thus asks, as it were, two questions: What is the value of this industrialized product of society and the economic rationale that produced it? What is the value of Warhol's equally industrialized product and the aesthetic rationale that produced it? Anthony's "naive" drawing may be seen as a superimposition upon Warhol's famous copy of copies, making the latter artistically unnecessary. Whether we choose to see Warhol's soup can as a disingenuous, kitsch celebration of technology or as a straightfaced parody of a commonly available image, Anthony's parody of it allows us at least to consider the possibility that pop art is a kind of extra-artistic phenomenon that exists solely in terms of "art history": i.e., here it is, so it must be art.

His satire works differently, as the reader of this book will see. One might say that his parody is located in the specific and his satire in the general. The sense of the ludicrous in one drawing is different from that in another. Yet in both, despite their superficial cheeriness, that nagging vision of man as a kind of supreme and undifferentiated moron persists. It is not, I think, that Anthony makes bizarre and crippled images of mass-man that disturbs; the drawings are, most obviously, not images that have any pretensions to the realistic. What comes through these works is the psyche of mass-man, his mind and soul. If one were to ask exactly how the "mind" of a game show or the "mind" of a mass demonstration in Peking might be objectified, an Anthony drawing would surely answer.

I see the evocation of this nightmare world as William Anthony's private purpose as an artist. Through the public façade of what seems a silly and labored primitivism, the artist permits his true message registration. It is as if the essential meanness and stupidity of the Zeitgeist, as exemplified by the lives and faces and poses of mass-man, has asserted itself, finally, without the mask of the ordinarily familiar to obscure it. Looking at Anthony's copy of the well-known photograph of the peace officers who killed Bonnie and Clyde, we see what they looked like, but the drawing acts too as a gloss upon that naked photo: we see that their differences are less than their samenesses—their *spirit* is a whole and it is the spirit of inane cruelty.

To take this a little further: It may be that beneath and behind the much-photographed and -reproduced images of our most "famous," visible, public people, lies an understructure of insipidity; that under the famous smile and famous eyes and famous profile one can almost, but not quite, discern a dim-witted visage in repose. This hidden visage is, of course, never really seen. What is "seen" is the public face, and the "life" as manufactured by public-relations departments and press agents and reporters. This "life" is reimagined in Anthony's drawings, reimagined so that we may descry it as the hidden visage rendered pure. The "star" is caught with his blankness showing, yet—and this, I think, is what makes Anthony's drawings unique—this pure face, this Anthony face, reveals no embarrassment at the exposure, is, in fact, quite pleased. It is this pleased, smug face, this idiotic face, this true face that the flesh conceals, that Anthony constructs. The suddenly glimpsed face, either of a real subject or of a ubiquitously recognized type, exposes the bankrupt soul; is, in fact, its surrogate. The artist presents this as a joke but it is a very serious joke indeed, like those in Baudelaire.

Bible Stories appears to be lighter, perhaps because Anthony is here dealing with the historical and mythical. But what sharper comment on the Exodus than Anthony's drawing? It says all that there needs to be said about the worship of false idols.

We have in William Anthony's drawings a remarkable art that can be apprehended on various levels. Like all good satirists, his targets are precisely located; like all good parodists, he is thoroughly aware of all the facets and ramifications of his original; and like all angry and humane men, he cannot help but show us what we are beneath our pretenses. In his last great poem, "L'Imprévu," Baudelaire writes:

> Célimène roucoule et dit: "Mon coeur est bon,
> Et naturellement, Dieu m'a faite très-belle."
> —Son coeur! coeur racorni, fumé comme un jambon,
>   Recuit à la flamme éternelle!

In William Anthony's drawings we find, over and over again, Célimène and her stunted heart.

Bible Stories, 1978

47

Genetic Coding

Anyone who has read my fiction can isolate, with a greater or lesser degree of accuracy, the writers who have influenced me, or, more precisely, can see, to use Butor's terms, my fiction as the particular "knot" formed within the "cultural texture" from which I have emerged. With Butor and other writers, I do not believe in Originality but consider writers a kind of "collaborative" band, each adding a stratum to the work done by others, each stratum possible only because of that work. My novel *Mulligan Stew* is not truly intelligible unless it is seen as dependent on the work of Joyce and Flann O'Brien, as well as on the shiftings and permutations of the Zeitgeist of the past half-century, its rubbish and ephemera. The novel is, or was meant to be, the end of that process we call modernism; and its ultimate roots are in *Bouvard and Pécuchet*. Edward Sapir, in his brilliant 1931 paper "Fashion," notes that "a specific fashion is utterly unintelligible if lifted out of its place in a sequence of forms." If I substitute "literary work" for "fashion," I might say, then, that *Mulligan Stew* is *only* intelligible when in place in the sequence of forms known as the modernist movement.

But this is by the way. It interests me only insofar as it allows me to ask a question of myself: Why these particular influences? What I am trying to get at is this: does a writer choose his influences, or are they, so to speak, lying in wait for him, so that when encountered they are seen to be destined for him? I think this must be the case, and if it is, it means that one's influences are deeper than the "merely" literary, are, indeed, at the core of one's life.

My mother was Irish on her mother's side and Welsh-Irish on her father's. My maternal grandmother was Roman Catholic, my maternal grandfather "Church of Ireland"—an Orangeman. My father's father was born in Salerno, my father's mother in Sciacca, Sicily, as was he. That side of my family is wholly Roman Catholic. This is a common mixture of blood among many people of my generation and class in the large industrial cities of the North, but none the less remarkable because of its ordinariness. Neapolitans are extroverted, demonstrative, masters of bravura, and expert in the niceties of social intercourse; Sicilians are withdrawn, proud, "Byzantine" and convoluted in their mental processes, and equally expert in the niceties of social intercourse. The Irish are a people who suffer from what Vivian Mercier calls "life-hatred"; from this comes their incredible sense of the comic futility of human existence, especially as it relates to the great mysteries of sex and death. To the Irish, there is nothing to be done about them, and hence they are ruthlessly mocked.

Both the Italians and the Irish have an understanding of the essential idiocy of living, the former possessing the Mediterranean tragic sense of life in a pure state, and the latter cloaking their despair under violent, savage, and heartless comedy, comedy that is grounded in what Beckett calls the "mirthless laugh . . . the laugh of laughs, the *risus purus*, the laugh laughing at the laugh." Both have a cynical contempt for authority beyond the family and "clan" and are, to put a nice face on it, bemused as well as amused by it. As far as their art goes, well, now we may begin to see something of that toward which I am, as best I can, digging. In brief, their art is complexly unrealistic: life is not enough for it.

Italian art is, generally speaking, the art of layering: one adds and adds and then adds some more, until the initial impetus, the base upon which the work rests, is almost unrecognizable. We see this in Dante, Cavalcanti, Pirandello, Calvino, Fellini; in the statues of saints in New York churches; in cuisine and pastry; in the elaborate rituals of manners played out by Italians who are introduced to strangers. It is a conscious gilding of the poor thing offered up as "reality." And Irish art is so far removed from nature that the latter is grotesquely distorted in it: in the Book of Kells, Swift, Sterne, Shaw, Wilde, Joyce, Synge, Yeats, O'Brien, we see a withdrawal from the representative.

The Italians and the Irish hold reality cheap, and the brilliance of the art produced by these peoples is, by and large, the brilliance of formal invention used to break to pieces that which is recognizable to the quotidian eye. (That the objects that we think we see in the real world are the result of interactions between outer wave patterns and mental wave patterns—i.e., that we do not "see" the same world that the fish does, or the cockroach, or the eagle, but "see" a world that reflects the human mind—is the suggestion, perhaps not coincidentally, of Vasco Ronchi of the National Institute of Optics in Arcetri.) The hallmark of the art of both these peoples is a relentless investigation into the possibilities of form, a retreat from nature, a dearth of content. This is art made out of Yeats' "mouthful of air"; in the modern parlance, it is not "sincere"; that is, it is interested in how to say it, and not in what is said. "In the long run the truth does not matter," Wallace Stevens writes. It never has for either the Italians or the Irish, which may be why Italian rodomontade and verbal pyrotechnics are often thought of as transparent flattery or "charm," and why Irish stories are called blarney or bunk—as if the speakers were not fully conscious of themselves in the act of invention!

It is from this background that I come, and it is this background that allowed me to recognize those influences that were "mine" when I encountered them, that allowed me to use them: they were, indeed, "lying in wait" for me. They spoke to my genetic memories and permitted me to see my possibilities as an artist. And it was amazing to recognize that these two background streams were so much alike, so that Fellini, for instance, crammed with dreams, fantasies, mockery of modern life and sexual contretemps, grotesques and cripples, and over all, everpresent death, is oddly Irish; and Joyce, with his "unnecessary" swirls, his "self-indulgent" games, his strata of baroque decoration, his false clues and exaggerations, is almost Italian.

This is my "cultural texture" out of which the "knot" of my work, such as it is, emerges. I am, most helplessly, an American writer, but my formal concerns are rooted in my hereditary makeup, so that my Americanism is one of the materials to hand. Or, to put it another way, I am sure that had I been born and raised in France or Germany, I would have used *their* cultural and national materials in the same way that I use the American ones; i.e., I am closer to Laurence Sterne than I am to Henry Thoreau, and I "understand" Italo Calvino better than I do John Cheever.

So then. The writers who influenced me did so because of the deeper influence of genetic coding. They agreed with my own artistic necessities, which are: an obsessive concern with formal structure, a dislike of the replication of experience, a love of digression and embroidery, a great pleasure in false or ambiguous information, a desire to invent problems that only the invention of new forms can solve, and a joy in making mountains out of molehills.

I end with two stories, which may be read as glosses on this piece. The first concerns a man who goes into an Italian cobbler's shop with a pair of shoes to be heeled. He makes it clear that he must have the shoes that same evening, and that if the cobbler can't do the job, he won't leave the shoes. The cobbler swears that the shoes will be ready. That evening, the man returns to find that the shoes are not ready, and, exasperated, he asks the cobbler why he swore to him that they would be. The cobbler replies: "Telling you that they'd be ready, even when I knew they wouldn't, made you happy all day."

The second is the joke about the Irishman who comes home to his wife drunk every night. A priest tells her that she should throw a good scare into her husband to cure him, and that night, when he arrives at the door, his wife appears in a sheet, and screams at him: "I am the Devil, come to take you to hell!" The drunk looks at this figure, and after a moment, says, "I'm pleased to meet you. . . . I married your sister!" That this latter touches on the strange Irish affinity for the heresy of Manichaeism is another story.

In Praise of What Persists, 1983